The Digital Dialectic

New Essays on New Media

edited by Peter Lunenfeld

The MIT Press   Cambridge, Massachusetts   London, England

First MIT Press paperback edition, 2000

This book was set in Garamond 3 and Bell Gothic by Graphic Composition, Inc. and was printed and bound in the United States of America.

Library of Congress Cataloging-in-Publication Data

The digital dialectic: new essays on new media / edited by Peter Lunenfeld.
    p.   cm.—(Leonardo)
Includes bibliographical references and index.
ISBN 0-262-12213-8 (hardcover : alk. paper), 0-262-62137-1 (pb)
    1. Computers and civilization.   2. Technology—Social aspects.
3. Science—Social aspects.   4. New media theory.   I. Lunenfeld, Peter.
II. Series: Leonardo books.
QA76.9.C66D54   1998
303.48'34—dc21   98-25750
                                                CIP

10 9 8 7 6 5

To Gerald O'Grady
for what he built

Contents

Series Foreword

Editorial Board: Roger F. Malina, Denise Penrose, and Pam Grant Ryan.

We live in a world in which the arts, sciences, and technology are becoming inextricably integrated strands in a new emerging cultural fabric. Our knowledge of ourselves expands with each discovery in molecular and neurobiology, psychology, and the other sciences of living organisms. Technologies not only provide us with new tools for communication and expression, but also provide a new social context for our daily existence. We now have tools and systems that allow us as a species to modify both our external environment and our internal genetic blueprint. The new sciences and technologies of artificial life and robotics offer possibilities for societies that are a synthesis of human and artificial beings. Yet these advances are being carried out within a context of increasing inequity in the quality of life and in the face of a human population that is placing unsustainable burdens on the biosphere.

The Leonardo series, a collaboration between the MIT Press and Leonardo/International Society for the Arts, Sciences and Technology (ISAST), seeks to publish important texts by professional artists, researchers, and scholars involved in Leonardo/ISAST and its sister society, Association Leonardo. Our publications discuss and document the promise and problems of the emerging culture.

Our goal is to help make visible the work of artists and others who integrate the arts, sciences, and technology. We do this through print and electronic publications, prizes and awards, and public events.

To find more information about Leonardo/ISAST and to order our publications, go to the Leonardo Online Web site at <http://www.mitpress.mit.edu/e-journals/Leonardo/home.html> or send e-mail to <leo@mitpress.mit.edu>.

Acknowledgments

This collection grew out of "The Digital Dialectic: A Conference on the Convergence of Technology, Media, and Theory," which was held the weekend of August 5, 1995, at Art Center College of Design in Pasadena, California. All of the essayists and the interactive architect Christian Möller gave presentations. The best conferences have the value of engaging the whole of the human bandwidth: the talks, the imagery (from slides, video, Web sites, CD-ROMs, hypertexts, and digital movies), and the discussions that go on before, during, and after the presentations themselves—and it is often here that the real pleasure and edification take place. For supporting the conference, and thereby this book, I would like to thank David Brown, Art Center's president. Others at Art Center who deserve thanks include Linda Norlen, Steve Nowlin, Steve Weir, Mary Morris, William Cheeseborough, Mark Salazar, Doug Sutton, and Luis Valenzuela. My students in the Graduate Program in Communication & New Media Design at the time were immensely helpful during the conference: Roshi Givechi, Sarah Anastasia Hahn, Thomas Müller, Fred Nymoen, and Carolyn Sherins.

The conference was an extension of my experience organizing *mediawork:* The Southern California New Media Working Group, and there was obvious an crossover effect: Michael Heim, Florian Brody, Lev Manovich, and N. Katherine Hayles are all regular *mediawork* participants. I want to acknowledge the help and advice of others from *mediawork* who have become an essential part of my intellectual life: Steve Mamber, Vivian Sobchack, Carole Ann Klonarides, A. Michael Noll, Paul Harris, Jennifer Steinkamp, Coco Conn, Steve Diskin, and Norman Klein. Two more individuals stand out, deserving special credit for the interest they have shown in this project over the years: Ken Goldberg and Dan Harries. At the MIT Press, Robert Prior encouraged me to collect the essays, and when Douglas Sery took over the process, he gracefully shepherded the book through to completion. The comments of the Press's anonymous readers were much appreciated. This book would not have been possible without the enthusiasm of its contributors, and it is a source of pleasure for me that a number of these individuals have since become friends.

Richard Hertz, chair of the graduate programs at Art Center, deserves special mention. His vision is acute, and his support unyielding. Finally, I want to thank Susan Kandel, brilliant critic and editor whom I am lucky enough to have as house counsel. She reads every sentence I write, fixes the ones she can, and is tactful about the ones beyond redemption. She and our daughters, Kyra and Maud, tolerate my obsessions—including this book—with good humor. They know how much that means to me.

Contributors

Florian Brody

Florian Brody is President of Brody Inc., a publishing company based in Los Angeles and Vienna that is dedicated to the emerging information society. With a background in linguistics and computer science, he has worked for the Cinémathèque Française and the Austrian National Library and was technical director of the Expanded Book Project at the Voyager Company. He teaches at Vienna University and Art Center College of Design.

Carol Gigliotti

Carol Gigliotti is a practicing media artist, educator, and theorist who specializes in the aesthetics and ethics of interactive technologies. She is assistant professor in the Department of Art Education, and at the Advanced Computing Center for the Arts and Design, at Ohio State University. She lectures and publishes widely in the United States and Europe.

N. Katherine Hayles

N. Katherine Hayles, professor of English at the University of California, Los Angeles, writes on relations between science and literature in the twentieth century. She is the author of *Chaos Bound: Complex Dynamics in Contemporary Literature*. Her most recent book is *How We Became Posthuman: Virtual Bodies in Cybernetics, Literature, and Informatics*.

Michael Heim

Michael Heim is a Southern California-based philosopher who writes about the digital revolution. His books include *Electric Language*, *The Metaphysics of Virtual Reality,* and *Virtual Realism.* He consults for the computer industry and has organized six virtual reality conferences for military, government, and industry. He teaches at Art Center College of Design.

Erkki Huhtamo

Erkki Huhtamo is a media researcher and curator. He worked as professor of media studies, University of Lapland, Finland, between 1994 and 1996, and pursues his activities as a wandering scholar. His most recent book is *Virtuaalisuuden arkeologia (The Archeology of Virtuality).* He has written and directed three television series on media culture for the Finnish Broadcasting Company.

George P. Landow

George P. Landow is professor of English and art history at Brown University. His books range from studies of nineteenth-century literature, art, and religion to literary theory to educational computing. His publications on digital culture include *Hypertext 2.0: The Convergence of Contemporary Critical Theory and Technology* and *Hyper/Text/Theory.*

Brenda Laurel

Brenda Laurel is a researcher and artist. Her work focuses on human–computer interaction and cultural aspects of technology. She cofounded and became vice president for design of Purple Moon, a new media/play company for girls. She was a member of the research staff at Interval Research Corporation, where she conducted research on gender, technology, and play that led to the formation of Purple Moon. She codesigned and produced the Placeholder virtual-environment project at the Banff Centre for the Arts. She is editor of the book *The Art of Human–Computer Interface Design,* and author of *Computers as Theatre.*

Peter Lunenfeld

Peter Lunenfeld teaches in the Graduate Program in Communication and New Media Design at Art Center College of Design and is the founder of **mediawork:** The Southern California New Media Working Group. He writes on art, digital culture, and the history and theory of media. His column, "User," appears in *art/text.*

Lev Manovich

Lev Manovich is a theorist and critic of new media on the faculty at the University of California, San Diego. His book *The Engineering of Vision from Constructivism to Virtual Reality* is forthcoming from the University of Texas Press. He is currently working on a collection of essays on digital realism and a CD-ROM on the archaeology of digital media.

William J. Mitchell

William J. Mitchell is the dean of the School of Architecture and Planning at MIT. He is the author of *The Reconfigured Eye: Visual Truth in the Post-Photographic Era*. *City of Bits: Space, Place, and the Infobahn* examines architecture and urbanism in the context of the digital telecommunications revolution and the growing domination of software over materialized form.

Robert Stein

Bob Stein founded the Voyager Company. For 13 years he led the development of over 300 titles in the Criterion Collection, a series of definitive films on videodisc, and more than 75 CD-ROM titles, including the CD-ROM Companion to Beethoven's *Ninth Symphony* and the Voyager edition of *Macbeth*. His new company, Night Kitchen, Inc., is developing authoring tools for the next generation of electronic publishing.

Introduction

Screen Grabs: The Digital Dialectic and

New Media Theory

Peter Lunenfeld

Introductions to collections of essays about digital culture generally begin by justifying the perverse. They explain that electronics and cybernetics have so infiltrated the realms of art and the humanities that a hybridized discourse simply has to spring into being, and so they offer models, exemplars, and/or apologias. This introduction, however, starts from a different premise. At this moment, digital culture has been so thoroughly hyped in every forum from television to academic journals to the World Wide Web that new commentaries need justification less than they require the kind of logic and style we demand of serious discourse on anything else.

Another problem with introductions—of all sorts—is that they presume to tie disparate arguments together in the guise of overarching themes. As theorists of the postmodern have argued so persuasively, however, this is an era actively hostile to metanarratives, a climate that resists the urge to totalize. Thus, this introduction is titled "Screen Grabs," the first of many such liftings from technical manuals. A screen grab is a quick and dirty way to capture an image on the monitor, in order to save or print it. In many desktop computer systems, the screen grab is accomplished with a simple combination of keystrokes.

What is interesting is that this operation captures everything present on the screen at a particular moment—operating system menus, tool palettes, file labels, and so on—and creates a new image out of it. The speed and ease of the screen grab is counterbalanced by the fact that it saves things that one does not necessarily want or need. The screen grab, then, is a compromise, and the first embrace of ambivalence to be encountered in this collection. To embrace ambivalence, contrary to what this might intuitively seem, is to sacrifice neither rigor nor sense. It is to lodge oneself in the dialectic, where reversals are not simply expected but required. But this book is called *The Digital Dialectic*, which I define as grounding the insights of theory in the constraints of practice. Before we ask what practice, and which theory, we need to ask what the digital is, and what the dialectic is—for us.

The digital is more than simply a technical term to describe systems and media dependent on electronic computation, just as the analog, which preceded it, describes more than a proportional system of representation. Examine Alexander Graham Bell's telephone. In this pioneering system, a caller spoke into the phone and a signal was created in direct relation to the sound pressure of the speaker's voice. The transmission voltage, being proportional to this pressure, activated the speaker on the receiver's end to re-create the sound. Or, for another nineteenth-century example, take black-and-white landscape photography. Here was an analog system in which a smooth gradient scale of gray tones was used to capture an image of the exterior world. In both the analog phone call and the analog photo, there is a proportional, continuously variable relationship between the original and the mediated copy (of the voice and of the vista, in these two examples).

Yet both the telephone system and much of photography have since "gone digital." What does this mean, both technically and aesthetically? Digital systems do not use continuously variable representational relationships. Instead, they translate all input into binary structures of 0s and 1s, which can then be stored, transferred, or manipulated at the level of numbers, or "digits" (so called because etymologically, the word descends from the digits on our hands with which we count out those numbers). Thus a phone call on a digital system will be encoded as a series of these 0s and 1s and sent over the wires as binary information to be reinterpreted as speech on the other end. The digital photograph is perhaps better recast as an electronic photo-graphic. The digital photograph, rather than being a series of tonally continuous pigmented dots, is instead composed from pixels, a grid of cells that have precise numerical attributes associated with them, a series of steps rather than a continuous slope.

We have, in fact, come to expect a certain crispness from digital media precisely because of this stepping, leading some to categorize the analog as somehow natural, less polarized, more curved. Yet the aesthetic effect of the movement toward the digitization of everything from telephony to photography to text delivery systems to the cinema goes far beyond a taste for either the curved or the crisp. It is the capacity of the electronic computer to encode a vast variety of information digitally that has given it such a central place within contemporary culture. As all manner of representational systems are recast as digital information, then all can be stored, accessed, and controlled by the same equipment. This is the true basis of the "multimedia" revolution. It is because of this similarity at the level of binary coding that this collection of essays can take on text, photographic image, sound, and cinema in one, ever bubbling electronic stew.

The digital is linked to other terms: electronic, cyber, telematic. These terms are more than technological nomenclature. They are being tested to serve as overarching descriptions of a moment. No one could ever quite define what they meant by "modern," but to speak of the "modern moment" was at least a comprehensible statement. Even harder to pin down was the word "postmodern," but it, too, served for a time to describe a set of often conflicting tendencies, movements, and artifacts. I would maintain that "digital" has a similar function as a placeholder for whatever term we or posterity chooses to describe our immediate present. The collection promises "New Essays on New Media," but the very term "new media" is ambiguous. Is video still a "new" medium? Are operating systems media? Is hypertext a different medium than the electronic book? In the end, the phrase "new media" turns out to be yet another placeholder, this time for whatever we eventually agree to name these cultural productions.

If the digital is difficult to delineate because of its relative freshness, the challenge of defining the dialectic derives from its advanced age; the word is encrusted with centuries of conflicting meanings. My screen grab of the dialectic is intended to introduce the term rather than to limit its use. In fact, the dialectic is treated by some of the authors included in this volume as a philosophical system, by others as a method of disputation, and by still others as an analytical tool. The word itself shares its etymology with the Greek phrase for the art of conversation (*dia logou*), and the Socratic dialogue—where the teacher draws out the truth from a student by a method akin to a cross-examination—comes the closest to that conception.

The dialectic, though, predates Socrates and has remained central to Western philosophy ever since (whether celebrated or reviled); for centuries it was even synonymous with logic itself. Today, the dialectic is commonly understood to be a dynamic process in which one proposition is matched against another (often its opposite) in order to bring a third, combinatory proposition into being. Formulaically, the dialectic is the thinking or acting through of the thesis and the antithesis to reach a synthesis.[1] Screen grabs from the history of philosophy: for Zeno of Elea, the dialectic's ideal object was the "Paradox"; for Immanuel Kant, it was "Illusion." G. F. W. Hegel devoted himself to its relation to the "Spirit"; Karl Marx concentrated his dialectical thinking on "Matter." Paradox; Illusion; Spirit; Matter: these are just four of the objects to which the West's critical tradition has applied the dialectic.

The dialectic as we use it today, however, is inextricably linked to the philosophies of Hegel and Marx. For Hegel, who was interested in the realms where philosophy and the spiritual begin to fuse, the dialectic involved ideas that "supersede themselves, and pass into their opposites," and only then are transformed into the achievement of a higher unity. One of Hegel's examples of dialectical thinking is found in his discussion of mortality:

We say, for instance, that man is mortal, and tend to think that the ground of his death is in external circumstances only; so that if this way of looking were correct, man would have two special properties, vitality and—also—mortality. But the true view of the matter is that life, as life, involves the germ of death, and that the finite, being radically self-contradictory, involves its own suppression.[2]

For Marx, the spiritual realm was of less interest than the physical, and we call his philosophy "dialectical materialism" to acknowledge this. Dialectical materialism hopes to account for the seeming contradictions of economic and historical development; Marx attempts to explain opposing forces, tendencies, or principles in terms of a common causal condition of existence—that is, by looking at the overall movement of history.

Both Hegel and Marx organize the dialectic teleologically, which is to say, with a goal in mind. For Hegel that organizing goal is the Spirit, which can be interpreted either as God or as the force that impels man toward God. For Hegel, history is the story of man's inexorable move toward God, and thus we speak of his transcendental dialectic. Though profoundly influenced by him, Marx wrote in contradiction to Hegel, replacing "spirit" with "matter." For Marx, history did not move toward God but rather toward a utopia of the proletariat. His history moved forward from feudalism through capitalism to communism.[3] Not all dialectical thought, however, shares this teleological bent.

Frankfurt school theorist Theodor W. Adorno saw within the dialectic a way to weld together identity and the contradiction of thought, unfolding "the difference between the particular and the universal."[4] Capable of indicating two possible states or conditions—"0" or "1" or "off" or "on"—the binary mode of cybernetic calculation might appear to resemble this duality, which is, in essence, the dualism of thesis and antithesis. Resemblance is not identity here, however, and conflating the digital with the dialectic is a mistake. On the digital frontier, the endless alternation of off/on, a system of closed and open switches, never generates a true synthesis; it merely impels the regeneration of the system. Yet this inability to come to synthesis may be turned to our advantage. It may prevent us from falling prey to a newly devised teleology for the digital age: the techno-utopia that cyberlibertarians promise once the markets are unfettered and the world is fully virtualized. The digital dialectic's universals, to return to Adorno's formulation, are far less bombastic, averse in the end to such rosy metanarratives.

The digital dialectic shows its strengths in its attention to the particulars. If there is a central dialectic that draws together the essays in this collection, it is the relationship between theory and practice. A critical theory of technological media will always be in inherent conflict with the practice of creating these very media. For if theory demands from its objects a certain stability, theory is itself free to break the tethers of its objects, to create a hermetically (and hermeneutically) sealed world unto itself. The pressures of the market and the innovations of the laboratory combine to make stability impossible within the practice of digital media, however. Yet both the market and the technologies themselves are bound by a series of constraints that theoretical texts can elide with fuzzy forecasting and the bromides about the future. The digital dialectic offers a way to talk about computer media that is open to the sophisticated methodologies of theory without ignoring the nuts and bolts or, better yet, the bits and bytes of their production. To repeat, the digital dialectic goes beyond examining what is happening to our visual and intellectual cultures as the computer recodes technologies, media, and art forms; it grounds the insights of theory in the constraints of practice.

A few final words on this: no matter how much digital systems resemble film or television, they are fundamentally different. The computer, when linked to a network, is unique in the history of technological media: it is the first widely disseminated system that offers the user the opportunity to create, distribute, receive, and consume audiovisual content with the same box. Thus, theorists have to strive to create new models of commentary that consider more than consumption or spectatorship. These models must take into account such things as the trade-off between speed and immersion, potential in the lab versus viability in the market, the social dynamic of the user group, the demo or die aesthetic, the Byzantine mechanisms of distribution, and, of course, the inevitability of machine failure. All this and more begin to get at the constraints of practice particular to these new media.

The essays in this collection, then, offer conceptual tools based on an intimate understanding of how these media are created and work. This grounding prevents the slide into what I have referred to as a "science-fictionalized" discourse.[5] Too many contemporary observers churn out theories that offer fantasies of fully accessible, fully immersive virtual realities where gender and identity are untethered from the body; that literalize the metaphor of cyborg life; that obsess on the ever-titillating concept of teledildonics. The trend is to discuss the implications of technologies (especially where something could go) rather than to analyze the technologies themselves (where they are). This is not to say that the contributors to *The Digital Dialectic* are completely immune to the delights of amateur futurism. Few choose to involve themselves as fully as they have with these technological systems without some hope for the future, and the digital dialectic as practiced here is a redemptive endeavor, not simply an exercise in critique. On the whole, the authors search for those aspects of digital culture worthy not only of analysis but also of nurturance. But they are as aware of the limitations of these systems as they are of the potentials, and in fact see these limitations as formative.

This is as appropriate a place as any to deal with the inevitable question: "Why publish a book dealing with the culture of an era that has supposedly transcended the printed page?" We still will publish in book form that which we deem to have lasting significance. Nothing ages faster and becomes inaccessible quicker than electronic media. The silver oxide is falling off the tapes that constitute our archive of the pioneering era of video art. Good luck trying to find a system that can access computer files that are a mere decade old (especially if they were composed on now-abandoned operating systems). And bit rot (a lovely, though all too appropriate, coinage to deal with the digital's always already dated qualities) is almost immediate on the World Wide Web, with sites popping up and falling away like flowers in the desert.[6]

Rather than thinking of the digital media and environments mentioned herein as though they possessed the stability of painting or architecture, better to embrace their mercurial qualities and conceptualize them as being somehow evanescent, like theatrical performances or dance recitals. We encourage the theater critic to evoke a great performance without expecting to be able to attend it, much less recall it from the archive. We accept dance's transience as no small part of its power. We should do the same for digital culture, at least for now.

The dialectic is, as noted earlier, the sibling of the dialogue. This sense of the dialectic as conversation helps to explain the vortices around certain texts, concepts, and figures. Grab these screens to freeze Hegel and Marx, *Neuromancer* and *Understanding Media*, digital video and *Myst*, immortality and obsolescence, the Luddites and *Wired*. These systems and references swirl through the essays. Four loose dialectical pairings—"The Real and the Ideal," "The Body and the Machine," "The Medium and the Message," and "The World and the Screen"—structure the essays and serve to define areas of common interest in the wider conversation that is the book as a whole. Each section opens with a short essay laying out the specific dialectic and weaving together the contributors' ideas.

The late photographer, filmmaker, and digital artist Hollis Frampton engaged in a series of dialogues with the sculptor Carl Andre early in their careers. In an example of E-mail correspondence in advance of the technology, the two artists met in Andre's apartment every weekend over the course of a year from 1962 to 1963. One would bang away at the typewriter while the other lay on the bed, reading. They would then switch, in this way creating a *written* dialogue: a mediated, immediate, and intimate text-based conversation. It was in the midst of this process that Frampton commented, "There may have been a time when talk was literature, but we understand the two things differently now."[7] It is my hope that this book can capture some of the flavor of the dialectic as dialogue, those moments when talk seems as heady as literature.

The Digital Dialectic

Part I

The Real and the Ideal

In the long history of philosophy, the oldest dialectical pairing is likely to be the real and the ideal. If the real has been categorized as something that exists independent of the vicissitudes of sensory experience, and the ideal as that which exists in the mind as a perfect model, then what are we to make of a decade during which the phrase "virtual reality" (VR) went from technical arcanum to journalistic cliché? The new medium of VR developed in science and engineering laboratories removed from the decades of intense debates in the humanities over how to describe, much less claim to know, the real. The theory wars of poststructuralism, deconstruction, and postmodernism were often arguments about language and the way we use it to represent reality. The essays in this section engage with these battles, in that they are intimately concerned with the language we are developing to describe new media, but they do not restrict themselves to a discourse about discourse. There are questions posed about language here, but they are questions regarding the tools needed to analyze objects, systems, and media, rather than another recycling of attacks on the real.

This is not to say that a generation's battering of the real bolstered the ideal. Though much has been made of the relationship between the archetypes floating outside of Plato's cave and the computer's virtual spaces and immaterial objects, the ideal has also been rocked by digital technologies. If idealism is seen as fundamentally spiritual—with the ideal standing somehow outside and beyond the realm of the material—then the materialistic rationalism that leads to the development of digital technologies would seem to undermine our confidence in *an* ideal, much less *the* ideal.

My essay, "Unfinished Business," introduces the ideal of the digital and the real of its production: digital movies, CD-ROMs, hypertexts, Web sites, and intelligent architectures. In an astonishingly short period of time, the computer has colonized cultural production; a machine that was designed to crunch numbers has come to crunch everything from printing to music to photography to the cinema. But in so doing, the computer has followed the law of unintended consequences: the box that came to be seen as the conclusive media machine has made conclusions themselves more difficult to reach. The open structure of so many electronic environments not only allows for constant incremental changes but demands them. The three sections of the essay—"Unfinished Spaces," "Unfinished Stories," and "Unfinished Time"—sketch an open-ended aesthetic for digital media, an aesthetic that accepts the limitations, and perhaps naïveté, of inherited concepts of "finishing" a work.

At first glance, philosopher Michael Heim's contribution seems, if not conclusive, at least complete. As the author of groundbreaking works on word-processing and virtual reality, and as a developer of Web-based distance learning environments and Internet services, Heim is well equipped to explicate "The Cyberspace Dialectic." His essay offers the most fully fleshed assessment of the dialectical method that he seeks to rescue from the brute application of "DIAMAT" (the Soviet acronym for dialectical materialism). Liberated from totalitarianism, the dialectic becomes for Heim a tool to ferret out irony and cut through hype. He is bemused when the fans of the Unabomber, the antitechnology terrorist, post their thoughts on the World

Wide Web. In this unintended humor, there is a reflection of the dialectical struggle between two camps: naïve realists and networked idealists.

The naïve realists are those who would ground the essence of humanity outside the realm of the technological, refusing to concede that technologies manifest human creativity. The networked idealists are those who would brush aside any concern with the debilitating qualities of new technologies and media, the blithe futurists who echo Candide's mantra that this is the best of all possible worlds—and that the digital will only add to its bounties. Heim offers up "virtual realism" as a synthetic position that brings together the innate criticality of naïve realism and the zeal of networked idealism. His virtual realism is itself "an existential process of criticism, practice, and conscious communication."

One way that the process of criticism remains dynamic is by responding to pressures from without. Carol Gigliotti's "The Ethical Life of the Digital Aesthetic" offers a different assessment of how to deploy the digital dialectic and to what ends. If Heim's strategy is to steer between absolutisms to develop a grounded method of technological analysis (what he calls "technalysis"), then Gigliotti hopes that dialectical reasoning will strengthen efforts to "undertake a form of moral imagination" with regard to the digital era's cultural production, economic organization, and political structures.

Gigliotti has worked as an artist, a curator, and a theorist, and has been actively crafting art education strategies to draw upon new media systems. In all facets, she attends to ethical questions, no matter how they might be communicated, embodied, or disembodied. Here, she moves from the ever-inflammatory (and hence always popular) issue of pornography and the Internet to the challenges presented the art world by the World Wide Web, from the rhetoric of digital revolution to the politics of access. Throughout this free-ranging investigation, Gigliotti stresses a holistic continuum: not the real versus the ideal, but rather a worldview that can consider both from that all-important ethical vantage point.

1

Unfinished Business

Peter Lunenfeld

Unfinished Introduction

The business of the computer is always unfinished. In fact, "unfinish" defines the aesthetic of digital media. The great cybernetic anthropologist Gregory Bateson speaks of the metalogue—a conversation in which the form of the discussion embodies the subject being discussed: a metalogue about the nature of passion is impassioned. The metalogue offers a means to engage with language without resorting to a metalanguage.[1] While what follows does not uphold the form of the metalogue, it does follow in its spirit: it is an unfinished and unfinishable essay about the electronic times and places in which we live.

Consider the taint of failure that inhabits the word "unfinished." In the Renaissance, *The Battle of Anghiari* was never more than the full-scale cartoon for the mural left unfinished when Leonardo abandoned the Florentine commission to return to Milan in 1506. We know it today only from the drawings of later artists like Peter Paul Rubens (1605). "Unfinish" also encompasses the unrealized. The Age of Reason un-reasonably offers us the most famous monument of unbuilt architecture in Etienne-Louis Boullée's Memorial for Isaac Newton (1784). Boullée's paper architecture of "majestic nobility" was so imbued with pictorial lyricism that its function was inspiration rather than habitation.[2] In the photomechanical age, Orson Welles incarnates Hollywood's unfinished business with scripts, plays, films, books, and other projects never begun, left incomplete, or wrested away from him at the crucial moment.[3]

Not just failure, but death, encircles unfinish. A composer dies "before his time" and we are left with Franz Schubert's "Unfinished Symphony." Walter Benjamin, in despair over Europe's impending immolation and his own situation, commits suicide on the border between Vichy France and neutral Spain; we struggle to jury-rig simulations of his great Arcades Project from notes and archives.[4] AIDS leaves us wondering where artist Keith Haring, novelist Paul Monette, and critic Craig Owens were heading next.

I have raised music, art, architecture, literature, film, criticism, yet not a single word about the computer. That may well be because at this very moment, the computer is swallowing—with stealth or bombast, it matters not which—all of these disparate endeavors. Cybernetics is the alchemy of our age: the computer is the universal solvent into which all difference of media dissolves into a pulsing stream of bits and bytes. It is a curious thing that a calculating machine we forced to become a typewriter only a decade and a half ago now combines the creation, distribution, and spectatorial functions of a vast variety of other media within one box—albeit tied into a network. But this is the present state of affairs, and things are likely to become more complicated before they become less so.

So how can it be that the computer will compel us not only to confront our fears of unfinished business but also to embrace an aesthetic of "unfinish"? First off, we would be remiss to ignore those aspects of unfinish that can be sexy. Would James Dean and Marilyn Monroe have the same thanapoptic appeal if they had grown old in an age of Twelve-Step redemption? The unfinished work or person allows us to read our own desires into a not yet fully formed object—opening up more space for pleasure and identification than any "complete" work or person can ever offer.

But this sexiness is not the specific pleasure of unfinish that the computer offers. Nor do I mean to conjure up the half-baked, the incomplete, or the anarchic, as did the Surrealists. To celebrate the unfinished in this era of digital ubiquity is to laud process rather than goal—to open up a third thing that is not a resolution, but rather a state of suspension. To get to that unresolved third thing—that thing in abeyance—we need first to acknowledge the central effects the computer has had on art and culture. A coherent conceptual vocabulary is an invaluable tool as we deal with a staggering amount of "newness": platforms, tools, softwares, and delivery systems that rapidly develop, proliferate, obsolesce, and are replaced. As hypertext visionary Ted Nelson has hyperbolized, "Everything changes every six weeks now."[5]

The question becomes how to categorize such a fast-moving set of objects and concepts. My own thinking involves generating operating paradigms—or threads, as I prefer—with which to make meaning. The three threads I weave here are story, space, and time. These threads are obviously broad enough to cover just about anything, but they also tie in specifically to the notion of unfinish.

Unfinished Spaces

Perhaps no other aspect of the new technologies has opened such a wide-ranging set of investigations as the advent of virtual environments and on-line matrices, with their recalibrations of physicality and seemingly boundless realms. It is obviously important to discuss how we explore these realms, but this is a different sort of exploration than the far-flung sort offered by Marco Polo, Christopher Columbus, and Sally Ride. Instead, consider the meander. It involves the pursuit of less grandiose dreams; it is the exploration that goes on almost in spite of itself. The meander is a distracted form of motion. It is the recataloging of the local environment we perform when we walk around, the reenvisioning of our domestic geography that occurs as we pass through the streets and alleys of our neighborhoods. Yet this is an urban model of exploration, and we are supposed to be living in a posturban age. So where does the wanderer venture? I am not the first to observe that he goes inward, into on-line realms, spreading out through the World Wide Web.

Take the case of Justin Hall, who at twenty years old served as an exemplar of the distracted electronic explorer. Starting in January 1994 (fairly early in the World Wide Web boom), he began publishing a personal Web page called "Links from the Underground" that offered a mix of Web site reviews, tutorials, articles, and autobiographical content. His site, essentially a map of his wanderings and a collection of his intertextualized ruminations, received at its height an astonishing quarter-million raw hits a day. Some might explain this by pointing out that Justin Hall had one of the earliest extensive listings of pornographic sites, but that would be to ignore the fact that we long have expected our explorers to come back with stories about sex. Justin Hall, as well as many more like him—including, of course, Jerry Yang and David Filo of Yahoo (Yet Another Officious Oracle) fame[6]—are spread across the globe, but all are found on the Web (often indexing each other's indexes). Yet, as they develop new habits of "unfinish," and innovative modes of exploration, it becomes interesting to seek out precedents for their activities.[7]

I am thinking of the midcentury, avant-garde movement known as the Situationist International, SI for short. Best known for its critique of the society of the spectacle, and for inspiring the student revolt in France in May 1968, the SI offers a remarkably sophisticated theorization of urbanism, a new vocabulary to describe and engage with the city as an open-ended place of play and investigation. The SI was interested in constructing "psychogeographies" of urban environments—creating mental correspondences for physical locales—going through a city block by block, neighborhood by neighborhood, building a revolutionary sense of mutable space and creative engagement. One of its techniques was termed the "dérive," which translates roughly as a "drifting." It is "a technique of transient passage through varied ambiances."[8] I would propose that if we were to strip the dérive from its original context, it describes precisely what people like Justin Hall were and are doing on the Web. They are practicing a "digital dérive," a dérive not through what my students now refer to as "realworld," but rather a dérive through that technopsychological environment of the matrix/Web/cyberspace.

As Hall and others like him surf through computer-generated image worlds, creating their hot lists and recording their observations, they are surfing through two-dimensional HTML documents, though—following Ted Nelson's six-week rule—they will soon be meandering through 3D virtual environments. When this becomes commonplace, the digital dérive will engender a psychogeography less of space than of the "consensual hallucination" William Gibson prefigured in *Neuromancer.* The digital dérive is ever in a state of unfinish, because there are always more links to create, more sites springing up every day, and even that which has been cataloged will be redesigned by the time you return to it.

The Web as it is presently constituted is essentially a collection of two-dimensional data spaces with a limited visual palette. We have to anticipate that those few prototypes of three-and-more-dimensional virtual spaces will eventually proliferate and coalesce into what Marcos Novak so elegantly refers to as the liquid architecture of cyberspace.[9] Where will the aesthetic of unfinish lead us in these yet to be designed realms?

Before answering that, I want to a step back and examine the impact that the computer is having on our very conception of what constitutes architecture. At the Vienna Architecture Conference in 1992, Coop Himmelblau remarked that "General interest in tangible, three dimensional architectural creations is steadily decreasing. . . . Virtual space is becoming the sphere of activity for the life of the mind."[10] Their statement, published under the apocalyptic title "The End of Architecture," is symptomatic of architecture's movement into the dis-incorporated realm of display and simulation. This transformation leads to an interesting inversion of a number of architectural prejudices.[11]

One of the curious aspects of contemporary architectural practice has indeed been that since the general slowdown of building in this country dating at least back to the 1970s, and intensifying during the recent economic downturn, certain outposts of the architectural profession have turned increasingly to a paper, rather than a brick and mortar, practice. The visionary Boullée, whom I mentioned earlier, becomes a new avatar.

Bernard Tschumi, dean of the School of Architecture at Columbia University, has seen a good number of his designs reified as standing buildings, but his renown rests at least as much on his theoretical work and sketches, plans, and unfinished paper projects. He responded to a series of critiques, the most pointed in the *New York Times,* by defending his and his program's attention to theoretical discourse, and the prevalence of paper architects on his faculty. He maintains that theory and practice have never been more fruitfully engaged, and argues "that what is unprecedented in certain architectural work over the past decade is the use of theory to develop concepts that inform the actual making of buildings as well as to examine concepts excluded from the domain of architecture by its inherited and prospective dualities of form and use."[12]

I would argue that virtual space blurs the distinction between form and use. As paper architecture becomes virtualized, it adopts the fluid states of liquid architecture. Perhaps we will have to recalibrate our concept of the digital dérive, taking it even farther from its Parisian origin, and move with it to an electronic Atlantis where merpeople can float as well as meander, opening up new vectors of exploration.

That liquid architecture and the digital dérive should adopt an aesthetic of unfinish is to be expected, but what of the computer's effect on built environments? As video walls, LCD panels, video projections, and large-scale computer graphic displays become greater and greater parts of our lived environments, we enter a new era of architecture, one in which the design of our lived spaces reflects and incorporates the electronic information and imaging technologies that are ever more central to our lives. Oddly enough, the lessons taught by these dematerialized imagescapes may end up having a beneficent effect on the hardscapes of built spaces. Stewart Brand offers some insights into this question in *How Buildings Learn: What Happens After They're Built.* He writes that in popular usage, the term "'architecture' always means 'unchanging deep structure.'" Yet his book is an impassioned plea to remember that "a 'building' is always building and rebuilding."[13] The central thesis of *How Buildings Learn* is that finishing is never finished. Brand identifies as a major problem the way that contemporary architecture is judged just once—at the moment just before the client takes possession, before it makes the ineffable shift from volumetric sculpture to inhabited space.

The computer industry could never function this way. Software is never finished, and early users of a new product always expect difficulties, followed

Unfinish: A grain silo in Akron becomes . . .

The Quaker Square Hilton.
Photos by Bruce Ford, City of Akron.

Peter Lunenfeld

by upgrades.[14] We can anticipate that the mix of liquid and built architecture will offer a similar process of refinement and give-and-take between designers—be they programmers, architects, or both—and the users who will dwell in these hybrid imagescapes and hardscapes.

So back to where we were. If we are to establish the creative potential of unfinish in the era of liquid architecture, we must defend computer-generated environments as being and offering a more fully spatialized experience than those offered by the image commodities on television. That is, we must defend the digital dérive as more than channel surfing. To do so, we will have to build these cyberspaces to ensure that what we give up sensually in the dérive of the *quartier, sestiere,* borough—that is, smell, atmosphere, and light—can be compensated for by the release from the constraints of physical movement. Vivian Sobchack speaks of the dialectic between carnal phenomenology on the one hand and arbitrary semiotic systems on the other—that is to say, the differences between the way we find and situate ourselves in realworld and the ever unfinished signscape that fills our media environments with simulations, morphing, and Net surfing.[15] One way we find our way through is by telling stories of where we have been.

Unfinished Stories

I have a word to tell you/a story to recount to you . . . /Come and I will reveal it.

This is an invitation. It speaks of the seductive power of narrative.

All right, then, so tell us a story then.

This is a command. It speaks of the demands of those who have surrendered to narrative's seductions.

These two quotations, which are on one level so close, are divided by over thirty-four centuries and a technological shift that is almost unimaginable. The first is from a poetic celebration of the god Baal composed in ancient Canaan and inscribed in cuneiform on clay tablets.[16] The second is an excerpt from Stuart Moulthrop's *Victory Garden,* a hypertext fiction created to be read on a computer.[17]

Human beings are hardwired into the storytelling process—whether they are the ones spinning the tales or those listening to them. As mentioned earlier, one of the links between the Age of Exploration and the era of the digital dérive is the propensity of those who venture out to return with stories of what they have seen. The difference between the eras is reflected in the way these stories are structured.

One of the most often noted qualities of hypertext is the way it offers a never-ending variety of ways through material. Hyperfictions encourage play and challenge our received critical vocabulary. Is a reader reading, or is a user using? The revolutionary qualities of an active engagement with open-ended narratives—whether as reader or user—have been well covered by others, most notably George Landow. I do not want to restate the well-rehearsed analyses of hyperfictions as instantiations of Roland Barthes's "writerly" textuality, wherein the reader does not encounter a work with a preconstituted meaning, but rather (re)writes the text through the process of reading.

I am concerned, instead, with situating open-ended hypernarratives in a broader context of unfinish. Just as the text has multiplied its own paths toward an internal form of unfinish, so the boundaries between the text and the context have begun to dissolve in the aforementioned universal solvent of the digital. Technology and popular culture propel us toward a state of unfinish in which the story is never over, and the limits of what constitutes the story proper are never to be as clear again.

French literary theorist Gérarde Genette refers to the "paratext": the materials and discourses that surround the narrative object.[18] Genette generated his theories from a study of literature and considers the paratext in terms of the publishing industry: cover design, book packaging, publicity materials, and so on. I would say, however, that the transformation of the publishing industry in the past two decades—the melding of publishers with moviemakers, television producers, and comic book companies, and the development of media conglomerates like Time Warner, Disney/ABC, and Sony—has bloated the paratext to such a point that it is impossible to distinguish between it and the text. Digital forms are even more prone to this, for who is to say where packaging begins and ends in a medium in which everything is composed of the same streams of data—regardless of whether the information is textual, visual, aural, static, or dynamic?[19] In addition, the backstory—the information about how a narrative object comes into being—is fast becoming almost as important as that object itself. For a vast percentage of new media titles, backstories are probably more interesting, in fact, than the narratives themselves.

As the rigid demarcations between formerly discrete texts become fluid liminal zones, and then simply markers within an ever-shifting nodal system of narrative information, the Aristotelian story arc, with its beginning, middle, and end, becomes something else again. Look at the cross-, trans-, inter-, para-, et cetera textualities that developed around the Sony Corporation's media "property" of Johnny Mnemonic—or, rather, the blurring boundaries between a number of Johnny Mnemonics. This proliferation of paratextuality was occasioned by the 1995 release of *Johnny Mnemonic,* a film directed by the artist Robert Longo. At <www.mnemonic.sony.com>, Sony marketed all of its Johnnys in one virtual place:

Way back in the 1980s, award-winning author William Gibson laid the foundation for the cyberpunk genre with fast-paced technothriller stories like *Johnny Mnemonic* and *Neuromancer.* Today, Sony presents Johnny Mnemonic in a variety of media: hence, we witness the arrival of *Johnny Mnemonic,* the movie starring Keanu Reeves . . . *Johnny Mnemonic,* the movie soundtrack . . . *Johnny Mnemonic,* the award-winning CD-ROM game from Sony Imagesoft (available for PC Windows and Mac) [not starring Reeves]; a plethora of assorted Johnny Mnemonic merchandise (T-shirts, caps, mugs); and, because it's the hip communication medium of the '90s, the *Johnny Mnemonic net.hunt,* a scavenger hunt on the Internet offering over $20,000 in prizes.[20]

To round it all out, there was a cover story in *Wired* that promised to return us to William Gibson for his take on "the making of" the movie.[21] Welcome to the digital revolution, brought to you by Sony. The result of such dubious corporate synergy is the blending of the text and the paratext, the pumping out of undifferentiated and unfinished product into the electronically interlinked mediasphere. Final closure of narrative can not occur in such an environment because there is an economic imperative to develop narrative brands: product that can be sold and resold. This is the justification for sequels, and not only for those narratives that are designed for sequels— as *Johnny Mnemonic* so obviously was—but even for the expansion of formerly closed narratives into unfinished ones. For that, see the recent trend in book publishing to unfinish *Gone with the Wind, Casablanca,* and even *The Wind in the Willows.*[22]

In the present moment, then, narratives are developed to be unfinished, or unfinishable. And if anything, narrative itself is being phased out in favor of character. Thus, the hope was that Johnny Mnemonic would take off as a

Going on-line in the film version of *Johnny Mnemonic*.

character, and that a never-ending series of narrativized and seminarrativized products could then be developed around him (the film flopped, however, stopping the process in its tracks). It is this phenomenon that accounts for the contemporary moment's inundation in comic book figures. A character like Batman is a narrative franchise. His story is always unfinished because one can never be certain that the narrative stream will not be invigorated by new tributaries in the years to come. The entire American comic book industry serves as a model of the perpetually suspended narrative: different artists, different writers, even different companies take the same characters, constantly reusing them, putting them into new yet similar narratives, and never closing them—for these creators are always working on someone else's product.[23]

This is the fate of the creative professional working for the postmodern image factory. What of other, more exploratory projects? Take David Blair's *Waxweb* as a work or, better yet, set of works, that makes the aesthetic of unfinish its own. Blair created the first important desktop video science fiction film in 1991, a curious hybrid called *Wax, or the Discovery of Television Amongst the Bees*. This dreamlike eighty-five-minute narrative blended video, computer graphics, and cinema. Since its release, there has been much

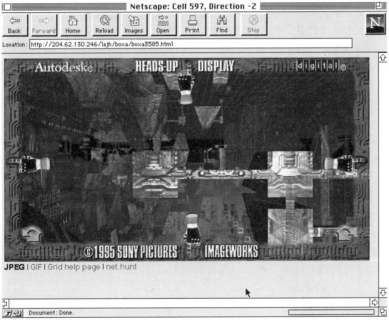

The CD-ROM game *Johnny Mnemonic*.
© Sony Imagesoft.

The *Johnny Mnemonic net.hunt*.

discussion of the film's remarkable visual style and looping narrative about Jacob Hive-maker, the nuclear testing sites in Almagordo, New Mexico, and how the bees guard the souls of the dead inside the moon.

Blair delivered *Wax* through a variety of channels, taking advantage of this era of proliferating networks. He blew up the video into a film print to show in theaters, sold cassettes by mail, and was the first artist to digitize and distribute a feature-length project on the Net. From there he went on to develop *Waxweb,* an interactive, intercommunicative feature film on the World Wide Web.

The original digital video is joined by 3,000 Web pages connected by 2,500 hyperlinks; 5,000 color stills; soundtracks in English, French, Japanese, and German; and more than 250 VRML-format 3D scenes, each in turn composed of thousands of hyperlinked parts.[24] All of this functions as a visualized MUD or, better yet, a MOO. In his book *The Virtual Community,* Howard Rheingold offers some definitions: "MUD stands for Multi-User Dungeons—imaginary worlds in computer databases where people use words and programming languages to improvise melodramas, build worlds and all the objects in them, solve puzzles, invent amusements and tools, compete for prestige and power, gain wisdom."[25] MOOs are object-oriented MUDs, and whereas MUDs generally follow fixed gaming rules, MOOS are more open. Users can reconfigure the spaces of MOOs, creating new rooms, and make many more modifications—down to the level of coding. As Blair puts it, "MOOs are network-based tools for computer supported collaborative work (and play), which allow realtime intercommunication in a multi-room virtual space, as well as the sharing of network information resources."[26]

Waxweb has created a community of users, hybrid reader/writers participating in an ever-changing, and thus never finished, process of reception, creation, and broadcast. It offers a chance to participate in a process, not to reach a goal. The multiplatform *Johnny Mnemonic* text/paratext is not a process but a product—undifferentiated and blurred, to be sure, but a product all the same. *Waxweb* offers a very different vision of how narrative can function in an age of unfinish.

Unfinished Time

The "Unfinished Introduction" to this essay proposes that the third thread to be followed is time. But, to be honest, I am not finished with narrative.

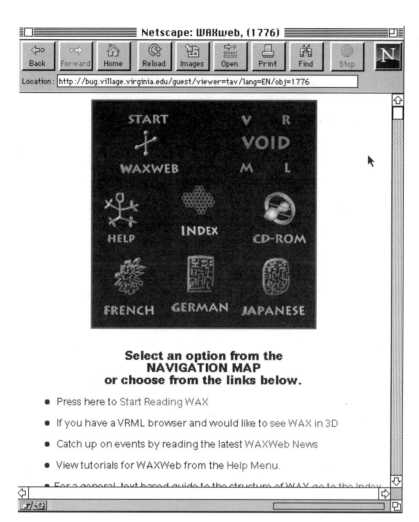

Netscape: WAXweb, (1776)

| Back | Forward | Home | Reload | Images | Open | Print | Find | Stop |

Location: http://bug.village.virginia.edu/guest/viewer=tav/lang=EN/obj=1776

START   V   R
               VOID
WAXWEB   M   L

HELP   INDEX   CD-ROM

FRENCH   GERMAN   JAPANESE

**Select an option from the
NAVIGATION MAP
or choose from the links below.**

- Press here to Start Reading WAX

- If you have a VRML browser and would like to see WAX in 3D

- Catch up on events by reading the latest WAXWeb News

- View tutorials for WAXWeb from the Help Menu.

- For a general, text based guide to the structure of WAX go to the Index

The opening screen of *WaxWeb*.
Courtesy of David Blair.

In fact, I cannot think about time without thinking about narrative. I am not the only one. Curator, author, and new media publisher Michael Nash notes: "The impulse to 'narratize' experience is endemic to the structure of consciousness and takes root from our mortality. Every heart has a fixed number of beats, and that absolute rhythm propels the story of our lives from one perception to another, linking units of meaning in a finitude so that all roads lead to where we are."[27]

I want to explore the linkage between narrative and time, and to look at how the shift in narrative toward an aesthetic of unfinish affects our sense of time, even our sense of death. Novelist Don DeLillo makes the connection explicit: "There is a tendency of plots to move towards death . . . the idea of death is built into the nature of every plot. A narrative plot is no less than a conspiracy of armed men. The tighter the plot of the story, the more likely it will come to death."[28] The question then becomes, Will loosening the plot—as the aesthetic of unfinish implies—affect this trajectory toward mortality?

Italian critic Carlo Levi offers this spin on the relationship between time, narrative, and mortality: "If every straight line is the shortest distance between two fated and inevitable points, digressions will lengthen it; and if these digressions become so complex, so tortuous, so rapid as to hide their own tracks, who knows—perhaps death may not find us, perhaps time will lose its way, and perhaps we ourselves can remain concealed in our shifting hiding places."[29]

It is this utopian dream that urges me to overcome my fears of unfinished business. So what will we have in an era of unfinished MOOs and ever-expanding narratives of communication? Will the final conflict be forever forestalled? Will we exist within a world of Scheherazades, always stretching out our stories for that one extra night of life? Technology does not develop independent of the rest of society, and is in fact inextricably bound up with its social context. And I have been watching with a certain fascination how the notion of unfinished time has been adopted by some of the farther reaches of digital communities.

The Incident: An International Symposium to Examine Art, Technology and Phenomena brings together artists and theorists interested in new media technology, and researchers and enthusiasts in areas such as UFOs, parapsychology, drugs, and dreams and other psychic and paratechnological explorations of human consciousness.[30] Regardless of one's feelings about any of these phenomena—and I am completely skeptical of all paranormal claims—a convergence like The Incident is wonderfully appropriate to the present millennial moment. I've long seen the UFO obsession as a projection of our dreams of the divine, its politics concerned with seizing the revealed wisdom of the higher powers from the government. Enough of Einstein has trickled down that space travel and time avoidance (if not full stabs at immortality) have become fully intertwined. The hopes that religion offers for life eternal have been augmented by the promises of digital technology—promises to make even the human spirit a part of the digital's unfinished time.

Marshall McLuhan once noted that "Today in the electric age we feel as free to invent nonlineal logics as we do to make non-Euclidean geometries,"[31] and I would add to this, free to invent nonlineal illogics. Look at the peculiar philosophies of Southern California's Extropians. This group, founded by Tom Morrow and Max More (then a graduate student in philosophy at the University of Southern California), is technopositive, with an unswerving belief in the ameliorabity of all human problems.[32] More and his group follow a program based on a concept they call extropy—the opposite of entropy—a refusal to accept the running down of the universe. One of their central beliefs is that eventually we will develop core memory technologies so sophisticated that we will be able to upload (their more positive and upbeat version of download) our consciousness into the ethereal realm of pure information, leaving our bodies behind and slipping from the clutches of death.

This is not far from the claims of alchemy, and if, as noted earlier, we take cybernetics to be the alchemical science of our age, it is worth exploring alchemy further. The Western variety of this protoscience has a twofold nature, one outward, or exoteric, the other hidden, or esoteric.[33] The exoteric nature of alchemy concerned finding the Philosopher's Stone that could transmute base metals into gold. The esoteric aspect of alchemy concerned the transformation of men's souls, stripping the impurities from them and enabling them to live far beyond their natural life spans. Alchemy, then, promises the unfinished life, and if it is an impossible promise, it is no less a productive one, for it forbids us to rule out anything—any idea, any movement, any space, any story. If this is truly to be an essay about unfinish, how can I end it? Impossible, but I choose to rest here.

Alchemical symbolism from the Ripley Scroll.
Courtesy of the Henry E. Huntington Library and Art Gallery.

2

The Cyberspace Dialectic

Michael Heim

Cyberspace floats now in a cultural limbo. The limbo is a zigzag holding pattern that professional philosophers call "the dialectic." This dialectic is a social fever characterized by wide mood swings between utopian fantasy and hateful cynicism. Hyperbole alternates with attack, and the status of cyberspace hovers uncertain: commercial jukebox? neodemocracy? the end of broadcasting? monster information swamp?

Cyberspace has always been provocative, but it has not always been controversial. The word, and the concepts it came to represent, burst on the scene like gangbusters in William Gibson's 1984 science-fiction novel *Neuromancer,* and then gained academic gravity in the early 1990s through conferences and books like Michael Benedikt's anthology, *Cyberspace: First Steps.*[1] Then in the mid 1990s, cyberspace became celebrated in daily newspapers and television spots, and the tenth edition (revised) of Merriam-Webster's *Collegiate Dictionary* confidently defined it as "the on-line world of computer networks." Politicians sought to extend legislative power over "the information highway" by dredging up on-line obscenities, pursuing hacker felons, and declaring cyberspace a federal "superhighway" where the speed of telecommunication would fall under congressional jurisdiction. Today, naïve questions like What is it? and How do I connect to it? have evolved into trickier questions like Am I for or against cyberspace? What position do I take regarding its social benefits? Now that we have crossed the electronic frontier, how does our society measure cyberspace? This is where most of us could learn from the dialectic.

Originally, the word circulated among the ancient Greeks, who used *dialektikē (tekhnē)* to mean the art of debate and conversation. *Dialegesthai* means "talking something through" or "organizing a subject matter." In other words, transformational dynamics first appeared as part of the art of conversation. The ancient Greeks gave dialectic its classical expression in written dialogues. There, in the Greek language, the word "dialectic" was born, and its twin sibling was the word "dialogue."

Jumping ahead several millennia, the idea of dialectic in modern times has come, through G. F. W. Hegel and Karl Marx, to signify the transformational dynamics of social history. Hegel developed his notion of the dialectic to include the back-and-forth process of social movements where one advance in freedom evokes its opposite reaction, which in turn calls forth another and opposite reaction, and so forth. Dialectic was not simply an abstract template of "thesis-antithesis-synthesis" to be applied in a doctrinaire manner to politics. Dialectic was, rather, the concrete movement of social history itself. Marx, the next signpost in the development of the dialectic, identified history with the history of civil wars and violent revolutions, but Hegel's dialectic originally included the more subtle shifting forces of social change that propel human evolution.

In those systems that adopted Marx's philosophy, the dialectic became the cornerstone of official ideology. In the Soviet Union, for example, millions of students in Communist schools carried textbooks bearing the stamp "DIAMAT," short for "Dialectical Materialism." The dialectic in its Marxist–Leninist form belonged to materialistic philosophy as a rigid set of doctrines defining the socioeconomic struggle between capital and labor. The straight party line of communism largely eroded the original meaning of "dialectic" as a term to describe historical dynamics. This was particularly ironic, for, as we have seen, dialectic resists stability, finding its form in the unsettling, the changing, the shifting.

Both historical and critical discussion of the dialectic runs through this paper, but it is important to acknowledge that the present taint of the word "dialectic" is due to its centrality to Marxist thought and policies. As a result, many people automatically recoil against dialectic and fail to see its usefulness in weighing the new reality layer. It is true that networked computer media have launched an information space that ill befits the materialistic mold of Marxism, based as it was in the reading of early industrial capitalism. I believe, nonetheless, that we can still use dialectic as a tool to move beyond the polarity of fear and fascination that characterizes the continuum binding the fans of the antitechnology Unabomber to the millions who use computers to surf the Internet.

The dialectic I have in mind is that which preceded Marxism and can be clearly described. I want to show that dialectic can indeed illuminate the paradoxes of the current debate about the value of cyberspace. Though bound by an underlying ontology, the dialectic can still illuminate the confusion and tension created by new media. There is something of the joke or paradox that propels all dialectical thinking. We live in a most appropriate era to savor the dialectical joke. An appropriate joke, indeed, for an era when people express their support for anarchist-inspired attacks on technology by posting messages to the World Wide Web.

Unabomber Backlash

The figure of the Unabomber (and the concerns he came to represent) is one side of the cyberspace dialectic.[2] An extreme provokes the full force of its opposite. To be sure, the Unabomber's fervor cannot be understood in isolation from the one-sided enthusiasm that pervades a commercial culture that sells millions of computers every year. The Unabomber's extremism became clear to the public in September 1995, when the *Washington Post* published his 56-page, 35,000-word manifesto, "Industrial Society and Its Future."[3] Under the pressure of bomb threats against airline passengers, the newspaper carried the manifesto in its morning edition. By evening on the East Coast, you could not find a single copy of the *Post* with its 8-page manifesto insert. The next day, however, the 200-kilobyte text of the manifesto turned up on the Internet. It appeared on a World Wide Web site sponsored by the Federal Bureau of Investigation. Desperate to be published, the Unabomber now had his own "home page," illustrated with "wanted" posters and maps pinpointing the series of explosions he had caused, all in a high-tech, HTML format.

Search the Unabomber Manifesto and you find the word "computer" frequently used in conjunction with "control" and "technology." The serial bomber blames technology, especially computers, for a vast variety of social ills: the invasion of privacy, genetic engineering, and "environmental degradation through excessive economic growth." The Unabomber Manifesto borrows from an older school of social critics who followed the French writer Jacques Ellul. Ellul's *Technological Society,* a bible in the 1960s, demonized an all-pervasive technology monster lurking beneath the "technological-industrial system."[4] Ellul took a snapshot of technology in the 1960s, then projected and expanded that single frozen moment in time onto a future where he envisioned widespread social destruction. Ellul's approach—what economists and futurists call "linear trend extrapolation"— takes into account neither social evolution nor economic transformation. Ellul did not take into account the possibility that economies of scale could develop that would redistribute certain forms of technological power, allowing individuals, for instance, to run personal computers from domestic spaces and, in turn, publish content on an equal footing with large corporations.

The dark future portrayed by Ellul appears throughout the Unabomber Manifesto, but the Unabomber goes further by linking the technology

Police sketch of the Unabomber, hooded and wearing aviator sunglasses.
Courtesy of the Federal Bureau of Investigation.

Michael Heim

threat explicitly to computers. This killer–critic sees computers as instruments of control to oppress human beings either by putting them out of work or by altering how they work. The manifesto states:

It is certain that technology is creating for human beings a new physical and social environment radically different from the spectrum of environments to which natural selection has adapted the human race physically and psychologically. If man does not adjust to this new environment by being artificially re-engineered, then he will be adapted to it through a long and painful process of natural selection. The former is far more likely than the latter.[5]

The dilemma outlined by the Unabomber can be found in writings of other extremist critics. Many share the Unabomber's views without harboring his pathological desperation. The no-win dilemma they see is either to permit evolution to wreck millions of lives or to use technology to forcibly reengineer the population. Laissez-faire evolution or artificial engineering seem to be the sole options: Either manipulate humans to fit technology, or watch technology bulldoze the population until all that remains is a techno-humanoid species of mutants. The Ellul school of criticism posits a monolithic steamroller "technology" that flattens every activity, and the Ellulian view allows only a static fit between technology and society. Recent alumni of this school, like Jean Baudrillard, nationalize the alien technology monster and call it "Americanization."[6] They fear the ghostly "representations of representations" that inject Disneylike simulacra into every facet of cultural life. Cultural life floats on a thin sea of representations that represent other representations whose active content has been exploited until they are empty images without meaning.

We need not look outside the borders of the United States, of course, to find antitechnological, Luddite theory. The Unabomber Manifesto reveals concerns raised by American critics. Some authors—Kirkpatrick Sale, for instance—felt compelled to distance themselves from the Unabomber Manifesto because they in fact use many of the same arguments to reject technology and they share with the Unabomber some common critical sources like Ellul. While agreeing in principle with what the Unabomber says, they want to distance themselves from terrorist practices. Such critics grew in numbers during the early 1990s, when information technology extended

Kirkpatrick Sale smashing a computer.
© Neil Selkirk for *Wired*.

into every area of life, spawning a multimedia industry and virtual reality companies. Computer networks like the Internet came into general use in the early 1990s, and economic forecasts indicated that the computerized infrastructure was transforming the national economy as well as the American culture. Not surprisingly, critics took a look.

The computer's impact on culture and the economy mutated from a celebration into what I call the cyberspace backlash. A cultural pendulum swings back and forth, both feeding off and being fed to a sensation-hungry media.[7] The media glom onto hype and overstatement culled from marketers and true believers. When the media assess the technoculture, a trend climbs in six months from obscurity to one of the Five Big Things—complete with magazine covers, front-page coverage in newspapers, and those few minutes on television that now constitute the ultimate in mass appeal. After the buildup, the backlash begins. The process is as follows: (1) simplify an issue; (2) exaggerate what was simplified; (3) savage the inadequacies of the simplification. Cyberspace was no exception, and the reverse swing against cyberspace was inevitable.

The backlash is not simply the product of a fevered media economy; it taps into people's real attitudes toward an ever more technologized culture. This runs from those who are frustrated by the frequent need to upgrade software to those who experience "future shock" as a personal, existential jolt. While futurologists Alvin and Heidi Toffler preach "global trends" from an economist's overview, the individual suffers painful personal changes in the workplace and the marketplace. Waves of future shock may intrigue forward-looking policy makers, but those same swells look scary to someone scanning the horizon from a plastic board adrift in the ocean. The big picture of evolutionary trends often overwhelms and silences the personal pain of living people. Those people will eventually find their voices in a backlash against the confident soothsayers in business suits.

A streak of the Unabomber's Luddite passion weaves through the cyberspace backlash. The titles of several books published in the past few years give a glimpse of the breadth of the backlash. Among the books are *Resisting the Virtual Life,* by James Brook and Iain Boal; *Rebels Against the Future: The Luddites and Their War on the Industrial Revolution,* by Kirkpatrick Sale; *Silicon Snake Oil: Second Thoughts on the Information Highway,* by Clifford Stoll; *The Age of Missing Information,* by Bill McKibben; *The Gutenberg Elegies,* by Sven

Birkerts; *War of the Worlds: Cyberspace and the High-Tech Assault on Reality,* by Mark Slouka; and *The Future Does Not Compute,* by Steve Talbott. Obviously, these books show infinitely more grace than the Unabomber's crude, coercive manifestos, but they all reject, to varying degrees, the movement of life into electronic environments.[8]

These critics tend toward what I call "naïve realism." Many naïve realists take reality to be that which can be immediately experienced, and they align computer systems with the corporate polluters who dump on the terrain of unmediated experience. The elaborate data systems we are developing still exist outside our primary sensory world. The systems do not belong to reality but constitute instead, in the eyes of the naïve realist, a suppression of reality. The suppression comes through "the media," which are seen to function as vast, hegemonic corporate structures that systematically collect, edit, and broadcast packaged experience. The media infiltrate and distort non-mediated experience, compromising and confounding the immediacy of experience. Computers accelerate the process of data gathering and threaten further, in their eyes, what little remains of pure, immediate experience. The naïve realist believes that genuine experience is as endangered as clean air and unpolluted water.

The purity of experience was defended by the New England transcendentalists in the nineteenth-century. Thinkers like Henry David Thoreau, backed by the publicity skills of Ralph Waldo Emerson, proclaimed a return to pure, unmediated experience.[9] Thoreau left city life to spend weeks in a rustic cabin in the woods at Walden Pond, near Concord, Massachusetts, so he could "confront the essential facts of life." Far from the social and industrial hubbub, he spent two years contemplating the evils of railroads and industrialization. Although railroad tracks and freeways now circumscribe Walden Pond, many contemporary critics, such as Wendell Berry, seek to revive the Thoreauvian back-to-nature ethic and take up the cause represented by his Walden retreat.[10]

In the eyes of the naïve realist, computer networks add unnecessary frills to the real world while draining blood from real life. Reality, they assert, is the physical phenomena we perceive with our bodily senses: what we see directly with our eyes, smell with our noses, hear with our ears, taste with our tongues, and touch with our own skin. From the standpoint of this empirically perceived sensuous world, the computer system is at best a tool, at worst a mirage of distracting abstractions from the real world. The mountains, rivers, and great planet beneath our feet existed long before computers, and the naïve realist sees in the computer an alien intruder defiling God's pristine earth. The computer, say the naïve realists, should remain a carefully guarded tool, if indeed we allow computers to continue to exist. The computer is a subordinate device that tends to withdraw us from the primary world. We can and should, if the computer enervates us, pull the plug or even destroy the computer.

The naïve realist speaks from fear. There is fear of abandoning local community values as we move into a cyberspace of global communities. There is fear of diminishing physical closeness and mutual interdependence as electronic networks mediate more and more activities. There is fear of crushing the spirit by replacing bodily movement with smart objects and robotic machines. There is fear of losing the autonomy of our private bodies as we depend increasingly on chip-based implants. There is fear of compromising integrity of mind as we habitually plug into networks. There is fear that our own human regenerative process is slipping away as genetics transmutes organic life into manageable strings of information. There is fear of the sweeping changes in the workplace and in public life as we have known them. There is fear of the empty human absence that comes with increased telepresence. There is fear that the same power elite who formerly "moved atoms" as they pursued a science without conscience will now "move bits" that govern the computerized world. By voicing such fears, the naïve realist sounds alarms that contrast sharply with the idealistic good cheer of futurists like Alvin and Heidi Toffler.

Naïve Realists vs. Network Idealists

Futurists describe and advise a culture shaken by future shock. But the shock they describe comes in macroeconomic waves, not in personal, existential distress. In this sense, futurists like the Tofflers are idealists. Idealists take the measure of individuals by placing them within the larger economic or political contexts to which they belong. Most futurists look to the economically and politically global, not to the individually existential. Their big idea absorbs individuals. The "digerati" celebrated by *Wired* magazine welcome the digital revolution and offer a central warning: you had better join soon, or be crushed by the wheels of history. Many of the celebrated digerati come from institutions of technology that are dedicated to advancing the cybernetic control systems of society. Such institutions came to prominence not by educating through the liberal arts but by subordinating education to the advancement of government-sponsored technical research. When Alvin Toffler writes about a "powershift," he uses a prophetic style that underlines the assumptions of the power group to which his futurist rhetoric belongs.[11] Drowning the individual in the "waves" of social development has been a consistent theme in the history of idealism, from the conservative F. H. Bradley in England to the liberal-monarchic idealism of Hegel in Germany.[12]

Such idealism goes back to the early pioneers of computing. Seventeenth-century rationalists like Gottfried W. Leibniz and René Descartes pushed computation and mathematical physics far ahead of ethics and feelings. The Cartesian revolution in philosophy put mathematical physics at the top of the list of priorities while ethics became the incidental victim of skeptical reasoning. The Cartesian faith in progress relied on the reduction of thinking to systems of rational logic. So great was the optimism of seventeenth-century rationalists that they became easy targets for satirists like Voltaire, the French philosopher and writer whose works epitomize the Age of Enlightenment. In his novel *Candide* (1759), Voltaire caricatured Leibniz in the character of Professor Pangloss. Pangloss's tortured young student Candide meditates: "My Master said, 'There is a sweetness in every woe.' It must be so. It must be so."[13]

The idealist points to evolutionary gains for the species and glosses over the personal sufferings of individuals. Idealists are optimists, or, on bad days, they are happy worriers. The optimist says, "This is the best of all possible worlds, and even the pain is a necessary component." In the eyes of naïve realists, the idealist is selling snake oil. No accident that Leibniz, who was caricatured in Pangloss, was the same Leibniz who worked on the protocomputer and pioneered the binary logic that was to become the basis for computers and digital culture.

The cyberspace backlash strikes at idealistic–futurist flimflam as much as it reacts to felt personal–existential changes. Postmodern theory, with its often glib talk of "cyborgs," "software cities," and "virtual communities," provokes its opponents by flashing a brand of intellectually sophisticated terror. Postmodern rhetoric, lacking a compassionate basis in shared experience and common practices, aims to frighten the insecure and to train commandos who attack common sense. After all, linguistics, semiology, and structuralism combined to make it virtually impossible to see language as anything but a code or system, never as a living event through which we are all responsible to one another. Since Ferdinand de Saussure, the communicative power of language, its ability to build community, has become suspect to the point of ridicule for sophisticated theoreticians.[14]

And what of those who ignore the theoreticians and insist on building a community around the new words, the new structures thrown up by the computer's wake? There is, of course, a certain jaded idealism that also enjoys poking common sense in the eye with hot purple hair, revolutionary verbiage, and cyberpunk affectations. A cybervocabulary promotes confusion as a fashion statement. Wave the banner of confusion, however, and you provoke a return to basics. Naïveté then seems a blessing. Yet the dialectical story does not end so simply, because the futurist vision is not without cogency. What the futurist sees is precisely what frightens others.

Nerds in the Noosphere

The futurist sees the planet Earth converging. Computer networks foster virtual communities that cut across geography and time zones. Virtual community seems a cure-all for isolated people who complain about their isolation. Locked in metal boxes on urban freeways, a population enjoys socializing with fellow humans through computer networks. Shopping, learning, and business are not far away once we enhance our telepresence abilities. The prospect seems so exciting that you see the phrase "virtual communities" mentioned in the same breath as McLuhan's "global village" or Teilhard's "Omega Point."

Pierre Teilhard de Chardin, a French Jesuit paleontologist, envisioned the convergence of humans into a single massive "noosphere" or "mind sphere" (Ionian Greek *noos,* "mind").[15] This giant network would surround Earth to control the planet's resources and shepherd a world unified by Love. Teilhard's catholic vision ranged from evolutionary physics to world religion (though his views received more suspicion than support from Church orthodoxy). He saw in the physical world an inner drive for all substance to converge into increasingly complex units. Material atoms merge to create higher-level units. Matter eventually converges to form organisms. The convergence of organic life in turn produces higher-level complexities. The most complex units establish a new qualitative dimension where consciousness emerges. On the conscious level, the mind—and then the networking of minds—gives birth to a new stage of spirit.

As in Hegel's nineteenth-century philosophy, Teilhard sees the birth of spirit as the inner meaning or cosmic purpose of the entire preceding evolution. Convergence toward greater complexity, even on the subatomic material level, exemplifies the principle of Love (agapic rather than erotic love). Only later, with the dawn of intelligence, does Love come into full consciousness and self-awareness. For Teilhard, this is the Christ principle that guides the universe. "In the beginning was the Logos." Only at its culminating point does history reveal its full meaning as the mental sphere becomes dominant. Teilhardians see ultimate convergence as the Omega or EndPoint of time, the equivalent of the Final Coming of Christ.

Teilhard, like Marx before him, absorbed much about evolutionary dynamics from Hegel, the father of German idealism. Hegel's centrality to the discourse of Western philosophy is such that his work on the dialectic deserves another telling in this context. Hegel applied the Christian notion of Divine Providence to the recorded events of civilized history in order to show a rational progression. His elaborate encyclopedias and multivolume histories of Western civilization affirmed a hidden evolutionary will driving with purpose toward a single culmination. The fulfillment of history, according to Hegel, was a unity harmonized in diversity, a oneness that later interpreters described as a "classless society" (as with Marx) or as "social progress" (as with William Torrey Harris and the American Hegelians).[16]

Hegel's genius was to see a divine Idea unfold in the material world of historical events—even to the point of squeezing all recorded history into a Procrustean logic of progress. The famous "Hegelian dialectic" changed from its original meaning of logical conversation to its new meaning of social movements and improvements. The motor that powered the movement of history was a series of internal civil wars, each bringing the entire society a little closer to perfection. The culmination of all revolutions, for Hegel, produced Western constitutional democracies where the individual and the individual's rights are recognized by the social collective. Just what this heavenly harmony looks like in practice appeared differently to the various proponents of Hegelian idealism. While Marx's advocates dressed in the worker's garb of political economy or in the revolutionary's guerrilla fatigues, Teilhard's vision blended synthetic physics with Christian communitarianism. It is especially the communitarianism that attracts network idealists.

This link between the communitarian impulse and the cult of technology may seem incongruous at first glance, but we must not forget that the organized, durational community is itself a by-product of agricultural technology, of the development of machines. At first, and for millennia, machines functioned as stand-alone tools under supervision of a single human operator—the hoe, the plow. With larger-scale projects and manufacturing, machines increasingly functioned in an ensemble—the mill, the boatyard. The shift from isolated work tools to the components of larger systems became one of the defining characteristics of the industrial era, with railroads, fuel distribution, and highway systems being the obvious examples. The interconnection of one machine with another extended into the sphere of human society and cultural production with networks: first radio, then television, and now computers. The recent convergence of all three media has created a situation in which a vast variety of machines plug into seemingly limitless networks, all with the computer as the controller switch.

The network idealist builds collective beehives. The idealist sees the next century as an enormous communitarian buzz. The worldwide networks that cover the planet form a global beehive where civilization shakes off individual controls and electronic life steps out on its own. In that networked world, information circulates freely through the planetary nervous system, and intellectual property vanishes as a concept. Individuals give and take freely. Compensation is automated for the heavenly, disembodied life. Electronic angels distribute credit. Private territory and material possessions no longer divide people. Digital mediation does away with the battle of the books, and proprietary ideas give way to free exchange and barter. Cooperative intelligence vanquishes private minds. Extropian idealists (who define themselves as the enemies of entropy) encourage their members to entrust their deceased bodies to cryonic storage until scientists can one day either revive the repaired body or upload the brain-encased mind into silicon chips. The Teilhardian Internet is optimism gone ballistic.

Realists remain unimpressed. They are uneasy with the idealists who celebrate an electronic collective. I know people in rural communities who hear wishful thinking in the phrase "virtual community." It sticks in their craw. For many, real community means a difficult, never-resolved struggle. It is a sharing that cannot be virtual because its reality arises from the public places that people share physically—not the artificial configurations you choose but the spaces that fate allots, complete with the idiosyncrasies of local weather and a mixed bag of family, friends, and neighbors. For many, the "as-if community" lacks the rough interdependence of life shared. And here is where the naïve realist draws the line. The direct, unmediated spaces we perceive with our senses create the places where we mature physically, morally, and socially. Even if modern life shrinks public spaces by building freeways, and even if the "collective mind" still offers much interaction among individuals through computers, the traditional meeting places still foster social bonds built on patience and on the trust of time spent together. Here is the bottom line for realists.

No surprise, then, for realists when they hear the Internet Liberation Front is bringing down the Internet's pipeline for six hours, when anti-Semitic hate groups pop up on Prodigy, when *Wired* magazine gets letter-bombed, or when neo-Nazis work their way into the German Thule Network. The utopian *communitas* exists as an imagined community, as the Mystical Body. Real community exists, on the contrary, where people throw their lot together and stand in face-to-face ethical proximity. Computer hardware may eventually allow us to transport our cyberbodies, but we are just learning to appreciate the trade-offs between primary and virtual identities. Put the New Jerusalem on hold until we phone security.

Reclaiming the Idea of Dialectic

Both network idealism and naïve realism belong to the cyberspace dialectic. They are two sides of the same coin, binary brothers. One launches forth with unreserved optimism; the other lashes back with a longing to ground us outside technology. Some enthusiastically embrace the commercial development of the Internet, while others vehemently oppose it. While everyone agrees that information technology is transforming postmodern society, not everyone agrees that we can make any sense out of the transformation at the present moment. A third group insists that cyberspace is going through a confusing birth process, like every other important earlier technology, and they believe that all attempts at understanding the process, no matter how intelligent, remain pointless. This third group regards the cyberspace dialectic as irrational guesswork and hyperbole. All bets are off, as far as they are concerned. They support their skepticism by pointing to the histories of other media, like television and film, illustrating their viewpoint with the scribblings of critics of yore who attacked prior technologies but whose screeds are now amusing because they failed utterly to understand how the future would choose to use the technology.[17] This skeptical view results in a let's-wait-and-see attitude because rational criticism has, according to this view, never worked in the past. Such skepticism kills dialectic by rejecting social evaluation as baseless futurism.

Skepticism cannot guide us through a dialectical situation. We must make some sense of the future as we make decisions in the present. Cyberspace is contested territory, and those who reject the contest will not meet the challenge of the present. The battle between the telecommunications legislators and the Electronic Frontier Foundation confirms the fact that cyberspace is contested territory.[18] The cultural struggle over cyberspace signals the need to rethink dialectic so that we can enter it properly.

The cyberspace debate reveals a subtle groundswell presaging the pulse of the next century. Some historians, in fact, gauge the twentieth century as one of the shorter centuries, one of those epochs that ends before its official centennial birthday. They mark the end of the twentieth century with the 1989 fall of the Berlin Wall. Many historians count the advent of personal computers and worldwide information systems among the causative factors leading to the overthrow of Marxism–Leninism and the changes in world history that are ushering in the twenty-first century.

If Marxism has expired as a political and economic model, its characteristic dialectic has evinced an intellectual afterlife in the work of German-influenced French thinkers and their American disciples. From structuralism to semiotics to hermeneutics to poststructuralism and deconstruction, the dialectic of Marxism persists as an unspoken model of how correct-thinking and postmodern people should regard society. Critical theory has often been just another name for Marxian analysis incognito. Through virtuoso verbalism, critical theory often refuses to submit its covert social assumptions to clear argumentation. Earlier variants—the Frankfurt School with Max Horkheimer and Theodor Adorno's "negative dialectics,"[19] and Jürgen Habermas's theory of ideal communication[20]—were willing and able to address their Marxian roots. When Horkheimer and Adorno spelled out what they called the "dialectic of the Enlightenment," or Herbert Marcuse continued their work by advocating the "No" or Great Refusal ("drop out") in the face of the industrial–technological system, they were engaged in an avowedly Marxian critique of the West's capitalist society.[21] But the obscurantism of recent French theory conceals under its narcotic smoke screen a whole host of Marxist assumptions about social revolution that do not spell their meaning clearly in this era of information.[22] We need to know more explicitly what kind of dialectic we move in, if we are moving in a dialectic at all. Once the dialectic no longer swings between the socially oppressed and the power of big capital, we must ask where and how dialectic comes into play. If our social developments begin to manifest outside the mode of material production, what does the mode of information mean for social change?

We keep returning to the same core questions: What is dialectic? How does the dialectic apply to the struggle over cyberspace? While we definitely need to recognize the cyberspace dialectic, we do not want a replay of the violent civil wars that attach to Marxist dialectical materialism. Perhaps we need to return to the earliest incarnation of the dialectic, starting with its appearance in the *Dialogues of Plato,* which are actually the dialogues of Socrates written down and polished by Plato (with "dialogue" having its root in the Greek *dia logou,* "through words or argument"). The dialectic—the "working through words or argument" of the *dialegesthai*—was an integral part of Plato's *Dialogues.* Dialectic refers to the logical side of what occurs in the *Dialogues.* Dialectic emphasizes the oppositions found within dialogue. Dialogues between people achieve more than mutual recognition and shared feelings; dialogues also expose conceptual and attitudinal differences as they apply to the issues under consideration. The interplay of differences about issues constitutes the original meaning of dialectic. It is this meaning of dialectic—an ongoing exchange between polar positions—that I wish to emphasize for and in cyberspace.

You could say, then, that dialectic is the conceptual exchange that happens in dialogue. Dialogues can contain banter, jokes, irony, and shared feelings, but any serious, sustained dialogue will sooner or later reveal a dialectic in play. Dialectic is the inner logic of differences exposed over an extended period of interchange. We should not, in other words, associate dialectic exclusively with conflict and flat-out contradiction. Dialectic comes from human differences as they become articulate—not from the confrontation that breeds revolution and civil war. What more fitting support to dialectic could we have than the technological medium we call cyberspace?

Hegel would have appreciated a mutual opposition while betting on an eventual synthesis. Right now, a cyberspace synthesis is not in sight, certainly not in the near future. But a collision or the collapse of one of the sides may not be the only end point to look for. We may have to learn to live with the dialectic as the art of permanent exchange. We might learn to balance the idealist's enthusiasm for computerized life with the need to ground ourselves more deeply in the felt earth that the realist affirms to be our primary reality. This uneasy balance I have elsewhere called "virtual realism."[23] Virtual realism is the middle path between naïve realism and network idealism. On the middle path, the dialectic becomes electric. The cyberspace dialectic sustains opposition as the polarity that continually sparks the dialogue, and the dialogue is the life of cyberspace.

Virtual Realism

Virtual realism walks a tightrope. The delicate balancing act sways between the idealism of unstoppable Progress and the Luddite resistance to virtual life. The Luddite falls out of sync with the powerful human push that has been promoting rationality for three centuries, and that now seems ready either to blossom or to blow up in the next century. The idealist falls for the Progress of tools without content, of productivity without satisfaction, of ethereal connections without corporeal discipline. Both inclinations—naïve realism and futurist idealism—belong to the current of our time. The long, thin rope stretches across the chasm of change and permits no return. Indifferent standstill is even more dangerous. The challenge is not to end the oscillation between idealism and realism but to find the path that goes through them. It is not a synthesis in the Hegelian sense of a result achieved through logic. Neither is it a synthesis arising from the warfare of the two sides. Rather, virtual realism is an existential process of criticism, practice, and conscious communication.

What is the path of virtual realism? Virtual realism parts with realism pure and simple. Realism often means lowered expectations. "Being realistic" often implies reducing or compromising ideals. Historically, in fact, realism often follows periods of high idealism. The pendulum swings back because it had swung so high in the first place. No movement of history begins, however, without an initial affirmation, without a first postulate affirming that it has cleared the mist and found reality. Realism begins as a sober criticism of overblown, high-flown ideals. Yet at the core of realism is an affirmation of what is real, reliable, functional. Today we must be realistic about virtual reality, untiringly suspicious of the airy idealism and commercialism surrounding it, and we must keep an eye on the weeds of fiction and fantasy that threaten to stifle the blossom.

At the same time, we have to affirm those entities that virtual reality presents as our culture begins to inhabit cyberspace.[24] Virtual entities are indeed real, functional, and even central to life in coming eras. Part of work and leisure life will transpire in virtual environments. Thus it is important to find a balance that swings neither to the idealistic blue sky where primary reality disappears, nor to the mundane indifference that sees just another tool, something that can be picked up or put down at will. The balancing act requires a view of life as a mixed bag, as a series of trade-offs that we must discern and then evaluate. Balancing means walking a pragmatic path of involvement and critical perception.

In *Electric Language: A Philosophical Study of Word Processing,* I developed a theory of cultural trade-offs as they happen during ontological shifts.[25] There I describe in detail the trade-offs between the computerized and the traditional ways of doing things. For *Electric Language,* this meant the specific trade-offs between electronic and printed texts. The method used was phenomenology, a way of describing the first-person modes in which we read and write, specifically to contrast reading and writing with computers and with traditional books. Such descriptions highlight the psychic frameworks of two very different modes of reading and writing—not from the viewpoint of economic, or social, or legal products but from the viewpoint of living through the activity itself.

These trade-offs belong to what I called "the ontological shift." This ontological shift has been referred to by others in shorthand as a move from "managing atoms to managing bits." But I would argue against this pat reduction. Our practical use of symbols never did move in the element of atoms, for atoms are scientific abstractions. The abstractions of science about the atomic level have, of course, had an enormous impact on history, but that impact came not from a change at the core of culture but from the pressure that bore down on the surface of politics, warfare, and energy production. Culture took the atomic age into account only slowly. Atoms are abstractions, just as bits and bytes are abstractions. But while bits and bytes abstract from a computational process, they touch information, and information reaches to the core of culture.

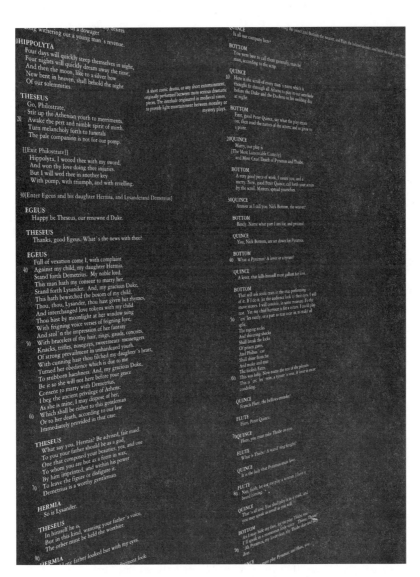

Electronic text: David Small's *Virtual Shakespeare*.
Courtesy of David Small, MIT Media Lab.

The ontological shift described in *Electric Language* occurs in what I called "the tectonic plates of culture," the unnoticed cultural element that supports—at different times, in different ways—the symbols of language. No longer papyrus or paper, the new element is digital information. The element belongs to the psychic framework of life, not to the abstractions of physics or the sciences. The symbol element is where much of practical culture transpires. It is where we store our memory, where we record our history, and where the sacred things are preserved. Most important to virtual realism is the sense of history behind the ontological shift. We need the large perspective on cultural change and the way symbolic elements mutate in history. The big picture is crucial for virtual realism, for only from that broad perspective can we envision the trade-offs that occur in historical drift.[26]

An important component of virtual realism is what I call *technalysis*. Technalysis—as the term suggests—is the analysis of technologies, and the analysis proceeds from a critical but practical standpoint. It is a critical strategy for describing specific technologies, a style of thinking appropriate for walking the fissures of a culture in transition. Technalysis accepts the ontological fact that we move in a new layer of electronic reality. In the technologized West, fewer and fewer discussions or oppositions occur without leaving traces in cyberspace. Today, the Unabomber's fans as well as the network idealists meet on-line. The dialectic of cyberspace is happening *in cyberspace*. This dialectic, if sustained, can become technalysis, a new kind of social self-awareness.

Whether right or wrong in its conclusions, each attempt at technalysis brings to language the human encounter with specific technologies. Detailed analysis of specific technologies has major advantages over the wholesale rejection of technology found in writers from Ellul and Baudrillard to the Unabomber. The wholesale suspicion of technology as a monstrous Leviathan supposes that we can extricate ourselves sufficiently from automobiles, telephones, and computers in order to arrive at a negative assessment and eventual disengagement. The suspicion directs its gaze at a monster whose features must remain vague and remote. Fear of the giant technology monster blinds the critic to detail in daily life as we install technologies and as we install ourselves in technological environments. Blind to details, such critics close off the possibility that their analysis might contribute something of value to the concrete planning of future systems. Instead, they must maintain a posture of hostility—a posture that requires considerable effort but delivers no constructive dividend.

The advantage of technalysis—the detailed phenomenology of specific technologies—resides in its working alongside "human factors" engineering, which, however remote from its participants, places the human being at the center of technology.

Virtual realism, then, seeks to support the cyberspace dialectic as an ongoing exchange, as a mutual penetration of the opposite poles of discussion. Virtual realism meets destiny without being blind to the losses of progress. It strives to enrich the unfolding future from a personal standpoint by referring to moments when we have been at our best. It explores the need to ground ourselves in the earth, not naïvely, but in a way that draws on the growing knowledge we are obtaining from a global garden of human practices, from the body energy cultivation of Taoism and yoga to the new green therapy that insists on our spending time outdoors. As we look beyond alphabetic writing, increasingly away from symbolic processes and toward virtualized processes, our path must be one of virtual realism.

The Ethical Life of the Digital Aesthetic

Carol Gigliotti

In these final years of the twentieth century, the aesthetics of the digital realm are playing a large role in determining the future of our ethical life. The extravagance of this theoretical claim appears to be supported by, among many other practical examples, the ferocity of current debates over pornography on the Internet. Should there or should there not be pornography on the Internet? The arguments gravitate toward two opposite poles. Yes, because any kind of censorship in this new communication medium implicates its exploitation by the powers that be. No, because it offers easily to children what should be available only to adults desiring it. Yes, because with the advent of software programs developed to block children's access to material on the Net found to be offensive by their parents, the danger of children coming into contact with such material is minimized. No, because the real issue is the damage to the identity of women and children that this new medium for distribution will perpetuate. The argument goes on and on until the child, over whom this volley of positives and negatives is being hurled, walks to the nearest television set and turns on a talk show about teenage girls who have been molested by their stepfathers.

The problematic environment surrounding attempts to answer such questions attests to both the necessity and the difficulty of working out this culture's contradictory relationship with the assumptions about the content of the conflict, as well as the method by which the conflict is put forward, the manner in which it is engaged, and in what way possible solutions are engendered and practiced. Whether pornography should be permitted on the Internet is akin to asking if laboratory animals should or should not have their cages cleaned. Assumptions about the content of the question, coupled with the contrapositional framing of the question, encourage catastrophically unhelpful answers. In the case of laboratory animals, posing the problem in this way only obscures deeper ethical questions concerning our relationship with animals and confounds the possibilities for knowledge offered by the involvement in answering those questions.

In a similar way, focusing only on whether or not pornography has a place on the Internet obscures deeper ethical questions concerning this culture's conflicted relationship with its own physical nature. In fact, the relationship between pornography and the use of animals for research has been undergoing a thorough investigation by feminist theorists.[1] From Aristotle on, rationality—thought to be absent or minimally present in women, along with nonwhite males and animals—has been the defining characteristic of those

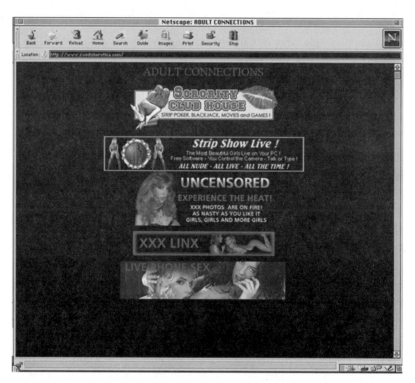

Web pornography's ubiquitous banner advertisements.

deserving of moral consideration. The underlying justifications, whether conscious or unconscious, for both pornography and the use of animals in experimentation can be traced at least to a definitive historic perspective in this way. The more deeply rooted somatic reasons for the need for such a justification deserve even more sustained investigation, as some, though admittedly few, theorists have attempted.[2]

Modeling this kind of in-depth inquiry offers a more productive approach to questioning the assumptions inherent in the polarization of views most often put forth concerning pornography on the Internet. As we look more carefully at the four arguments representing particular polarized positions, intrinsic relationships among them begin to emerge. The first position, that any kind of censorship in this new communication medium implicates its exploitation by the powers that be, brings to mind questions such as What are the goals of the powers that might be said to exploit the distributive power of the Internet? Do these goals for the growth and direction of the Internet differ from those of individuals or groups who consider themselves to be without power, and if so, how? Do groups and communities having access to the Internet fall into only two categories, having and not having power, or is there a continuum of power along which they might reside? What about those groups who have no access to the Internet? Are any of these groups' goals only economically based, or are they vehicles for a social and cultural environment in which various segments of the population would find themselves more or less privileged? Is it possible to separate economic, social, and cultural goals for the development of the Internet and still make them viable? What would be the benefits of doing that?

The second position, that pornography should be kept off the Internet because it offers easily to children what should only be available to adults who desire it, brings forth related questions of access and power. Assumptions about the rights of children, or rather their lack of rights, are evident in an argument that hopes to curtail the content of what is accessible to adults on the Internet, based on what other adults believe should not be available to children.

The third position, advocating the use of software programs developed to block children's access to material on the Net found to be offensive by their parents, and seemingly a contrasting argument, actually blends into the first. It mirrors the second position's assumption of the lack of the rights of children to be involved in decision-making influencing their life. Jon Katz, however, sees the use of such software as a false security: "Blocking deprives children of the opportunity to confront the realities of new culture: some of it is pornographic, violent, occasionally even dangerous. They need to master those situations in a rational, supervised way to learn how to truly protect themselves."[3] Katz's approach is more helpful, in that it focuses on questioning the goals of those on both sides of the argument. Are we interested in bringing up responsible people who are able to choose for themselves, or is our primary interest free speech and action at a cost? What if that cost is the limiting of children's access to experiences that are essential to their ability to choose for themselves? Both the second and the third position take for granted "consenting adults'" involvement in the production of pornography.

The fourth position, viewing pornography on the Internet as one more vehicle perpetuating continuing damage done to the identity of women and children, questions this assumption. This position sees that consent as a form of acquiescence to a male worldview that most women feel powerless to change.

Several themes consistently emerge in this analysis. Two of these, desire and power, however, take innumerable forms, some of which are obscured by the initial framing of the oppositional arguments above. Indeed, the relationship between desire and aesthetics, of which pornography is one example, is a historically contradictory one in Western culture. Terry Eagleton places the break between these two concepts in the late eighteenth century, when "with the emergence of the early bourgeoisie, aesthetic concepts (some of them of distinguished historical pedigree) begin to play, however tacitly, an unusually central intensive part in the constitution of a dominant ideology."[4] The current struggle over the representation of sexuality, whether it be of women, men, or children, is an example of this continuing breach and its part in today's dominant conservative ideologies, driven in the most part by a market mentality.

A distressing example of this is the simultaneous depiction of teenage sexuality in various media as both stimulating and commodifiable, and decadent and unmanageable.[5] In this way, it confiscates the capacity of an entire segment of the population to create their own cultural identity. A segment, it is important to note, that has as much or more right to the definition of the future as the adults who seem able to view the argument only from their own current interests.

At the very least, in making decisions about topics considered to be public territory, we need to be aware of the simultaneously contradictory and convergent relationships concerning the content of the conflict. In the case of pornography on the Internet, this step involves locating and listening to issues—among others, of desire and power—separated, for a time, from the question of the Internet. In this case, the Internet becomes not only a vehicle for the distribution of pornography but also a form of mediation of the pornography itself, a form adding more layers of confusion and contradiction, more hidden agendas of desire and power, unless we are clear about the original conflict.

Unfortunately, public arguments framed and carried out in the more oppositionally constructed, former way are widely accepted as examples of the daily ethical life of our cultural identity. They are accepted as, after all, particular judgments based on the moral and ethical tradition of this culture. A particular argument is found to be either right or wrong. This method of argument, however, limits knowledge rather than uncovering it, and characterizes the complicated and contradictory nature of much of our cultural identity, as well as the content and manner in which we build that identity.

Personal experience, as well as indirect experience offered by the media, reminds us of the ongoing struggle over cultural identity, its content and form. Certainly we understand that identity to be multiple. Even more reason why the questions relating to the impact of digital aesthetics on the future of our ethical life need to clarify rather than obscure: What are we about when we speak of the aesthetic of the digital environment? How do we define the concept of aesthetics for use in today's culture? Upon what and whose notions of value is it developed? Who decides how the digital aesthetic, pervasively moving to define the logistics and mechanisms of a large portion of the culture of which we are a part, represents the people who daily communicate through it? The fundamental question becomes What is the ethical content of the cultural identity we are building with the digital aesthetic?[6]

The interrelated challenges of answering that question are threefold: How can we technologically acknowledge the oppositional environment in which this culture's individual and communal identity is constructed? How can we bridge this acknowledgment with changing and interlinked practices of aesthetics and ethics? How can we clarify the possibilities and limitations of the digital medium in working toward the first two tasks?

The Dialectical Challenge

The contradictions and oppositions evident in these questions call up a fourth challenge, one that is composed of the most difficult obstacles in solving the first three challenges or, depending on how one perceives the role of opposition in solving problems, offers enormous resources for cooperation and growth. The dialectical method, in all its incarnations, still flourishes in Western thought. Revising that method, instead of completely throwing it out for something else, is one way of opening up possibilities of something better emerging, both in a method of thought and in the digital aesthetic.

The dialectical process involved in answering these questions will be helpful if we are unafraid of revising it to fit our needs. We need a dialectic drawing upon the morally imaginative methods of Socrates, the grounding of ethical life in the cultural contexts of Ludwig Wittgenstein, and a disregard for contentious argument for its own sake. This dialectical challenge is one upon which the other three challenges must depend. Pitting one method, one idea, one object, one person, one culture against another for the purpose of canceling one of them out is, though efficient, not particularly healthy. As Wittgenstein reminds us, "If you use a trick in logic, whom can you be tricking other than yourself?"[7] What is needed is a dialectical process based on the goal of one position enlarging the other, offering it possibilities for improvement that an insider might never have guessed. This consideration of the dialectic is one that runs through the following descriptions of cultural identity, both aesthetics and ethics, and the digital environment.

The Challenge of Cultural Identity

The challenge of acknowledging the oppositional environment of cultural identity includes not only finding ways in which multiple and oppositional identities are represented, but also finding ways in which individuals and communities might be free to grow into other identities of their own choosing. In *The Ideology of the Aesthetic,* Terry Eagleton describes this process:

All "oppositional" identities are in part the function of oppression, as well as of resistance to that oppression; and in this sense what one might become cannot be simply read off from what one is now. The privilege of the oppressor is his privilege to decide what he shall be; it is this right which the oppressed must demand too, which must be universalized.[8]

The importance of this process seems to be lost on the highly visible political and corporate concerns in the United States that have embraced the metaphor of a "digital frontier." Newt Gingrich, whose tenure as the Speaker of the House had encompassed an impassioned embrace of virtualized politics, characterizes these technologies as a force that "decentralizes and transforms all power."[9] Left unstated is exactly what cultural identity will emerge from this decentralization. That the rhetoric involves values that seem already to have been determined not just for the United States

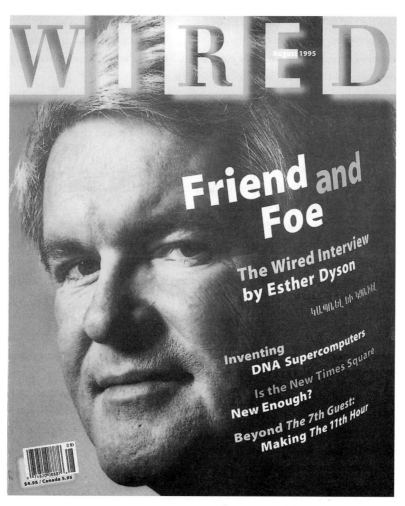

Newt Gingrich on the cover of *Wired*.

but for the entire human race, prior to the widespread distribution of these technologies, is another clue that those speaking have perhaps not thought deeply enough about what they are saying. Or perhaps they are extremely conscious of the subterfuge this rhetoric allows.

Whether or not one agrees with "postliberal" leaders on the American right and their insistence on the values of "prosperity, freedom and safety" as those by which America, through decentralization and the replacement of the welfare state, will lead the world, one thing is clear.[10] Their approach in utilizing technology at face value assumes two widely held and contradictory views: technology is deterministic and it is value-neutral. Assuming either of these views for whatever technological program we might propose is a mistake. Assuming them both simultaneously is a mistake of more profound proportions. It is one, however, that offers an opportunity to situate the apparent contradictions between them, uncover motives and purposes hidden in their dissemination, and use that knowledge to assist in answering the questions asked above.

Viewing technology as deterministic implies the inevitability of technological design. The characterization of aspects of technology, in this view, is as self-generating and a naturally occurring progression. Investigation of "technological rationality" and the tradition of which it is a part permits us an alternative view. This view sees the rationality that permeates current digital hardware and software design as not inevitable and not value-neutral, but as characteristic of the historic contexts in which it has been developed. Those contexts have been the advancement of the project of modern science and, more recently, the continuation of corporate goals. As Andrew Feenberg points out:

Technologies are selected by these interests from among many possible configurations. Guiding the selection process are social codes established by the cultural and political struggles that define the horizon under which the technology will fall. Once introduced, technology offers a material validation of the cultural horizon to which it has been preformed. I call this the "bias" of technology: apparently neutral, functional rationality is enlisted in support of a hegemony. The more technology society employs, the more significant is this support.[11]

Characterizing technology as both deterministic and devoid of embedded values, then, can be seen as a political method to obscure the possibility of choice. Accepting these assumptions or simply ignoring them means that we accept barriers to cultural transformation, at least any transformation other than that desired by the established hierarchy.

Michel Foucault's theories of the integral nature of power and knowledge describe how the characteristics embedded in the particular design of the technologies used obscure the possibility of the act of choice in order that the social order seems justified.[12] Donna Haraway's employment of cyborg imagery goes much further in offering an example of dialectic imagination that refuses to produce one universal theory and also refuses "an anti-science metaphysics, a demonology of technology, and so means embracing the skillful task of reconstructing the boundaries of daily life, in partial connection with others, in communication with all of our parts."[13]

The Challenge of the Ethical Aesthetic

The act of choice is central to the practice of both ethics and aesthetics. Ethical questions, as well as aesthetic ones, involve judgment. The idea of judgment in both ethics and aesthetics is an all-encompassing function. Involving our entire being, it is the way we choose among many possibilities. Those choices commit us to paths that are more or less consistent with our nature and the rest of our lives.[14] The accountability of our judgments is "part of the condition of our existence as social, integrated, affectionate, language-using beings."[15] Since the late eighteenth and early nineteenth centuries ethics and aesthetics have been called on to play the role of colonizing the senses.[16] The separation of moral and intellectual thought since then has influenced much of our thinking about judgment and its place in making ethical and aesthetic choices.

At the heart of all ethical and aesthetic investigations is the fact of our embodiment. This central fact and the social nature of our existence offer us possibilities for developing a process by which ethical digital aesthetic choices may be made. The point about the current insistence on the centrality of the body in discussions concerning aesthetics and ethics is not that we must transcend this envelope of skin in order to act morally, but that the body allows us to be of and in the world at the same time. We may act, think, grasp, be individual and yet part of the whole. We collaborate with the world, and at the same time we are the world. This embodiment is something we share, and is the primary way we share experience of the world.

This understanding allows us to imagine paths to making ethical and aesthetic decisions that are alternative to paths determined by classical theories that discount the body's central role in human reasoning. Ethical and aesthetic choices are entwined in the digital realm, as they are in countless areas of our life. In working with and becoming involved in the aesthetic development of digital systems, we are either accepting or rejecting, stabilizing or altering, our assumptions about the necessity of our human judgment and human worth. As we have made aesthetic choices, we have assumed certain ideas about the purposes and values of artmaking. Those assumptions have changed over time and have come from various sources, both internal and external to the artmaking process, but they have had primary impact on what was communicated by the art and about the art of any particular time.

Ethics and aesthetics both can be defined in terms of judgment. It is this partnership that allows us to grapple conceptually with both areas of thought at once. But it is their active involvement in the artmaking process that allows us to understand the consequences of that partnership.[17] The aesthetic choices we make as artists, programmers, developers, and educators have the possibility of influencing the formulation of public policy concerning the digital medium due to the pervasiveness of that medium throughout disparate forms of contemporary human activity. Specific aesthetic decisions made by anyone involved in the development of digital technology in any discipline or any area of application bring with them the possibility of standard acceptance in any other discipline or area of application. Allowing various forms and content of feedback instead of only a particular kind, and encouraging the users of a computer application to reorganize material as they see fit, become ethical choices as well as aesthetic ones. For digital aesthetics this means a constant acknowledgment and inclusion of the realities of use.

Ironically, this also means that the idea of a universal digital aesthetic is not possible. Aesthetics is no longer theory-driven but is developed from what is. That is why the art world has fought the inclusion of digital work for so long. Unable and unwilling to grasp the concrete way in which the digital realm has accomplished the breaking up of the aesthetic canon through its ability to create, reproduce, and distribute, outside the economic circles on which the art world is based, the art world as a whole, until very recently, has seen digital art as a rather embarrassing and banal distant cousin. The recent change in a great deal of the art world's take on the art produced digitally has more to do with finding out that that cousin has come into a large amount of money, than with any abiding interest by the art world in the possibilities this medium may provide for a truly communal construction of an aesthetic, digital or otherwise.

The World Wide Web has become the focus of this commercial expedition by museums, galleries, independent curators, and art consultants into digital territory. Faced with an opportunity to become involved with the development of a new aesthetic in ways that might encourage the construction of a positive cultural identity for the community at large, most museums, galleries, and curators have chosen to view these developments as a means to continue the established hierarchy of the art world, a hierarchy based on marketable products.

Early involvement in the Internet by the art world emerged from reaction to right-wing attacks on the NEA. Artswire, the first on-line art network, founded in 1988 by the New York Foundation for the Arts, offered communications about grants and exhibitions, but was primarily an alternative to the contemporary art world, from which many nonprofit subscribers felt excluded. According to Barbara Pollack, this began to change in the mid-1990s:

Interest in on-line art heated up—not because thousands of artists went digital— but because a group of curators and gallery directors announced that they were leaving the artworld for the Internet. Armed with savvy and credentials—all dressed up in the shrinking art market of the early 1990's—they viewed the Internet as a new venue for, among other things, career advancement.[18]

As Pollack points out, the quality of the Web that most interests this group is its ability to distribute information about buying art.

It is particularly telling that museums and centers of art in the United States have mirrored the emphasis on market-driven activities on the Web taken by the commercial art world. I choose to focus on museums and art centers, since that is where my own experience lies, and as public institutions they symbolize this country's ongoing conflict over the place of art in the larger identity of this culture. Many museums and centers of art have chosen two main pathways to become involved in the digital aesthetic, both of which have contributed toward the continuation of the preestablished

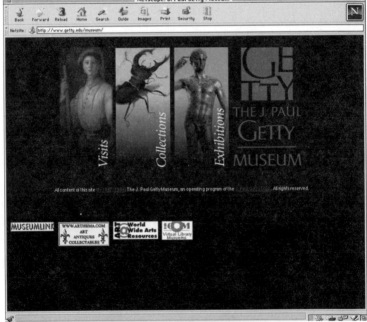

The Metropolitan Museum of Art Web site.

The J. Paul Getty Center Web site.

Carol Gigliotti

hierarchy of the art world. One pathway is linked to the embattled state of the arts in the United States and Canada, and the other pathway, more insidious in its repercussions, implicates the art world in its own demise.

The first pathway is one that mimics the commercial art world's use of the Web as a marketing tool. As in the commercial art world, "public education" is touted as the rationale for museums' and art centers' monetary and staff investment in developing Web sites. These investments are often paid for through public funding earmarked for educational purposes. Like the commercial art vendors, however, most museums' and art centers' Web sites are hardly educational in nature. They provide one-way access to information about the programs, exhibits, and sales opportunities available to the public on-site. Some truly entrepreneurial museums, like the Museum of Modern Art, offer the viewer on-line purchase power, which, for most visitors to museum Web sites, as well as to many actual sites, is the only interactive opportunity.

During these times of decreasing public funding for the arts, the temptation on the part of museums and art centers to increase visibility through the use of the Web and, perhaps because of that visibility, increase the number and amount of funding sources, is understandable. But will these short-term objectives concerning the Web support or erode the long-term stated goals of museums and art centers? What are those goals? In order to answer that question, one might ask, What role does education play in today's art museum or art center? And, further, what role do these institutions see themselves playing in the education of this culture? These questions lead to others concerning education in general, and the role of art in education. Are we fundamentally interested in teaching consuming or making? In this situation, as in the questions asked about pornography on the Net, don't the consumers or makers of the future have the right to help determine this emphasis?

Markus Kruse, involved with the development of the Web as an educational medium since the early 1990s, sees the answers to those questions quite clearly:

The future success of Web sites for museums and art centers will only be manifested by a fundamental change of attitude: Control has to be shifted from internal and external marketing departments to a joint partnership between curatorial, educational and technical staff. All parties will furthermore have to accept the changing nature of the meaning of the art museum as a traditional institution in parts of the Western World and especially if they are to understand its meaning and purpose on the Web.[19]

One might add the public to that joint partnership. The idea that the art museum might truly see education as its central mission is one not readily acceptable to most museum administrators or curators. It is not surprising, then, that the Web is not viewed as an educational opportunity.

The second pathway to digital involvement taken by museums and art centers involves an emphasis on tenacious aspects of the modernist aesthetic tradition that is delivered under the guise of postmodern concerns. Rather than investigating the Web for artists whose work is integrally involved in the development of an interactive aesthetic, one that encourages the participation of the viewer in the process of creation, most curators have preferred to commission well-known artists, whose work has proved to be profitable, to develop, most for the first time, what might pass as an interactive, Web-ready work.

The fear that curators specifically, and museums in general, feel when they are confronted with the possibility of an aesthetics developed outside their control should not be a surprise to anyone who has spent much time in the art world. If interactivity is not defined only as a technological method for manipulating data, but if in defining it one insists on the placement of that method in an environment in which all parties concerned have the ability to contribute information as well as the potential to change outcomes, the level of fear and resistance may rise. The standard prescient image of such a predicament becomes either the museum's dismal and empty future, or an idealized dream of art for all. The reality of what the Web has to offer the development of an interactive aesthetic falls somewhere in between those two extremes, and is based entirely upon the ethical choices we, as well as museum administrators and curators, are faced with in encouraging that development. Douglas Crimp states this most succinctly when he says:

It is upon this wresting of art from its necessity in reality that idealist aesthetics and the ideal museum are founded; and it is against the power of their legacy that we must still struggle for a materialist aesthetics and a materialist art.[20]

The belief that the construction of the digital aesthetic might be an interactive democratic project can be meaningful only if it is "materialistic," as

Crimp uses it here, and if the parts of this project reflect those notions as well as the whole. Inclusion and democracy may well be touted as the rationale behind the enormous amounts of money, time, and energy showered on the development and distribution of electronic media, but what needs continuous monitoring and work is the concrete daily decisions constituting that overall program. The ethical life, as we are beginning to understand, is not developed as one unified abstract concept and then implemented easily, but is constantly being worked out in the face of competing needs and desires.

Assumptions about judgment underlying moral absolutism and extreme moral relativism arise from the same Enlightenment sources as similar assumptions about judgment in aesthetics. Again, the fact of our embodiment reminds us of ethical choices alternative to those that adhere to an absolute objectivity or an absolute subjectivity. It is important to note current theories on moral imagination, some of which utilize research in cognitive science. These theories help to explain how both moral absolutism and moral relativism are based on the same false understanding of objectivity.[21]

According to Mark Johnson, in light of empirical investigations by second-generation cognitive science researchers on the structure of human conceptualization and reason, our understanding of morality must change from one that takes universal reason for granted. Instead of relying on classical theories concerning categories and concepts that insist on the essential quality of rational logic and reason, the very stuff of what we have assumed objectivity to be made, cognitive science investigations have been widened to include the imaginative character of human reason. Empirical findings have substantiated the integral role imagination plays in the development of human thinking. Metaphorical understanding, narrative, frame semantics, prototypes, and basic-level experience exemplify the kinds of structures and systems revealed by these findings. All share a reliance on the imaginative ability to conceive of other than what is traditionally accepted as an objective viewpoint.

Johnson offers a differing view of human objectivity involving moral as well as other kinds of imagination:

This dialogue of different perspectives—this dialectic of transperspectivity—is not merely an intellectual endeavor carried out through conscious reflection and argument. It is, rather, a process of individual and group experience. It is worked out through the experience of a people over long periods of time. It is a form of cultural and transcultural experimentation, which ultimately tests a culture's imaginative resources.[22]

This approach allows us, unburdened by argument with the unhelpful and unrealistic fears of either moral absolutist views or extreme moral relativistic views, to phrase questions that might guide us in directing the impact of the digital on how and why we act in the world. Could the question Should or should there not be pornography on the Internet? be rephrased in another way? What and whose needs are being met by distributing what some in this culture consider to be pornography on the Internet or through any form of media? Why does the concept of pornography exist in this culture? What if it did not? What do we, as a culture, receive from its existence? To undertake the dialectic method is to undertake a form of moral imagination. Combining the reason of this method with the metaphoric possibilities offered by the digital realm creates an environment in which to discover the moral content of our desires, our needs, and our plans.

The Challenge of the Digital Dialectic

One of the most fascinating qualities of our involvement with the digital realm is our relationship with the dialectic structure that seems to be its very life blood. The yes, no, yes, no, yes, no, yes pumps away like a beating heart. The image that comes to mind is that of the child curled in the womb, listening intently to the whooshing of the mother's internal rhythm. To the child, that sound means safety. To us, adult children in a world where safety no longer exists, the yes and no of the digital structure offers us, or so we think, an unqualified soothing answer to the vagaries of life. Can this structure offer an opportunity for a wider understanding that comes from recognizing both positive and negative repercussions of differing positions? Further, if it does, then how to practice, in the real world of which we are a part, what is easily clarified in the digital world and seemingly so possible in the theoretical one?

But these questions miss the central and often overlooked idea: the digital realm is a humanly constructed environment. As such, it remains based on the physical and material nature of our existence. Construction of the digital environment, what we may call the digital aesthetic, mirrors back to us all the same nagging questions about how to act in the physical, natural world of which we are a part. This construction gives us a chance to test out particular theories and, given the gift of human imperfection, a chance to learn from our mistakes.

The digital certainty provides us with a dialectical opportunity, the opportunity to imagine the consequences of a particular course of action and, at the same time, solidify those consequences by the nature of its pervasiveness in every form of our life. The challenge of the digital dialectic is to imaginatively work out the consequences of a particular course of action while constantly considering the responsibilities of that imaginative work. What goals do we use to choose a certain dialectical path: freedom, justice, truth, subjectivity, equality, compassion, responsibility, and care? Neither useless nor solved, the questions accompanying those goals still need to be debated and constantly revamped.

What is the moral content of the cultural identity we are building with digital media? Determining how we might answer that question is far from a theoretical issue. Cultural identity emerges from decisions made person by person, bit by bit, moment by moment, experience by experience. Determining what any aesthetic decision may mean for the future development of the digital medium, all-encompassing as it will be for our ethical identity as a culture, is a daily practice that demands our commitment, responsibility, and a trust in the practicality of our imagination.

Part II

The Body and the Machine

"Body" and "machine" are fighting words. Within themselves they contain myriad dialectics. At the turn of the century, people talk of training their bodies into machines at the same time that they give pet names to their hard drives. The body is both sacred (made in the image of God) and profane, for it suffers from all the ills and perturbations of the flesh; the machine is both the product of human ingenuity and the emblem of soullessness. How societies integrate and segregate human from machine has been central to philosophical and popular discourses about technology. Like nature and culture, the body and the machine have traditionally been opposed; but the twentieth century has been rich with fusions of the two. Mechanized transport brought with it bicycles, motorcars, and airplanes. These machines in turn drew their operators into tighter and tighter intermeshings between flesh and metal. The electrified communications media of the telegraph and the telephone obliterated distance between bodies and moved rapidly from novelties to necessities. Mass media like radio, cinema, and television offered narratives and news, creating surrogate communities from the bodies of their users.

The computer, after vacuuming up other communication media and their forms, adds the promise of human/machine interactivity to the mix. This combination helps fuel the new myth of the fully integrated machine body: the cybernetic organism—or cyborg, for short. From eyeglasses to artificial hearts, from hearing aids to bioengineered proteins, the body becomes hybridized. These prostheses offer both the potential for liberation and the menace of enslavement. The cyborg, mixed-breed offspring of the body and the machine, is tailored for an era of ambivalence, slippage, and technological ubiquity; it is a figure that haunts the margins of all three essays in this section.

N. Katherine Hayles, a literary theorist with a background in the life sciences, sets out to define a specific condition of the body in the era of smart machines: "the cultural perception that material objects are interpenetrated by information patterns." Hayles, best known for her pioneering work relating literary studies to chaos theory, here looks to biology, information theory, and contemporary electronic art to trace what she calls "The Condition of Virtuality." She notes that the dialectic between presence and absence has been superseded by the shifting continuum between pattern and randomness. In this, the either/or choice that so many see implicit in digital environments—either the body or the machine—becomes a quest for both/and—both the body and the machine. Technologies do not evolve autonomously. The choices to develop, deploy, and value digital media not only shape the technologies themselves but also are part of a feedback loop affecting the culture that creates them. "We already are cyborgs in the sense that we experience, through the integration of our bodily perceptions and motions with computer architectures and topologies, a changed sense of subjectivity."

If Hayles offers the most complex theoretical apparatus of any essay in this collection, Finnish media theorist and curator Erkki Huhtamo offers the most fully wrought historical investigation, an analysis of our culture's distrust of and infatuation with cybernation—the use of computers coupled with machines to control and carry out complex operations like manufacturing. "From Cybernation to Interaction" justifies its subtitle, "A Contribution to an Archaeology of Interactivity," by offering a perspective on digital interactivity built from the earliest discourses on automation and cyber-nation. Huhtamo's dialectic is one that pits the worker's enslavement to the machine against automation's promise to liberate the individual from the machine entirely.

In this archaeology of the recent past, Huhtamo also finds the remnants of robotics. Here the anxiety over the impact of cybernetic systems on the workplace—fear of the worker's replacement—mutates into disturbed fantasies about the conscious automaton—fear of the body's displacement. That it has been decades since cybernation was on the media's list of hot technotopics is incidental to Huhtamo. If anything, he appreciates the distance from the heat of the debate, which opens a space for him to compare the arguments over cybernetics on the factory floor to contemporary battles over the computer in the home and office.

Like Hayles and Huhtamo, William J. Mitchell is concerned with the body, but his concerns are specifically spatial, as befits an architect and architectural theorist. Mitchell deals with the ways the new medium of the World Wide Web is "Replacing Place," reconfiguring the body's social and architectural contexts. Mitchell, who writes widely about digital issues ranging from postphotographic technologies to electronic urbanism, here offers what amounts to a report from the front lines. Reviewing a vast number of Web sites, he offers an analysis of how people are using the metaphors and paradigms of built space to inform their constructions of electronic agoras. For Mitchell, the Web is the first serious contender to do some of the things that architecture has always done: creating places to do, places to see, places to be seen.

4

The Condition of Virtuality

N. Katherine Hayles

Virtuality is the condition millions of people now inhabit. What it means to be in a condition of virtuality was whimsically demonstrated with a device developed at Xerox PARC and exhibited at a recent SIGGRAPH show, the huge computer graphics convention where developers come to hawk their latest wares, hard and soft. From the twenty-foot ceilings of the Art Show exhibit dangled thin red cords, like monstrous strings of spaghetti left behind by naughty giants who got in a food fight. Sometimes the strings hung quiescent; at other times they writhed like lively plastic snakes. Connected by transducers to data lines, the cords were sensing devices that measured the flow of information moving through the room. The more bits being sent over the wires, the more the cords gyrated. They were information weather vanes. Inside the walls of the gigantic Los Angeles Convention Center, a sprawling complex larger than many small towns, which way the wind blows had ceased to be a concern of the ordinary citizen. But how currents of information were flowing—who had access, at what baud rate, to which data banks—occupied on a daily basis nearly every one of the fifty thousand people who had come to this show.

Let me offer a strategic definition. *Virtuality is the cultural perception that material objects are interpenetrated by information patterns.* Note that the definition plays off a duality—materiality on the one hand, information on the other. The bifurcation between them is a historically specific construction that emerged in the wake of World War II. When I say virtuality is a cultural perception, I do not mean it is merely a psychological phenomenon. It is also a mind-set that finds instantiation in an array of powerful technologies. The perception facilitates the development of the technologies, and the technologies reinforce the perception.[1] The analyses that constructed information and materiality as separable and discrete concepts developed in a number of scientific and technical fields during the 1940s and 1950s. The construction of these categories was far from arbitrary. The negotiations that produced them took into account existing technologies, and accepted explanatory frameworks and the needs of emerging technoscientific industries for reliable quantification. If the categories are not arbitrary, however, neither are they "natural." Whatever "nature" may be, it is a holistic interactive environment, not a reenactment of the constructed bifurcations that humans impose in order to understand it better.

One of the important sites for the construction of the information/materiality duality was molecular biology. In the contemporary view, the body is said to "express" information encoded in the genes. The content is provided by the genetic pattern; the body's materiality articulates a preexisting semantic structure. Control resides in the pattern, which is regarded as bringing the material object into being. The idea that reproduction might be governed by an informational code was suggested by Erwin Schrödinger in his influential 1945 book *What Is Life? The Physical Aspect of the Living Cell.*[2] In his analysis of the discourse of molecular biology as "rhetorical software," Richard Doyle has shown how, in the decades following Schrödinger's book, the gene was conceived as the originary informational pattern that produces the body, even though logically the gene is contained within the body, not the other way around.[3]

This "impossible inversion," as Doyle calls it, is aptly illustrated by a popular science book of the 1960s that Doyle discusses, George Gamow's *Mr. Tompkins Inside Himself.*[4] On a visit to his doctor, Mr. Tompkins is sitting in the waiting room when he hears a sucking sound and feels a strange sensation of constriction. Somehow he is drawn into a hypodermic needle and then injected inside his own body. This mind-bending scenario reenacts the same manuever that is carried out, in more stolid fashion, in the scientific discourse when DNA is conceptualized as the genotypic pattern that produces the body as its phenotypic expression. Doyle's point is that this conceptual inversion is a rhetorical rather than an experimental accomplishment. It is in this sense that the discourse functions as rhetorical software, for it operates as if it were running a program on the hardware of the laboratory apparatus to produce results that the research alone could not accomplish.

By the 1970s, this vision reached rhetorical apotheosis in Richard Dawkins's *The Selfish Gene.*[5] Although Doyle does not discuss Dawkins's text in detail, it provides a perfect illustration of his argument. In Dawkins's rhetoric, the genes are constructed as informational agents that control the "lumbering robots" we call human beings. Virtually every human behavior, from mate choice to altruism, is treated by Dawkins as if it were controlled by the genes for their own ends, independent of what humans might think. Although he frequently issues disclaimers that this is merely a colorful way of talking, the metaphors do more than spice up the argument. As I have argued elsewhere, they function like discursive agents that *perform* the actions they describe.[6] Through this discursive performativity, informational

Mr. Tompkins Inside Himself.

pattern triumphs over the body's materiality—a triumph achieved first by distinguishing between pattern and materiality and then by privileging pattern over materiality. The effect of this "impossible inversion" is the same whether it occurs in Gamow's cartoons, Dawkins's metaphors, or the lavishly funded Human Genome Project. *It constructs information as the site of mastery and control over the material world.*

It is no accident that molecular biology and other sciences of information flourished during the immediate post–World War II period. The case can be made that World War II, more than previous global events, made the value of information real. The urgency of war highlights the fact that information is time-dependent. It matters little what information one has if a message can move only as fast as a horse can run, for by the time it arrives at its destination, its usefulness often has passed. Shakespeare's history plays are full of messages that arrive too late. Only when technological infrastructures have developed sufficiently to make rapid message transmission possible does information come into its own as a commodity as important to military success as guns and infantry are. From this we can draw an obvious but nonetheless important conclusion: *The efficacy of information depends on a highly articulated material base.* Without such a base, from rapid transportation systems to fiber-optic cables, information becomes much more marginal in its ability to affect outcomes in the material world. Ironically, once this base is in place, the perceived primacy of information over materiality obscures the importance of the very infrastructures that make information valuable.

Nowhere is the privileging of information over materiality more apparent than in Hans Moravec's *Mind Children.*[7] Moravec argues that human beings are essentially informational patterns rather than bodily presences. If a technology can replicate the pattern, it has captured all that really matters in a human being. To illustrate, he offers a fantastic scenario in which "you" have your consciousness downloaded into a computer. Although the technology could be envisioned in any number of ways (since it is imaginary in any case), he significantly has the robot surgeon conducting the operation physically destroy your brain in the process. As "you" are transferred into a computer, the trashed body is left behind, an empty husk. Once "you" are comfortably inside in your shiny new body, "you" effectively become immortal. For when that body wears out or becomes obsolete, "you" can simply transfer your consciousness to a new model.

I will not bother to lay out all the reasons why this vision, in addition to being wildly implausible, is wrongheaded and dangerous. Let me instead point out a correlation that helps to explain the appeal of this fantasy (for those who find it appealing). In Moravec's text, and at many other sites in the culture, *the information/matter dichotomy maps onto the older and more traditional dichotomy of spirit/matter.* The underlying premise informing Moravec's scenario is the belief that an immaterial essence, which alone comprises the individual's true nature, can be extracted from its material instantiation and live free from the body. As this wording makes clear, the contemporary privileging of information is reinforced by religious yearnings and beliefs that have been around for a long time and that are resonant with meaning for many people.

There are, of course, also significant differences between a mind-set that identifies human being with the soul and one that identifies it with information. Spirituality is usually associated with mental and physical discipline, whereas the imagined escape of the soul-as-information from the body depends only on having access to the appropriate high technology. For Moravec, the difference means the problem of mortality has been rationalized so that it is possible to make steady progress toward achieving a solution rather than flailing around in mystical nonsense. This construction of the situation obscures the fact that his text is driven by a fear of death so intense that it mystifies the power of the very technologies that are supposed to solve the problem.

To probe further the implications of constructing information and materiality as discrete categories, let us return to the period immediately following World War II. In addition to molecular biology, another important site for articulating the distinction was information theory. In 1948 Claude Shannon, a brilliant theorist who worked at Bell Laboratories, defined a mathematical quantity he called information and proved several important theorems concerning it.[8] Jacques Derrida to the contrary, a message does not always arrive at its destination. In information theoretic terms, no message is ever sent. What is sent is a signal. The distinction that information theory posits between signal and message is crucial. A message has an information content specified by a probability function that has no dimensions, no materiality, and no necessary connection with meaning. It is a pattern, not a presence. Only when the message is encoded in a signal for transmission through a medium—for example, when ink is printed on paper or electrical pulses are sent racing along telegraph wires—does it assume material form. The very definition of information, then, encodes the distinction between materiality and information that was becoming central in molecular biology during this period.

Why did Shannon define information as a pattern rather than a presence? The transcripts of the Macy Conferences, a series of annual meetings where the basic principles of cybernetics were hammered out, indicate that the choice was driven by the twin engines of reliable quantification and theoretical generality.[9] Shannon's formulation was not the only proposal on the table. Douglas MacKay, a British researcher, argued for an alternative definition for information that linked it with the change in a receiver's mind-set, and thus with meaning.[10] To be workable, MacKay's definition required that change in a receiver's mind be quantifiable and measurable—an accomplishment that only now appears within reach through such imaging technologies as positron emission tomography. It certainly was not possible in the immediate post–World War II years. It is no mystery why Shannon's definition rather than MacKay's became the industry standard.

Shannon's approach had other advantages that turned out to incur large (and mounting) costs when his premise interacted with certain predispositions already at work within the culture. Abstracting information from a material base meant that information could become free-floating, unaffected by changes in context. The technical leverage this move gained was considerable, for by formalizing information into a mathematical function, Shannon was able to develop theorems, powerful in their generality, that held true regardless of the medium in which the information was instantiated.

Not everyone agreed that this move was a good idea, despite its theoretical power. Malcontents grumbled that divorcing information from context, and thus from meaning, had made the theory so narrowly formalized that it was not useful as a general theory of communication. Shannon himself frequently cautioned that the theory was meant to apply only to certain technical situations, not to communication in general. In other circumstances, the theory might have become a dead end, a victim of its own excessive formalization and decontextualization. But not in the post–World-War II era. As we have seen, the time was ripe for theories that reified information into a free-floating, decontextualized, quantifiable entity that could serve as the master key unlocking the secrets of life and death.

How quickly the theory moved from the meticulously careful technical applications urged by Shannon to cultural fantasy can be seen in Norbert Wiener's suggestion in 1950 that it would be possible to telegraph a human being.[11] We can see here the prototype for Moravec's scenario of downloading consciousness into a computer. The proposal implies that a human being is a message instantiated within a biological substrate but not intrinsic to it.[12] Extract the information from the medium, and you have a pattern you can encode into a signal and reconstitute in another medium at the end of the channel. The fantasy has not lost its appeal as the twentieth century races toward the next millennium; indeed, it now circulates so widely as to be virtually ubiquitous. Telegraphing a person to a remote location may have been startling idea in the 1950s, but by the 1990s it has achieved the status of a cultural icon. What is "Beam me up, Scotty," but the same operation carried out with a different (imaginary) technology?

Moravec's vision is extreme only in that it imagines "you" rematerialize inside a computer. If you had simply reoccupied your same body, nobody would have raised an eyebrow. Whether the enabling assumptions occur in molecular biology, information theory, or mass media, their appeal is clear. Information conceived as pattern and divorced from a material medium is information free to travel across time and space. Hackers are not the only ones who believe that information wants to be free. The great dream and promise of information is that it can be free from the material constraints that govern the mortal world. If we can become the information we have constructed, we, too, can soar free, immortal like the gods.

In the face of such a powerful dream, it can be a shock to remember that for information to exist, it must *always* be instantiated in a medium, whether that medium is the page from the *Bell Laboratories Journal* on which Shannon's equations are printed, the computer-generated topological maps used by the Human Genome Project, or the cathode ray tube that images the body disappearing into a golden haze when the *Star Trek* transporter locks onto it. The point is not only that abstracting information from a material base is an imaginary act. More fundamentally, conceiving of information as a thing separate from the medium that instantiates it is a prior imaginary act that constructs a holistic phenomenon as a matter/information duality.[13]

As I write these words, I can feel the language exerting an inertial pull on my argument, for only through the dichotomies constructed to describe it can I gesture toward the unity that the world is. Even as I point to the historical contingency of the terms, the very history that exposes this contingency reinscribes the information/materiality dichotomy I want to contest. This reinscription is complicated and exacerbated by the fact that the matter/information duality is enmeshed in a network of related dichotomies that help to support, distinguish, and define it. In order of increasing generality, these include signal/not-signal, information/noise, and pattern/randomness. Although I cannot avoid using these constructions, I want to show that they function as dialectics rather than dichotomies. For each of these dualities, the bifurcated terms tangle and interact with each other. The slashes turn out to be permeable membranes rather than leakproof barriers.

Consider, for example, the information/noise duality. In Shannon's theory, information and noise are defined by similar mathematical expressions. The similarity makes clear that noise is not the opposite of information. Noise *is* information, but it is information not encoded by the sender. Noise may actually increase a message's information content (a theme that Michael Serres played multiple riffs upon in *The Parasite*).[14] We can visualize this situation by imagining information and noise as balls careening through a channel. It is not the case that the noise balls are blue, say, and the information balls are red, and we can sort them by putting the blue balls in one urn and the red balls in another. Rather, all the balls are blue (or red). Some have been thrown in by the sender, some have popped into the channel through holes in its sides, and some have materialized from the channel's lining as it is pulled and twisted. The receiver ends up with more balls than the sender intended. (Here noise leaks into my own message as the language slips from one metaphoric network to another, illustrating how the situation grows yet more complicated when information is related to semantics). The only way to distinguish between information and noise is by comparing the message the receiver decodes with what the sender encoded.

The mathematical equivalence of information and noise points to a deeper ambiguity: whether information should be identified with pattern or randomness. The associations that the word "information" evokes suggest that information should have an inherent structure, and thus correspond to patterned communication rather than random bursts of noise. Yet as as early as 1968, John Arthur Wilson pointed out that such an intuition is not justified by the formal structure of the theory.[15]

We can understand this heuristically by comparing the information content of a nursery rhyme with that of a sequence of random numbers. After I have said the first line of a nursery rhyme—for example, "Mary had a little lamb"—you can guess the rest because it is so familiar. The remainder of the message is redundant and conveys no new information. By contrast, every one of the random numbers comes as a surprise. (Remember that in Shannon's theory, information has no connection with meaning.) Since randomness by definition implies an absence of pattern, you have no way to reliably guess what will come next. This line of reasoning suggests that the more random a message is, the more information it conveys—a result that conflicts with our cultural expectation that information should be structured.

This conundrum proved to be a powerful paradox within information theory. It led to the realization that in certain instances in which there is no access to the original message (for example, when analyzing the electromagnetic spectra of stars, where the stars are considered to be the message senders and humans who interpret the spectra are the receivers), the best strategy for interpreting the data is to maximize entropy (or randomness). This procedure, called Maximum Entropy Formalism, works well in such situations because it encodes the least number of assumptions about the results and so minimizes the chances for error.[16]

The point of detailing these developments within information theory is to indicate that although the theory relies for its articulation on such distinctions as information/noise and signal/not-signal, the dualities are not dichotomies but dialectics. In Derrida's phrase, they are engaged in an economy of supplementarity. Each of the privileged terms—signal, information, pattern—relies for its construction on a supplement—not-signal, noise, randomness.

As an electrical engineer employed by AT&T, Shannon had a vested interest in eliminating noise. One of his most important theorems proves that there is always a way to encode a message so as to reduce the noise to an arbitrarily small quantity. But since noise is the supplement that allows information to be constructed as the privileged term, it cannot be eliminated from the communication situation, only compensated for in the final result. We can arrive at the same conclusion through a different route by thinking more deeply about what it means to define information as a probability function. The definition implies that randomness always had already interpenetrated pattern, for probability as a concept posits a situation in which there is no a priori way to distinguish between effects extrapolated from known causes and those generated by chance conjunctions. Like information and noise, pattern and randomness are not opposites bifurcated into a dichotomy but interpenetrating terms joined in a dialectic.

I am now in a position to restate my major theme in a different key. As I have shown, the concept of information is generated from the interplay between pattern and randomness. Similarly, materiality can be understood as being generated by a dialectic of presence and absence. In each dialectic, one term has historically been privileged over the other. When the terms are inverted, assumptions become visible that otherwise would remain transparent. Deconstruction gained theoretical leverage by placing absence rather than presence at the origin of language; the Maximum Entropy Formalism gained theoretical leverage by regarding randomness rather than pattern as the generator of information. When information is privileged over materiality, the pattern/randomness dialectic associated with information is perceived as dominant over the presence/absence dialectic associated with materiality. The condition of virtuality implies, then, a widespread perception that presence/absence is being displaced and preempted by pattern/randomness.

Although virtuality is clearly related to postmodernism, it has distinctive features of its own. Table 4.1 summarizes some of these and compares them with parallel features in postmodern theory and culture. I will not have space here to develop the items in the table in detail, but a brief summary of a couple will serve to illustrate how virtuality both extends and modifies certain trends within postmodernism.

1. *Possession seriates into access.* Material objects are possessions. I cannot eat my cake and also give it away. By contrast, information is not a materially conserved quantity. When I copy information from my disk to yours, we both have it. The crucial issue with information is thus not possession but access. Access has already become a focal point for questions about how information as a commodity is going to be integrated into existing capitalistic structures. How can you publish something on the World Wide Web and get paid for it? When interactive television becomes a reality, how can access be controlled so consumers will pay for the information they tap? The shift of emphasis from possession to access has important implications for

Table 4.1 — A Comparison of Postmodernism and Virtuality

	Postmodernism	Virtuality
Defining Dialectic	Presence/Absence	Pattern/randomness
Integration into capitalism	Possession	Access
Psychological Crisis	Castration	Mutation
Theoretical Inversion Formalism	Deconstruction	Maximum Entropy
Creation of Narrative	(De)Construction of Origin	(De)Construction of Chaos

literature. Think of how issues of possession have driven literary plots, from the penniless younger brothers of Restoration comedies to the labyrinthine inheritance disputes in Victorian novels. How will literary forms shift when plots are driven instead by questions of access?

2. *Castration seriates into mutation.* The grounds for theoretical inquiry shift as postmodernism shades into virtuality. In Lacanian psycholinguistics, the focus is on inverting the traditional hierarchy of presence/absence, in much the same way and for similar reasons as it is in most deconstructive theory. Castration represents a moment of crisis because it bodies forth the subject's realization that absence interpenetrates and precedes presence. Absence drives the engine of desire, and desire drives the engine of signification and, therefore, of subjectivity. When the focus shifts to pattern and randomness, the nature of the precipitating crisis changes. In the pattern/randomness dialectic, mutation rather than castration is central, for mutation bodies forth the realization that randomness interpenetrates and precedes pattern. Mutation occurs when pattern can no longer be counted on to replicate itself, when pattern's disruption by randomness becomes visibly evident in the body. It is no accident that theorists concerned with virtuality, from Allucquère Rosanne Stone to the Canadian artist Catherine Richards, focus

on mutation as the decisive event precipitating a changed subjectivity in a virtual age. What theories of language and subjectivity will emerge when mutation is constituted as the catastrophic moment of self-recognition?

As these questions suggest, the impact of virtuality on literary theory and practice will be far-reaching and profound. At present, virtuality is largely terra incognita for the literary establishment. In *City of Bits,* William Mitchell has written insightfully about how technologies of information are forcing a reconceptualization of the city on many levels, from architecture to traffic flow and urban planning.[17] My interest lies in how these same technologies are forcing a reconceptualization of literary theory and practice. In the next section, I explore the effects on literature of the changing material conditions under which it is written and read in an information age. Part of what is at stake for me in this analysis is to show that materiality, far from being left behind, interacts at every point with the new forms that literature is becoming as it moves into virtuality.

The Virtual Book

We have seen it dozens of times—that moment in a film when a book is opened and the camera's eye zooms through the pages into the imagined world beyond. Once we are in the world, the page is left behind. It no longer appears on the screen, no longer frames the world we witness. The filmic convention captures a reader's sense that the imagined world of the text lives less on the page than in the scene generated out of the words by the mind's eye.

Virtual books—that is, books imaged on and through computer screens—operate according to a different convention. As with film, the user is sometimes given the illusion that she is moving through the screen into an imagined world beyond. But unlike film, this imagined world contains texts that the user is invited to open, read, and manipulate. Text is not left behind but remains in complex interplay with the perceived space into which the screen opens. Technically speaking, of course, the interplay is possible because the computer is an interactive medium.

My focus here is on how this interactivity is rendered through visual conventions. *Visually* it is possible because textual space is rendered as having depth—if not a full three dimensions, at least the "two and a half" dimensions of text windows stacked behind one another. Texts can play a part in the three-dimensional world of the screen image because in this interactive medium, they have similarly rich dimensionality. The correlation suggests that in electronic textuality, spatiality is of primary concern.

The changed conventions that operate with virtual texts are apparent in *Myst* (1993), the best-selling CD-ROM game. As the game opens, three-dimensional Roman letters spelling "MYST" appear. Then a book tumbles out of space and comes to rest in the foreground. Imagine that you are sitting at the keyboard with me so we can work together on solving the problems that *Myst* presents to us (a favorite way to interact with this challenging and complex game). As we peer at the screen, we notice that the same letters appear on the book. It comes closer, inviting us to enter. We plunge into it and find ourselves spinning through the air. Finally we come to rest on the island, the first of many worlds that *Myst* offers for exploration. We find that we have not left the book behind, for scattered about are pages giving important clues about the island's previous occupants. When we pick a page up (by clicking on it), it comes close enough for us to read.

The significance of the pages becomes clearer when we enter the library, perhaps the island's most important structure. In addition to the books lining the walls, the library features two podiums on which rest two books (one red and one blue, as if in recognition of red and blue balls flying through communication channels). When we open one of them (by clicking on it), we are greeted by a black rectangle inset on a white page. Inserting a nearby page into the book causes the rectangle to buzz into flickering life, and we realize it is a screen. Amid noise and static the image of a man appears on the screen. He tries to ask who we are, tries to communicate a message so broken up by static that we can catch only a few words asking us to find more blue (or red) pages and insert them into the book. When we do, the image gets progressively clearer and the messages become more intelligible.

To recapitulate: a book appears on the screen; we go through the book to the island, where we find fragments of more books. Reassembling the book in the library activates the screen inside the book; from the screen comes a message directing us back to the task of finding and reassembling the book. What are we to make of this extraordinarily complex interplay between screen and book? Here I want to point out something that is visually apparent to anyone who plays *Myst*. While the screens appear in a variety of high-tech settings, the books look archaic, with heavy leather bindings, watermarks, and ornate typefaces. Moreover, the screens are usually

The metaphor of the book in *Myst*®.
© 1993 Cyan, Inc. All rights reserved *Myst*® Cyan, Inc.

The virtual text worlds of *Myst*®.
© 1993 Cyan, Inc. All rights reserved *Myst*® Cyan, Inc.

N. Katherine Hayles

activated by solving various numerical or coding problems, whereas the books require physical reassembly. The visual richness of the books compared with the screens, their fragmentation, and their archaic appearance hint that books have become fetishized. When we open the book in the library, we do not find the information we seek imprinted on its pages. Instead, we interact with a screen emphasizing that the book has become fragmented and urging us to put it back together. Books are associated with the object of desire—finding out information—but metonymically, by a glancing connection based on proximity rather than a direct gaze.

The fetishistic quality of the books in *Myst* is consistent with their representation as anachronisms. Everything about their presentation identifies them as artifacts from the late age of print. Books still exist in this virtual world, but they have ceased to be ordinary, matter-of-fact media for transmitting information. Instead, they have become fragmented objects of vicarious desire, visually sensuous in a way that implies they are heavy with physicality, teasing us with the promise of a revelation that will come when we restore them to a fabled originary unity. The same kinds of transformation are evident at many sites where virtuality reigns. Let me give two more examples, this time from the Art Show at SIGGRAPH '95.

Roman Verostko's *Universal Turing Machine* illustrates how the function of the book changes when its materiality is conceived as interpenetrated by informational patterns. The title alludes to a conceptual computer proposed by Alan Turing in the 1950s.[18] The Universal Turing Machine is simply a string of binary code that contains instructions on how to read the code, as well as the code that describes itself. Verostko appropriated the code describing the Universal Turing Machine (which visually appears as a string of ones and zeros) and used a computer to print it out on thick parchment, formatted as if it were the text of a medieval illuminated manuscript. Then he fed the same string of code into a program for a line plotter and used it to generate the four illustrations surrounding the text, which look like not-quite-random nests of snaky red lines. In the centers of the side margins are two gorgeous gold decals that repeat, in simplified form, one of the motifs of the line drawings; Verostko noted that he intended the decals to suggest control points for the computer.

Like *Myst,* this work shows a keen interest in the physical and visual properties of the codex book, including its arrangement of space, its tradition of combining text and image, and its use of colored inks and gold leaf.

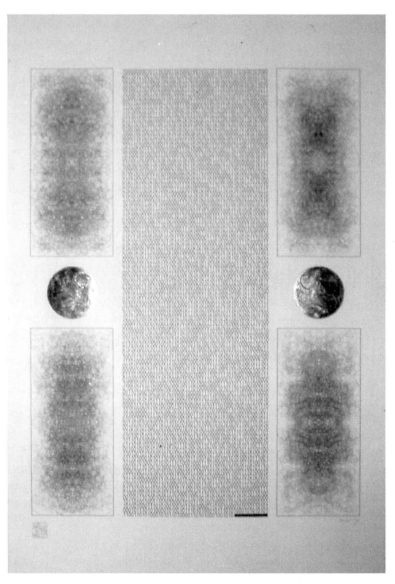

The Illuminated Universal Turing Machine.
Courtesy of Roman Verostko.

N. Katherine Hayles

But the book's traditional function of conveying verbal information has been given over to computer code. Just as illuminated manuscripts were used for sacred or canonical works, so Verostko uses his visually splendid work to enshrine the universal computer code that is universal precisely because it both explains and enacts its own origin. As with *Myst,* the materiality of the book is celebrated for its archaic and physical qualities, but it is a materiality interpenetrated by the informational patterns that generated it and that are rendered visually incarnate in the drawings. In this work commenting upon and exemplifying the late age of print, the book supplies image and visual form, while the computer supplies text and signifying code.

The materiality of the codex book is also celebrated in Andre Kopra's *The Ornament of Grammar,* although the properties selected for celebration are very different than in Verostko's work. Kopra intended his title to allude to Owen Jones's nineteenth-century text *The Grammar of Ornament,* a collection of decorative patterns from different cultures. Kopra's work consists of a collection of ten different texts bound in cheap, black, generic paper covers, printed on inexpensive paper, and displayed in an unpainted pine bookcase holding multiple copies of each of the ten texts. The pages of the books are filled with line drawings generated by computer programs. The drawings are laid out on a grid of thirty-six by thirty-six squares, yielding a total of forty-one different patterns. As one flips through a book, the drawings grow progressively more complex, an effect achieved by varying the parameters of the computer program generating them. Some of the books use rectilinear patterns; others feature curved lines. The patterns tease the eye, challenging the reader to discern in their visual form the algorithm that created them. Commenting on the tension between the underlying code and the visual surface, Kopra wrote that the "possibility of rationalizing visual imagery is called into question by an apparent encyclopedia of the arbitrary."[19]

The material qualities celebrated in this piece include the print book's sturdiness, its relative cheapness and portability, its technological robustness and ease of use, and its potential for mass production. (When I talked with him about the work, Kopra mentioned that several of the books had been stolen by the time SIGGRAPH ended, a fact that delighted him. He said the perfect ending of the display, from his point of view, would have been to have the bookcase emptied by bibliophilic thieves.)

Although he focuses on different material qualities, Kopra echoes Verostko in having the book's verbal content displaced by visual forms

The Ornament of Grammar.
Courtesy of Andre Kopra.

generated from a computer. The computer's role in producing the book is highlighted by the interplay between pattern and randomness in the visual forms. This interplay at once instantiates the dialectic of pattern/randomness and draws into question the ability of computer codes to produce significance, as if recollecting for the reader Shannon's move of divorcing information from meaning. Kopra's work has an ironic undertone that reflects, he says, his growing concern that we are drowning in an ocean of information that is produced not because it is meaningful but because it can be used to generate a profit. For him the SIGGRAPH context in which the work was exhibited was significant, for over the years he has seen SIGGRAPH itself change from a coterie of people who shared mutual interests to a huge commercial enterprise where millions of dollars are at stake.[20]

In an art show devoted to computer graphics, the focus on the book was remarkable. In addition to Verostko and Kopra, at least a dozen other artists produced works that were concerned with the interplay between print and algorithm. For them, the codex book functions as a crossroads at which one can see displayed the traffic between visual objects and computer programs, words and codes, images and language, fragmentation and wholeness, handwork and machine production, pattern and randomness, rationality and numerical permutations of the arbitrary. The overarching message is that the interpenetration of materiality by informational patterns is everywhere around us, even—or especially—in the books, at once virtual and physical, that are being produced in this late age of print.

Spatiality and Virtual Writing

Not all virtual books, of course, have their verbal content displaced by codes. Usually the codes work to introduce into the text's visual form a spatial dimensionality that operates in complex syncopation with language. The interplay between spatiality and text is central to electronic hypertexts. As most readers will know, hypertexts are electronic documents that are structured as networks of discrete units, or lexias, rather than as a linear sequence of bound pages. Hypertexts have encoded within them certain "hot spots" or interactive links. When a reader clicks on them, the link is activated and a new block of text comes up on the screen. As George Landow has pointed out, hypertexts are now becoming the standard way to convey information in many technical and engineering areas because they are easily updated, richly associational, and reader-directed. They can be found in everything from manuals for aircraft mechanics to electronic directories for museums. The World Wide Web is a vast hypertext, and most of the documents within it are hypertexts as well. Hypertext also provides a rapidly expanding arena for literary writing, both creative and critical.

In literary hypertexts, spatial form and visual image become richly significant. For hypertexts written in Storyspace (a hypertext authoring program developed by Mark Bernstein, Michael Joyce, and Jay Bolter), the map view shows how different lexias are linked to one another. The way they are arranged in space is used to indicate logical or narrative relationships. Some lexias may nest inside others; others may have multiple connections; still others may function as autonomous units or dead ends. Color coding also indicates various kinds of relationships, from highlighted text within lexias to different-colored links and boxes. In Toolbook (another authoring program), sound can be added to enhance textual or visual effects. As a result, space in hypertexts operates as much more than an empty container into which virtual objects are placed. Rather, it becomes a topography that the reader navigates by using multiple functionalities, including cognitive, tactile, auditory, visual, kinesthetic, and proprioceptive faculties.

Since I am focusing here on spatiality, let us dwell for a moment on proprioception. Proprioception is the sense that tells us where the boundaries of our bodies are. Associated with inner-ear mechanisms and internal nerve endings, it makes us feel that we inhabit our bodies from the inside. Proprioceptive coherence, a term used by phenomenologists, refers to how these boundaries are formed through a combination of physiological feedback loops and habitual usage. An experienced tennis player, for example, frequently feels proprioceptive coherence with the racquet, experiencing it as if it were an extension of her arm. In much the same way, an experienced computer user feels proprioceptive coherence with the keyboard, experiencing the screen surface as a space into which her subjectivity can flow.

This effect marks an important difference between screen and print. Although a reader can imaginatively project herself into a world represented within a print text, she is not likely to feel that she is becoming physically attached to the page itself. On the contrary, because the tactile and kinesthetic feedback loops are less frequent, less sensually complicated, and much less interactive, she normally feels that she is moving *through* the page into some other kind of space. The impression has a physiological basis. The physical stimuli the reader receives with print are simply not adequate to account for the cognitive richness of the represented world; the more the imagination soars, the more the page is left behind. This difference in the way that proprioceptive coherence works with the computer screen, compared with the printed page, is an important reason why spatiality becomes such a highly charged dimensionality in electronic hypertexts.

It makes sense, then, to insist, as Michael Joyce does, that virtual writing is also topographical writing.[21] He points to a number of assumptions that we absorb through our everyday work with electronic texts; together, they make our experience of electronic texts distinctively different from that of print texts. They include the following items, which I have adapted from Joyce's list and altered to suit my purposes here.

1. *Writing is inwardly elastic.* It expands and contracts; it allows the writer to work backward and forward; and it instantly adjusts the screen image to reflect these changes.

2. *The topology of the text is constructed rather than given.* Mechanisms that construct this topology include such humble devices as file names, as well as the more explicitly spatial commands used in hypertexts. As Joyce points

out, file names are more powerful than they may appear. They imply that writing done at different times is the same writing if it has the same file name, and that writing stored under different file names is different, even if it was done at the same time and contains the same text. File names also imply that writing is recognized as identical with itself through labeling rather than through spatial proximity within the computer. In contrast to printed books, where the physical location of the pages coincides with labeling conventions, in electronic texts, memory address and physical proximity have no necessary relation to one another. Topology is constructed by naming, not by physical assembly.

3. *Changes in a text can be superficial, corresponding to surface adjustments, or structural, corresponding to changes in topography.* Superficial changes are carried out through such formatting tools as spell checkers and font alterations, while structural changes involve such editorial functions as cut, copy, and paste. The different way these tools are organized within the authoring program, and the different coding operations to which they correspond, embody the assumption that the text possesses both surface and depth. Alterations in the surface are of a different kind than alterations in the topography.

The power of these assumptions lies in the fact that we do not need to be consciously aware of them to be affected by them. Like posture and table manners, they implant and reinforce cognitive presuppositions through physical actions and habitual motions, whether or not we recognize that they do so. As with any ritual, to perform them is on some level to accept and believe them.[22] The materiality of these interactions is one way in which our assumptions about virtual writing are being formed. Through mechanisms and procedures whose full impact we are only beginning to understand, virtual writing is being constituted as distinctively different from print. Even when its output is printed and bound into codex books, we know from the inside that it operates according to spatial principles and a topographical logic of its own.

The Physics of Virtual Writing and the Formation of the Virtual Subject

With all of this emphasis on spatiality, the reader may wonder how time enters into virtual writing. To understand the interaction between time and space in this medium, it is important to know something about the way the medium works. When computers speak their native languages—assembly code, and beneath that, machine language—they operate within a profoundly non-Cartesian space. Distance at this level is measured by clock cycles. The computer's CPU (central processing unit) has a characteristic clock rate. When you buy a faster computer, you are essentially buying a faster clock rate. Imagine a drummer on a Viking sailing ship, pounding out the beat for the rowers' strokes.[23] Every two beats, a rowing cycle is completed. The drummer's pace controls the rate that which the oars move, and consequently the speed at which the boat slices through the water. Similarly, inside the computer the CPU reads a byte of code every two clock cycles. The clock rate thus controls the rate at which computations occur. It follows that addresses at memory locations 1, 50, 1000, and 1001 are all equidistant. Each is exactly two cycles away if it is in local memory, and eight cycles away if it is in remote memory.

How does this non-Cartesian relation between time and space express itself at the level of the user's experience? It is relatively easy for a computer program to generate a two-dimensional array, for it simply assigns each pixel on the screen an address. But to build a three-dimensional representation, the program must layer a series of two-dimensional planes on top of one another, as if a mountain had been cut horizontally into very thin slices and was being reassembled by the computer. This means that three-dimensional representations take many more cycles to build than do two-dimensional maps. Hence the user experiences the sensory richness of a three-dimensional topography as a lag in the flow of the computer's response.

In *Myst,* for example, the user experiences movement through the represented three-dimensional space as a series of jumps interspersed by pauses. You click, the computer pauses, and then jumps to a point perhaps ten feet away where a flight of steps begins; you click again, the computer pauses, and jumps halfway up the steps. Distance within the screen is experienced as an inertial pull on your time as you navigate the topology. The result is an artifactual physics that emerges from the interaction of the computer clock cycle with the user's experience.

In this physics born of interactivity, the more complex the screen topography, the more inertial pull is exerted on the user's flow. The exact relation between the two is determined by the structure and programming of the underlying codes. Thus these codes, which normally remain invisible to the nonspecialist, are nevertheless felt and intuitively grasped by the user, in much the same way that the earth's gravity is felt and intuitively understood by someone who never heard of Newton's laws. Apples fall down; it takes effort to climb mountains. As inhabitants of cyberspace, we similarly understand in our muscles and bones that space belongs to the computer, and flow belongs to the user.

The physics of virtual writing illustrates how our perceptions change when we work with computers on a daily basis. We do not need to have software sockets inserted into our heads (as William Gibson envisions in *Neuromancer*) to become cyborgs. We already are cyborgs in the sense that we experience, through the integration of our bodily perceptions and motions with computer architectures and topologies, a changed sense of subjectivity.

Much has been written about how the transition from orality to writing affected subjectivity. In *Preface to Plato,* Eric Havelock initiates a fascinating line of inquiry when he asks why Plato is so adamant about banishing poets from the republic.[24] Havelock suggests that poetry is associated with oral culture, and consequently with a fluid, changing, situational, and dispersed subjectivity. Plato wants to establish a fixed, stable, unchanging reality, and to do this, he needs a fixed, coherent, stable subject to perceive it. So the poets have to go, for they produce through their linguistic interventions exactly the kind of subject that Plato does not want and cannot tolerate. Similarly influential has been the work of Walter Ong on the differences between oral and written culture, of Elizabeth Eisenstein on the effects of printing in early modern Europe, and of Marshall McLuhan on the effects of electronic technologies.[25]

We are only beginning to understand the effect of computers on culture and on subjectivity. Marsha Kinder has spoken about the importance of "shifting," the perception young children have when watching such programs as the Power Rangers that they can morph and shapeshift into various forms;[26] Brenda Laurel and Rachel Strickland have embodied similar perceptions in their virtual reality simulation "Placeholder";[27] and Allucquère Rosanne Stone, in *The War Between Technology and Desire at the Close of the Mechanical Age,* has written about the virtual subject as a "multiple" (analogous to someone who experiences multiple personalities) warranted by the body rather than contained within it.[28] Catherine Richards and Don Idhe have focused on proprioceptive coherence, looking at the way perception of body boundaries changes through technological interactions and interventions.[29] Michael Joyce, Jay Bolter, George Landow, David Kolb, and Jane Yellowlees Douglas, among others, have pointed out how navigating the topologies of electronic hypertexts creates new conditions for writing and reading, and thus for both producing and expressing new kinds of subjectivities.[30] Operating without any illusions about comprehensiveness or rigor, I venture in Table 4.2 to sum up a few salient comparisons between the oral subject, the written subject, and the virtual subject.

In the transition from the written to the virtual subject, deconstruction played a significant theoretical role, for in reinterpreting writing (emphasizing its instabilities, lack of originary foundations, intertextualities, and indeterminacies), in effect it made the written subject move much closer to the virtual subject than had traditionally been the case. This process is typical of what elsewhere I have called "seriation" (a term appropriated from archaeological anthropology), an uneven process of change in which new artifacts or ideas emerge by partially replicating and partially innovating upon what came before.

Although the shape of virtual subjectivity is only beginning to emerge and is therefore difficult to envision clearly, certain features are coming into focus. Proprioceptive coherence in interplay with electronic prostheses plays an important role in reconfiguring perceived body boundaries, especially when it gives the user the impression that her subjectivity is flowing into the space of the screen. When the interface is configured as keyboard and screen, the user will perceive that space belongs to the computer, and flow to the user. The symbiotic relation between humans and intelligent machines has complex effects that do not necessarily all point in the same direction. For example, it can evoke resistance and a privileging of human qualities that machines do not share, such as emotion, or it can lead to the opposite view that humans should leave to machines the things they do best, such as memory recall, and concentrate on the things humans do best, like language and complex pattern recognition. Whatever the symbiosis is taken to mean, it seems clear that the virtual subject will in some sense be a cyborg. These attributes are summarized below.

What Is to Be Done?

Should we respond with optimism to the products of virtual writing, or regard them (as an elderly gentleman informed me when he heard some of

Table 4.2 — Figuring Virtual Subjectivity

The Oral Subject
Fluid, changing, situational, dispersed, conflicting.

The Written Subject
Fixed, coherent, stable, self-identical, normalized, decontextualized.

The Virtual Subject
Formed through dynamical interfaces with computers.

When interface is keyboard and screen, space belongs to the computer, flow to the user.

Body boundaries extended or disrupted through proprioceptive coherence formed in conjunction with computer interfaces.

A cyborg.

these arguments) as abominations that are rotting the minds of American youth? Whatever we make of them, one thing is certain: Literature will not remain unchanged. It is sometimes difficult to convey adequately to an academic audience the very rapid pace at which computer technologies are penetrating virtually every aspect of our culture. In this respect, academe in general and literature departments in particular tend to lag far behind other sectors of the society. With some noteworthy exceptions, academe is not where it is happening as far as computer culture is concerned.

Yet academics can make, I believe, vitally important contributions to the development of these technologies. Perhaps the most crucial are interventions that provide historical contexts showing how and why the technologies developed as they did. Although certain paths of development may be over-determined, they are never inevitable. Other paths and other interpretations are always possible. The point I want to underscore is that it is a *historical construction* to believe that computer media are disembodying technologies, not an obvious truth. In fact, this belief requires systematic erasure of many significant aspects of our interactions with computers. It is almost never used as a working hypothesis by the people who are engaged in developing the technologies, for they cannot afford to ignore the materiality of the interfaces they create or the effects of these interfaces on their customers. If we articulate interpretations that contest the illusion of disembodiment, and if these interpretations begin to circulate through the culture, they can affect how the technologies are understood, and consequently how they will be developed and used. Technologies do not develop on their own. People develop them, and people are sensitive to cultural beliefs about what the technologies can and should mean.

Brenda Laurel has called recognizing the importance of embodied interaction an "endangered sensibility" that she believes the arts and humanities should fight to retain and restore. For me, this means being attentive to the materialities of the media and their implications. The illusion that information is separate from materiality leads not only to a dangerous split between information and meaning but also to a flattening of the space of theoretical inquiry. If we accept that the materiality of the world is immaterial to our concerns, we are likely to miss the very complexities that theory at its best tries to excavate and understand.

The implications of my strategic choice of definition now stand, I hope, fully revealed. Virtuality is not about living in an immaterial realm of information, but about the cultural perception that material objects are interpenetrated with informational patterns. What this interpenetration means and how it is to be understood will be our collective invention. The choices we make are consequential, for it is in the complex, doubly figured, and intensely ambiguous condition of virtuality that our futures lie.

5

From Cybernation to Interaction: A Contribution to an Archaeology of Interactivity

Erkki Huhtamo

"We are not destined to become a race of baby-sitters for computers. Automation is not a devil, a Frankenstein," the British industrialist Sir Leon Bagrit uttered in 1964, in one of his noted radio lectures on automation.[1] Whatever Bagrit may have thought about children and devils, his statement is a time trace, a textual keyhole through which to peer into another technological era. Amidst the current vogue for "interactive media" or navigating "the Net," the metaphor of baby-sitting a computer seems alien. The same might be said about the topic Bagrit was addressing: automation, or "cybernation." In the 1960s these concepts were widely debated as markers of a technological transformation that was felt to be shaking the foundations of the industrialized world. "Automation" and "cybernation" have long since ceased to be hot and controversial catchwords in public discourse.[2] Does this mean that such concepts, as well as the context in which they were molded, have become irrelevant for our attempts to understand technoculture, including fashionable phenomena like interactivity?

This chapter argues against such claims. One of the common features of many technocultural discourses is their lack of historical consciousness. History evanesces as technology marches on. This is not caused merely by some postmodern logic; rather, it is a reflection of the dominance of the "technorationalist" approach to culture. For a technorationalist the past is interesting only as long as it is useful for constructing new hardware and software. This attitude is echoed by the copy of the sales manager. Only the things that give "maximum performance," in practical use and in sales, are worthy of attention; the rest is obsolete. The history of the computer provides an example. Personal computers a few years old are good only for the dump; images of their forefathers, the mainframe computers of the 1950s, might just as well be from an old science-fiction movie. Did they really exist?

The technorationalist approach does not suffice to give a full account of the ways in which technology is woven into the fabric of culture. First, it does not explain how the users themselves have conceived their personal relationships to technology. As Sherry Turkle has so convincingly shown, their attitudes are complex mixtures of different ingredients (cultural, ideological, social, psychological) that make up personal life histories.[3] Second, cultural processes are multilayered constructions. The "progressing" layers (as exemplified by the spectacular advances in computer hardware) always exist in relation to layers that obey other logics. Technological discourses—

the conglomerations of fears, desires, expectations, utopias—do not always develop in tandem with hardware. There is no necessary sychronicity between the features of an invention, the ideas of its creators, and the meanings actually given to it in some cultural context.

The discursive aspects of culture are reiterative. Certain formulations keep coming back, again and again, always adapted to new situations. For their protagonists in the 1950s and 1960s, automation and cybernation represented a radically new and progressive relationship between the human and the machine. In Bagrit's view, it "is not a question of machines replacing men: it is largely a question of extending man's faculties by machines so that, in fact, they become better men, more competent men."[4] Very similar metaphors have been used in other times and places; recently they have been applied to interactive computing by its spokesmen—for example, Seymour Papert, in his description of the "Knowledge Machine," the (hypothetical) ultimate interactive computer that would unleash children's faculties for learning.[5]

Parallels can also be found on the "apocalyptic" side. Jacques Ellul, whose influential *La Technique* (1954) was translated into English as *The Technological Society* in 1964, warned against the effects of automation: "Man is reduced to the level of a catalyst. Better still, he resembles a slug inserted into a slot machine: he starts the operation without participating in it."[6] For Ellul, it was not a question of "causing the human being to disappear, but of making him capitulate, of inducing him to accommodate himself to techniques and not to experience personal feelings and reactions."[7] In his populist attack on interactive media and computer networking, Clifford Stoll has reenacted the fears of "capitulation," claiming that computers "teach us to withdraw, to retreat into the warm comfort of their false reality. Why are drug addicts and computer aficionados both called users?"[8]

In spite of their different emphases, Bagrit and Papert, Ellul and Stoll draw essentially similar conclusions: intercourse with the machine leads either to extending man's capacities, or to his dehumanization and alienation. The machine is either a friend or a foe. This observation merely shows that underneath the changing surface of machine culture there are tenacious and long-lived undercurrents, or "master-discourses," that get activated from time to time, particularly during moments of crisis or rupture.[9] Interesting as observing such "mytho-logics" is, it is also extremely important to show how such traditionbound elements (often manifested as polar opposites) function when (re-)activated in specific historical contexts, thus pointing out the interplay between the unique and the commonplace.

This chapter looks for a perspective on computer-mediated interactivity through the "eyes" of the early discourses on automation and cybernation. Instead of taking automation for granted, it will take a second look at some of its early manifestations, and the ways it was conceived by its champions and adversaries. The attention will be mainly on the modes of organizing the human–machine relationship. The chapter can be read as a contribution to an "archaeology of interactivity." It makes an effort to map contemporary interactive media by relating them to other manifestations of the human–machine encounter and by tracing some of the paths along which their principles have been formed.

From Automata to Automation

In the 1960s, Bagrit told the following anecdote: "I was talking to a man recently who said that automation was not new, that he had it in 1934. I said, 'How very interesting. What did you do?' and then he said 'Oh we had automatic machines even then' and he was convinced that this was automation."[10] The early spokesmen for automation made it clear that a distinction exists between "automatic machines" and "automation" as a general principle. An automatic machine is basically any machine with a sufficient self-regulating (feedback) mechanism to allow it to perform certain functions without human intervention. The classic example is the tradition of the automata, the often anthropomorphic mechanical curiosities that had been constructed and admired over the centuries. Automation, however, was defined in the preface to Bagrit's book quite precisely as "a process which substitutes programmed machine-controlled operations for human manipulations. It is the fruit, so to speak, of cybernetics and computers."[11]

The Spanish inventor Leonardo Torres y Quevedo may have been the first to take the conceptual step from the "useless" automata toward automation. In 1915 he presented the idea that automata could be turned into a "class of apparatus which leaves out the mere visible gestures of man and attempts to accomplish the results which a living person obtains, thus replacing a man by a machine."[12] In an interview in *Scientific American,* Torres claimed that "at least in theory most or all of the operations of a large establishment could be done by a machine, even those which are supposed to need the intervention of a considerable intellectual capacity."[13] The practical possibilities appeared gradually, reaching early maturity in the 1940s, with the development of the first computers, advanced servomechanisms with automated feedback functions, and new theories (cybernetics, information theory) explaining the functioning of such systems. The specific word "automation" seems to have been coined in 1947 at the Ford Motor Company, and first put into practice in 1949, when the company began work on its first factories built specifically for automation.[14]

Automation emerged in the context of military and industrial applications, and also became prominent in the vast field of administrative applications that came to be known as ADP (automatic data processing). In his overview in 1967, John Rose listed four categories of applications: control (from various industries to traffic and air defense), scientific (from engineering design and space travel to economic research and military logistics), information (from accounting and tax records to medical diagnosis and retrieval of information), and others (including pattern recognition and problem-solving).[15] Although some of these applications could be deemed inheritors of earlier mechanized operations (ADP was arguably a further development of the mechanical "business machines" of the 1920s and 1930s), the spokesmen for automation drew a sharp line between mechanization and automation.[16]

For Marshall McLuhan, "mechanization of any process is achieved by fragmentation, beginning with the mechanization of writing by movable types."[17] According to Siegfried Giedion, full mechanization was characterized by the assembly line, "wherein the entire factory is consolidated into a synchronous organism."[18] In the mechanized factory the manufacturing process was rationalized by dividing it into manageable "portions" that followed one another in a strictly predetermined order. Each task was accomplished by a worker coupled with a specialized machine tool. To facilitate and control the process, various methods were developed for the scientific study of work. The results of physiological studies on optimal body movements, proper use of human energy, and worker fatigue were seen by many as increasing the subordination of the worker to the mechanistic principles of the machine instead of easing his task. This was also Charlie Chaplin's interpretation of mechanization in his film *Modern Times* (1936). The human and the machine were hybridized as parts of a larger "synchronous organism." According to Anson Rabinbach's apt characterization, the worker was turned into a "human motor."[19]

The champions of automation pointed out that instead of enslaving the worker, automation makes him the real master. According to Bagrit, automation, "by being a self-adapting and a changing piece of mechanism, enables a man to work at whatever pace he wants to work, because the machine will react to him."[20] McLuhan elaborated the divide between mechanization and automation further by subsuming automation into his synthetic view on the cultural significance of electricity: "Automation is not an extension of the mechanical principles of fragmentation and separation of operations. It is rather the invasion of the mechanical world by the instantaneous character of electricity. That is why those involved in automation insist that it is a way of thinking, as much as it is a way of doing."[21] Automation thus became almost "automatically" one of McLuhan's new "extensions of man." Others, like the sociologist Daniel Bell, saw automation as a token of the passage from industrial to postindustrial culture.[22]

The demarcation line between mechanization and automation was never as clear as its spokesmen wanted to make one believe. This can be discerned even from Bagrit's scruples about using the word: "I am dissatisfied with it, because it implies automaticity and automaticity implies mechanization, which in its turn implies unthinking, repetitive motion, and this . . . is the exact opposite of automation."[23] Sir Bagrit preferred the word "cybernation," because "it deals with the theory of communications and control, which is what genuine automation really is."[24] The word "cybernation" had been used before—for example, by Donald N. Michael—to refer to "*both* automation and computers."[25] Although Michael justified the use of the new word (derived from Norbert Wiener's concept *cybernetics,* coined in the late 1940s) on purely linguistic and textual grounds, the choice can easily be interpreted as a strategic move on an ideological battleground: a make-believe attempt to clear the table of the crumbs of the past.

The Computer as a "Familiar Alien"

The machine as a physical artifact is always surrounded (and sometimes preceded) by the machine as a discursive formation. The "imaginary of automation" was greatly molded by the popular meanings attached to such "familiar but alien" artifacts as industrial robots and mainframe computers. The fashion for "things automatic" spread, however, to other, more accessible fields, such as household machinery and education (teaching machines), that, at least nominally, "brought automation to the people."[26]

The "automated housewife" and the "automated Socrates" are just two of the many discursive manifestations of this process.[27] The discourses on automation also merged with other discourses, like those related to consumerism and modernity, that held sway over the popular mentality in the industrialized world after World War II. The media, including the press, the cinema, and the novelty of the time, television (itself a piece of semiautomatic technology), played a major role in this dissemination. A case in point is an advertisement for the Bendix washing machine from 1946: "It's Wonderful!—how my BENDIX does all the *work* of washing! because it washes, rinses, damp-dries—even cleans itself, empties and shuts off—all automatically!"[28]

The imaginary around the robot is too wide a topic to be covered here.[29] As a self-regulating artificial system the industrial robot was, with the computer, the ultimate symbol of automation. Its roots went, of course, farther back into the mechanical era. In a typical 1950s fantasy, the cover story "Amazing Marvels of Tomorrow," published in *Mechanix Illustrated* in 1955, the robot has two roles. First, there are the "Robot Factories that are completely automatized without a single human workman inside."[30] Second, there is the "Robot Kit, Make Your Own Robot": "The kit has complete tools and parts for building your own metal robot, with an atomic battery guaranteed a century. Hearing and obeying all orders, the robot can be your servant. Or lonely people can train them to play checkers and cards, and even dance."[31] Other pieces of domestic automatic hardware mentioned in the fantasy are the "Meal-o-Matic" in the kitchen and the "Dream-o-Vision," an automatic "dream record" player.

The early imaginary about the computer also was greatly influenced by popular media. An important aspect of the media's appeal is the "surrogate presence" they create, giving access to spheres of life that are denied to direct experience. For the general audience the computer was for years an emphatically "nontactile," out-of-reach object locked behind the sealed doors of the control and engine rooms of the society. Its first public appearances were in television shows, newspaper cartoons, and popular science stories.[32] For example, there were game shows on TV featuring huge, room-sized "giant brains" to which a human (often a grandmother or a child) was allowed to pose questions. The computer would answer in some way, either with blinking lights or by spitting text through a teletypewriter. Another variation was the chess game between a human master and a computer. The motiva-

Cover of the March 1955 *Mechanix Illustrated*.

tion behind these "appearances" was to cash in on the novelty value of the computer (and automation), but also to humanize it to a certain degree. The "human face" was needed because most of the actual operations the early computers performed were so unexciting, or even hostile and destructive.

The media made the computer a "familiar alien." For example, it was frequently implied that the computer was in some way "alive," but even the "signs of life" were doubly mediated, first by the media and second by the computer's operators and programmers. The stereotyped little men in white coats standing by the huge machine (seen in countless cartoons) represented both a human presence and a distanced, mystified scientific priesthood.[33] Like priests, the operators and the programmers were dedicated to the "secret knowledge" about the computer and acted as mediators, both delivering questions to the computer and interpreting its answers. This atmosphere was beautifully described by Robert Sherman Townes in his short story "Problem for Emmy" (1952), told from the point of view of an assistant operator for a mainframe computer, Emmy:

When a problem was finally selected it was sent to the mathematicians—perhaps better, The Mathematicians. In keeping with the temple-like hush of the Room and our acolytish attendance on Emmy, there was something hieratic about these twelve men. They sat in two rows of six white desks, with small adding machines and oceans of paper before them, bent over, muttering to themselves, dressed in white (no one seemed to know quite why we all wore white), like the priests of a new logarithmic cult.[34]

Cartoons often emphasized the misunderstandings and communication breakdowns between these "priests" and the computers. In one typical example, two operators are standing by a mainframe. One of them says to the other, "Do you ever get the feeling it's trying to tell us something?" In another cartoon a similar-looking pair of operators is reading a tape output from the computer: "I'll be damned. It says, 'Cogito, ergo sum.'" The short story by Townes, mentioned above, deals with unexplainable reactions from the computer, ending in a mysterious message: "WHO AM I WHO AM I WHO AM I. . . . "[35] While these examples may simply reflect the public perplexity and the mystified position of the computer, they may also refer to real problems perceived in the relationship between the human and the computer, and thus in the idea of automation. John G. Kemeny reminisced:

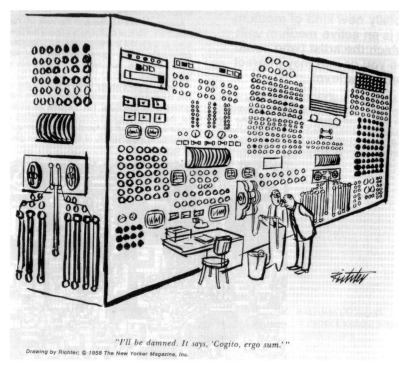

"I'll be damned. It says, 'Cogito, ergo sum.'"

The *Cogito* cartoon.
Drawing by Richter, copyright 1958, The New Yorker Magazine, Inc.

[Computers] were so scarce and so expensive that man approached the computer the way an ancient Greek approached an oracle. A man submitted his request to the machine and then waited patiently until it was convenient for the machine to work out the problem. There was a certain degree of mysticism in the relationship . . . *true communication between the two was impossible.* [36]

Many popular discourses stated outright that this kind of "true communication" was not needed anymore. Yet, there were also many instances of resistance to the idea of full automation. This became clear, for example, in reactions to the idea of the autopilot. Even Bagrit noted that "it is interesting to notice that we will often accept a limited degree of automation—the automatic pilot in an aircraft, for instance—but we are reluctant to see the human buffer—in the shape of the pilot—go completely." [37] This feeling was echoed in an anecdote retold in 1975 by Sema Marks: "This plane represents the ultimate in technological sophistication. All controls are handled automatically by our master computer. There is no human pilot aboard. Relax and enjoy your flight, your flight, your flight. . . . "[38]

Lev Manovich has emphasized that the very idea of automation as independent of a human agent is based on a misunderstanding: "It is important to note that automation does not lead to the replacement of human by machine. Rather, the worker's role becomes one of monitoring and regulation: watching displays, analyzing incoming information, making decisions, and operating controls."[39] Manovich sees here a new kind of work experience, "new to the post-industrial society: work as *waiting* for something to happen."[40] This observation leads him to claim that the real predecessor for this kind of a human–machine relationship is the experience of watching a film rather than working on a mechanized assembly line. For Manovich, the paradigmatic figure of this new work situation is the radar operator waiting for another dot to appear on the screen. It could, however, also be the "automated housewife" sitting by her automatic washing machine, adjusting its washing "program," and staring at its "screen" from time to time.

From the "Waiting Operator" to the "Impatient User"

Curiously, Manovich overlooks the role of variations within the new mode of work he has identified, particularly the significance of the differences in the rate of communication between the human and the machine system. According to Manovich, "it is not essential that in some situations [the user's] interventions may be required every second . . . while in others they are needed very rarely."[41] This aspect could, however, be considered extremely significant—as a question not only of quantity but also of quality—when we start tracing the gradual shift toward interactive media. Ideally, an interactive system is characterized by a real-time relationship between the human and the system, or, as the MIT Media Lab's Andy Lippman puts it, by "the mutual and simultaneous activity on the part of both participants, usually working toward some goal, but not necessarily."[42]

In an interactive system the role of the human agent is not restricted to control and occasional intervention. Rather, the system requires the actions of the user, repeatedly and rapidly. In his 1977 prophecy about the "home computer revolution," Ted Nelson gave a description of the emerging "impatient" user, a direct counterpoint to the "waiting operator" of early automation: "We are now going to see a new kind of user: slam bang, sloppy, impatient, and unwilling to wait for detailed instructions."[43]

Thus an interactive system is not based on waiting, but on constant (re)-acting. Interestingly, Harvard professor B. F. Skinner's description of the goals of the mechanical teaching machines he designed in the 1950s and 1960s approximated this idea: "There is a constant interchange between program and student. Unlike lectures, textbooks, and the usual audio-visual aids, the machine induces sustained activity. The student is always alert and busy."[44]

The human–machine relationships characteristic of mechanization, automation, and the more recent interactive systems don't have to be seen as absolutely clear-cut and mutually exclusive. Indeed, interactive media could be seen as a kind of synthesis of the two earlier models of the human–machine system: they adopt from mechanized systems the constant interplay between the "worker" and the machine, sometimes to the point of "hybridization." In the case of video games, virtual reality systems, and various interactive artworks—for example, Jeffrey Shaw's *Legible City* (1988) and *Revolution* (1990)—even aspects of physical exercise are reintroduced into the human–computer interaction. This "positive," active physical hybridization could, however, be traced to pinball machines and other mechanical coin-operated devices as well.[45] Computer-based interactive systems, however, incorporate innumerable automated functions.[46] As a consequence, different behavioral modes, including that of "waiting," can be included as built-in options of the system (in either hardware or software).

The procession toward today's interactive systems has taken place gradually with the development of more immediate and versatile computer interfaces, faster processing speeds, and larger memories. This technical development, with Ivan A. Sutherland's interactive drawing program *Sketchpad* (1963) as one of its early milestones, has been well documented.[47] It is, however, important to remember that this development has also been related to the broadening range of applications of computer systems. Early mainframe computers that were mostly used for complex mathematical calculations hardly required interactive features. These became necessary with the development of new uses for the computer, such as simulation, visualization, word processing, and gaming.[48] They were also connected with the gradual spreading of the computer away from the administrative and indus-

Ivan Sutherland sitting at his Sketchpad.

trial context into many different spheres of social life, including private use. Bagrit understood this development as early as 1964:

It is now possible to envisage personal computers, small enough to be taken around in one's car, or even one's pocket. They could be plugged into a national computer grid, to provide individual enquirers with almost unlimited information.[49]

Beginning from automation, Bagrit thus saw not only the coming of the personal computer but that of the Internet as well.[50] Almost at the same time, Marshall McLuhan observed the interactive and communicative potential immanent in automation: "Automation affects not just production, but every phase of consumption and marketing; for the consumer becomes producer in the automation circuit. . . . Electric automation unites production, consumption, and learning in an inextricable process."[51] With such views, the early idea of automation as a rather straightforward way of rationalizing and controlling industrial production and the handling of statistical data was already opening up to embrace more heterogeneous worlds. McLuhan foresaw "the creation of intense sensitivity to the interrelation and in-terprocess of the whole, so as to call for ever-new types of organization and talent."[52]

Conclusion

Those who had long worshipped silently now began to talk. They described the strange feeling of peace that came over them when they handled the Book of the Machine, the pleasure that it was to repeat certain numerals out of it, however little meaning those numerals conveyed to the outward ear, the ecstasy of touching a button however unimportant, or of ringing an electric bell however superfluously.[53]

These words from E. M. Forster's short story "The Machine Stops" (1928), which might be mistaken for a description of the priesthood of a mainframe computer in the 1950s, are by no means completely out of place in the world of interactive computing. The fact that computers have become ubiquitous, portable, and networked—and, indeed, have turned into media machines themselves—has not completely dispelled the feeling of awe toward them. New technocults have been created in the 1990s, whether in the form of a "lanierist" virtual reality priesthood or that of the "techno-pagans." The 1950s image of the human as a "baby-sitter" for a computer may have been turned upside down, the computers themselves now fre-quently serving as baby-sitters, but the notions and sentiments that guided the development of the computer decades ago are in many cases still current.

This chapter has argued that looking at "obsolete" phenomena like the early discourses on automation and cybernation may give us insights into the nature of the technologies surrounding us today. The now ubiquitous discourse on interactivity may seem to have appeared suddenly and very recently. The catchword "interactive media," to say nothing of "interactive shopping" and "interactive entertainment," was seldom used before the 1990s.[54] Magazines with "interactivity" in their title have begun to appear only very recently.[55] It is, however, important to see that the "cult of inter-activity" has been in the making for a long time. Even though today's pow-erful media machineries have the power to "make" things (instead of merely "presenting" them) almost overnight, these "things," including "interactive media," are not created out of nowhere.

Interactivity is part of the gradual development of the computer from ideas that were first discussed in connection with automation—a phenomenon that at first sight may seem to be its polar opposite. However, we should look even further, to earlier forms of the human–machine relationship. This chapter has only hinted at such phenomena as mechanical coin-operated games and teaching machines as important predecessors of at least some aspects of interactivity. At the same time, however, we should resist the teleological temptation of presenting the whole history of the human–machine relationship as leading toward our present idea of interactivity. This is certainly an illusion created by our observation post, and also by the cunning of history. The fabric of history consists of innumerable threads. It will present completely different visions for other "presents." We should resist the temptation to look at things in the past merely as an extended prologue for the present.

Thus, 1950s ideas about automation are certainly interesting not only from the point of view of interactivity. Another discourse closely related to it was the early development of artificial intelligence. After being eclipsed for a long time, it is regaining new vigor, but this time in the quite different-looking disguise of artificial life research. This may provide another good excuse to go back to the "basics," ideas concerning cybernetics and automation in the 1950s and 1960s.

6

Replacing Place

William J. Mitchell

Until very recently, the real estate business had no real competition. You always had to go places to do things. There was no alternative. You went to work, you went home, you went to school, you went shopping, you went to the theater, you went to conferences, you went to the local bar—or you just went out. But the alliance of electronic telecommunications and the personal computer has dramatically changed that. Now you can do these things, and more, without going anywhere—not to any physical place, anyway. You can do them in cyberspace.

"Cyberspace" isn't really some weird, new kind of space. It's a figure of speech that has emerged to cover a gap in our language. It allows us to describe, for example, the paradoxical situation that arises when you talk with a friend on the telephone. A naively curious child might ask, "Where does that conversation take place?" Obviously it's not just where you happen to be. And not just where your friend is. You can try to explain that it happens in two widely separated locations at once, or you can just say that it occurs in a special realm of electronic connections—in cyberspace.

As electronic telecommunication systems burgeoned, made the transition from analog to digital, and began to hook up to computers, this was a metaphor waiting to happen. And happen it did, in 1984, when William Gibson's novel *Neuromancer* introduced the term and vividly elaborated a vision of a computer-networked world of virtual places, disembodied consciousness, all-powerful global corporations, and hotshot hackers who cracked the corporate fire walls. Orwell's industrial-era dystopia of surveillance and Big Brother was replaced by a cool, postmodern, electronic Erewhon. Gibson's coinage quickly became general currency; before long, "cyberspace" was showing up everywhere, from the *Wall Street Journal* to the Modern Language Association. But the vision behind it was just cyberpunk fiction, right?

Worlds of Words

Well, no. Provisionally and imperfectly, the signifier started to sprout a signified; life began to imitate art. The growing Internet, and new commercial on-line services such as CompuServe and America Online, soon created a first approximation to Gibson's cyberspace by setting up numerous "places" and "rooms" that you could "enter" to interact with other people from your personal computer.

In an on-line "chat" room, for instance, you can converse by typing in your comments and seeing the responses of the other participants displayed on your screen. There isn't really any room, though—just some computer software that brings the participants in the conversation together and thus—in some abstract fashion—performs the basic function of a room. It is almost irresistible, then, to say that the software constructs a "virtual room."

MUDs (Multi-User Domains) and MOOs (MUD Object-Oriented) extended the virtual room metaphor by introducing the possibility of large-scale, collaboratively constructed, on-line environments—"virtual cities" that you could explore and within which it was possible (in some sense) to have a room of one's own.[1] These evolved from Dungeons and Dragons, the fantasy role-playing game that became a craze among high school and college kids at the end of the 1970s (hence the alternate acronym for MUDs, Multi-User Dungeons). The most popular have attracted tens of thousands, even hundreds of thousands, of participants. These participants enter textual descriptions of imaginary places that others can visit, and of objects and robotic characters that populate those places, awaiting scripted interaction with future visitors. The underlying software ties all the descriptions and scripts together to create a single, continually evolving environment and provides an opportunity for you to meet and interact with other participants within that environment.

The roots of MUDs and MOOs are literary. Like James Joyce's *Ulysses,* they textually construct complex places where the lives of many characters simultaneously unfold and interact, but they are collaboratively authored rather than the work of one person, and they are indefinitely in progress and constantly being extended—not closed and complete like a novel. Instead of turning pages, you explore them by typing commands or pointing-and-clicking to move around and evoke responses. If you look at the record of a typical session, you will see a curious commingling of several types of fictional prose; there are blocks of detailed description (that might come from a nineteenth-century novel) to set the scene at each location; there are third-person mininarratives describing the actions and speech of the characters that are encountered; and there are first-person interventions by the reader/protagonist. It's messy, but it works.

The World Wide Web

By the late 1980s, the World Wide Web had introduced (initially for the high-energy physics research community) another variant on the virtual place metaphor—one that was destined to become stunningly successful.[2] Its key innovation was provision of a simple, robust way to interconnect large numbers of independently created virtual places to form a single, continually growing and changing structure.

The Web presents to its users a world of information sites and links; you can explore it simply by clicking with a mouse to follow links from site to site, much as a tourist might explore a city by taking buses and taxis from attraction to attraction. With the emergence of popular graphic browsers such as Mosaic, Netscape, and Explorer in the mid-1990s, sites began to present themselves as collections of two-dimensional "pages" containing text, graphics, and clickable links. The Web quickly evolved into a vast, densely interlinked virtual structure with millions of active users.

Different imaginations appropriate it in different ways. For architects, urban designers, and the developers of on-line businesses, the Web is most naturally seen as an expanding virtual city with lots of new construction going on. For authors, scholars, and librarians it is an immense, all-encompassing, indefinitely extensible, lavishly illustrated reference work—the ultimate encyclopedia. If Denis Diderot had made it to the digital decades, he would have been delighted by it. For Trekkies following hyperlinks from site to site, without regard for physical distance, it can hardly fail to evoke the transporter.

As the Web expanded, major corporations and public institutions rushed to build elaborate Web sites—rough equivalents of imposing, downtown, corporate headquarters buildings. They employed professional designers, spent a good deal of money, invested in powerful servers and high-bandwidth connections, and felt that they had succeeded if they attracted large numbers of visitors. Simultaneously, commercial sites proliferated and routinely presented themselves as virtual "shops" and "malls." At the other extreme from these corporate and commercial efforts, hundreds of thousands of individuals built their own home pages on their personal machines, or by using server space rented from Internet service providers. Individual home page construction became—like the cultivation of suburban front gardens—a means of self-representation and a new form of folk art. Directories like Yahoo! have arranged sites into organized structures.[3]

Some directories have made the urban metaphor explicit in very literal ways. Singapore's National Computer Board, for example, calls its directory Cyberville. It opens with a clickable map showing the various "buildings" that you can enter, and heralds itself as "the first electronic township in South-East Asia . . . your one-stop, non-stop electronic village of today, with links to the major sights and sounds of cyberspace." (This turns out to be a particularly clean corner of cyberspace, of course—no virtual 42nd Street or Hollywood Boulevard.) The introduction is a narrative describing a walk-through, with clickable "stops" at various points along the way: "You begin your day by breakfasting at our *Cafe and Restaurant,* followed by a trip to the *News Stand.* . . ."

The very popular GeoCities directory is organized into "themed neighborhoods"—Athens, Bourbon Street, Broadway, Cape Canaveral, Capitol Hill, and so on.[4] These neighborhoods have chat spaces (playing the role of virtual agoras or village squares), commercial sites, residential districts organized into blocks of a hundred individual "homesteads," and search engines to help you get around. Each homestead is represented by an icon, in the form of a cozy suburban house, that you can click to enter. Somehow, it all comes across as a virtualized version of suburban Phoenix or Orange County.

Generally, though, the Web (in the form that it took as it grew explosively after the appearance of Mosaic and Netscape) is a two-dimensional, silent place with no people; you can explore it endlessly, but you can't meet anyone there. However, these limitations are not very fundamental; they are just more-or-less accidental consequences of the Web's original grounding in the computer and telecommunications technology of the 1980s, limitations on the bandwidth available to most users, its initial goal of providing a way to share scientific data, and the fact that the basic tool for building Web sites (HTML, HyperText Markup Language) is best suited to handling text and two-dimensional images. The limitations can be overcome by extending or completely rethinking the underlying software, and many efforts were soon under way to do this.[5]

Avatars and Habitats

During its brief and now legendary existence in the late 1980s, Lucasfilm's Habitat showed how to put people into virtual places—one way to do it, anyway. Running on the QuantumLink commercial network (which later evolved into America Online) and Commodore 64 personal computers, it was an on-line, two-dimensional graphic world populated by cartoon characters called avatars. The term "avatar" is appropriated from the Sanskrit, and originally referred to the Hindu notion of a deity descended to earth in an incarnate form.[6] The dominant metaphors here were of comic strips and Saturday morning animated cartoons. Like comic strips, the simplified graphics resulted from the strict limitations imposed by the medium.[7] Also like the cartoons, there were fixed scenic backgrounds across which objects and characters could move stiffly.

In Habitat, you could design your own avatar (the visual equivalent of a chat room or MUD pseudonym) to represent yourself in any way you wished—within the constraints of the medium and the catalog of available body parts and props. You could move your avatar around in a complex imaginary city called Populopolis, meet other people doing the same thing, and converse by typing messages that appeared on-screen in real time. Though Populopolis never had a population of more than a few hundred, and soon died (becoming one of the first lost cities of cyberspace), Habitat was a prototype that quickly spawned many successors. These include Club Caribe, which succeeded it on Quantum Link and grew much larger; Fujitsu Habitat,[8] running on the NiftyServe network in Japan and claiming ten thousand "citizens"; WorldsAway on CompuServe; ExploreNet on the Internet; and Time Warner Interactive's The Palace.[9]

In a rudimentary but effective fashion, WorldsAway appropriates the theatrical notions of costume, props and gestures. Characters can push the furniture around, sit on chairs, and carry objects in their hands. They can switch heads, bodies, and genders. Since bodies are virtual and readily dismemberable, there is in fact no clear distinction between body parts and props and costumes; here, your head is just a prop!

Unlike the original Habitat and its most direct progeny, which have been maintained on central computers and have depended on dial-in connections, The Palace is actually an evolving collection of linked, independently maintained, Weblike Internet sites. It presents a stage-set "architecture" of its world by replacing "pages" with elaborately rendered, two-dimensional color pictures of different kinds of "rooms"—the Palace Gate, Harry's Bar, the Red Room, the Study, the Spa, the Pit, the International Lounge, the Total Cosmic Cavern, Cybertown, the Space Station, Thatscape (a gay bar), the Village (where the conversation is in French), and so on. These rooms

Habitat's cartoon avatars.

A map to the WorldsAway virtual environment.

William J. Mitchell

are populated with avatars that—recalling their comic strip-character heritage—move around the frame and converse in speech balloons.

The Palace's browser software allows you to create your own avatar, teleport it from room to room, control its position within the frame, have it say things to the other avatars, and even have it trigger sound effects and preprogrammed animated gestures. Your avatar is born into the world as a simple colored sphere with a smiley face, but you can readily customize it by choosing from palettes of colors, expressions, and props, and by applying paint tools. So expression is not only textual but also a matter of makeup and mask management.

Technically, it is not difficult to use a photograph of your own face as your avatar in these sorts of environments. In systems for business use, such as the Art Technology Group's Oxygen virtual conference room, that seems appropriate.[10] But in more playful, social environments, users seem to enjoy the chance to dress up for going out.

You can surf into WorldsAway or The Palace at any time, just as you might drop into the local pub. You will always find some characters hanging out, ready to talk. Since they're all in disguise, though, and there's no possibility of identification or retribution, they're often tempted to spin some pretty tall tales to newcomers. (Regulars learn to be particularly suspicious of suggestively embodied females mouthing come-on lines; these usually turn out to be sniggering teenage boys in electronic drag.) These are not places where everyone knows your name—not your real name, anyway.

Sound, Expression, and Lip-Synch

Costume parties and masked balls can be amusing, and it can even be argued that they perform an important social function, but they aren't the best places to be when you want to be sure of the identities of your coparticipants, and when you need to see subtle nuances of expression. You wouldn't negotiate a contract or make an important emotional commitment there (though advice columnists sometimes get plaintive letters from those who have made just that mistake). So avatars and speech balloons don't always suffice, and there is a need to augment virtual worlds with sound and video—to turn them into places where you can see the look on someone's face, read his body language, and hear her tone of voice.

Unfortunately, the original Internet was not designed to carry live sound and video, and its basic structure did not really suit it to performing these tasks. But its capabilities could be stretched to accomplish them in limited ways, and the introduction of higher bandwidths and newer digital networking technologies will make high-quality sound and video increasingly feasible. Thus, by the mid-1990s, we were beginning to see prototype virtual places that provided more complete and realistic representations of their inhabitants.

For example, NTT's InterSpace[11] system added audio communication to an avatar-populated virtual space. In InterSpace, users speak into microphones at their computers, and the voices are mixed according to the angles and distances among their avatars in perspective-rendered three-dimensional spaces. Avatars are controlled by joysticks, and take the form of robots with video monitors for heads; these monitors—you guessed it—display live video images of the faces of their owners. It is still stiff and strange by comparison with being there in the flesh, but it represents a big step beyond Habitat. It's as if the phone handset becomes a remotely controlled, speaking-and-listening video popsicle.

A key to making speech believable, as ventriloquists and puppeteers have always known, is synchronization of facial expression—lips, in particular—with the sound. Careful sound synchronization can make even very crude, stiff facial motion seem natural—an old trick of cartoonists. So video-based systems like InterSpace become considerably less effective when bandwidth limitations result in slow, jerky, poorly synchronized video. On the other hand, animated avatar systems like OnLive!'s Utopia inexpensively gain verisimilitude through careful lip-synching combined with random gestures such as blinking.[12]

It's a replay of the movies. Silent virtual places came first, but by the mid-1990s they were being replaced by the talkies. And as this happened, forms of expression that depend on subtle nuances of expression (irony and sarcasm, attentiveness, reassurance, exchanging glances, flirting, pitching a project, conveying enthusiasm or skepticism, rolling your eyes, keeping your distance, the unspoken cold shoulder) became increasingly feasible in cyberspace.

3D Shared Spaces

This tale of technical development and associated extension of expressive potential does not end with sound and synchronization. At the point when the World Wide Web began to evolve into a new mass medium, three-dimensional virtual environments had long been familiar to designers who use CAD systems, computer animators,[13] users of flight simulators, and aficionados of virtual reality video games, so it was not hard to imagine incorporating virtual reality into the Web to create places that users could "walk" or "fly" around and doors they could pass through to follow hyperlinks to other sites.

Before long, then, VRML (Virtual Reality Markup Language) emerged to complement HTML, and extensions and elaborations of it were quickly used to construct a first generation of three-dimensional virtual places on the Web. Microsoft's V-Chat, Intel's Moondo, Sony's Cyber Passage Bureau, IBM's Virtual World, Lycos's Point World, AlphaWorld, Worlds Chat, The Realm, and Utopia were among the earliest.[14] Creation of these places began to look more like a job for architects and urban designers than one for graphic artists.

This was not the only 3D shared-space technology to emerge. At around the same time, for example, the Swedish Institute of Computer Science's Dive[15] (Distributed Interactive Virtual Environment) system was used to create some experimental cyberspace places. Dive environments have no centralized server; instead, they create the impression of a shared virtual world by sending multicast messages to coordinate software running simultaneously at many different network nodes. Users are represented by three-dimensional avatars. They can navigate through the shared world, meet and speak with other users, grab objects and manipulate them, and get together to collaborate in virtual conference rooms.

At the Mitsubishi Electric Research Laboratory, near the MIT campus in Cambridge, Massachusetts, researchers took yet another technical approach, pushed the envelope of computation and telecommunications capabilities, and did something even more spectacular. They created an extensive, elaborately detailed, fully three-dimensional, mile-square virtual place called Diamond Park.[16] As I wrote these paragraphs in 1996, it represented the cutting edge of networked, shared-environment research.

You see Diamond Park realistically displayed on a screen in front of you, and you "ride" around it by pedaling and steering a stationary bicycle that's wired to the computer. (This is a clever solution to the difficult problem of controlling a complex, highly articulated, three-dimensional character.) It's a marionette world, with the difference that you do not remain outside it

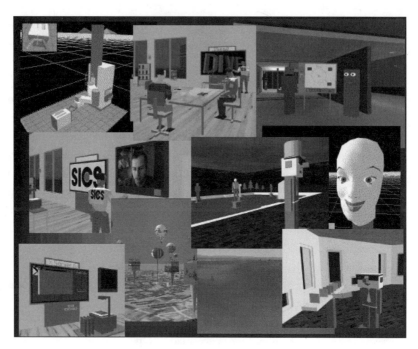

A collection of spaces from Dive.

pulling strings, but experience it through the eyes of your character—as if you were Gepetto inside the body of Pinocchio.

Diamond Park is physically engaging; when you go uphill, you have to pedal harder, and you can get quite a workout exploring the whole site. As you cycle around, you encounter others—represented as three-dimensional animated avatars—doing the same thing. (Actually, of course, the real people that they represent are all at their own stationary bicycles hooked to computers elsewhere in the network.) When they are close enough to be within earshot, you can speak to them and hear their responses. You can even race them round a virtual velodrome.

Could you dance in Diamond Park? Not easily or well, but the bicycles do provide a rudimentary means of bodily expression. To do more, you would need an interface that tracks subtleties of motion. And if you wanted to dance with a partner in any but the stiffest and clumsiest way, you would certainly need sophisticated force feedback—sufficient to tell you, for example, when avatar feet are stepping on avatar toes. (Keep in mind, though, that avatars don't necessarily have toes!)

With Diamond Park, modernism's quest for architectural lightness and transparency (originally pursued in steel and glass), and for the replacement of solidity by surface, had gone to the limit. And it seemed—to avant-garde enthusiasts, at least—that complex, three-dimensional virtual places, in which you could meet and interact with people from all over the world, might well be the new architecture of the twenty-first century. The architecture might be elementary, and your avatar might have a stiff and archaic look (like a Greek kouros), but it was easy to imagine that these limitations could be overcome with higher bandwidths and greater processing power.

Digital Downtowns and Cyber Siberias

Just as adequate building materials don't guarantee a successful work of architecture, though, so use of sophisticated networking technology and software doesn't guarantee that a virtual place will succeed. If you build one—no matter how fancy—they won't necessarily come. As with physical spaces, there are certain conditions of success. And if these conditions are not met, a virtual place is likely to remain unvisited and uninhabited, and thus to fail in its intended role.

First, like a shop, restaurant, or theater, a virtual place must be sufficiently accessible to potential users; if it is too much effort to get there, few will come. In physical space, accessibility is achieved by selecting a central location in a city or neighborhood, by locating at a transportation node, by choosing a site on a busy street or highway, or by building adjacent to an "anchor" attraction such as a large department store in a shopping mall. In cyberspace, accessibility is not a matter of physical location, but of the number of intermediate locations that must be visited, and of the number of hyperlinks that must be followed, in order to arrive there. Your cyberspace "neighborhood" is the collection of sites directly linked to yours; it may be large and densely populated with busy sites, or it may be small, isolated, and seldom visited. Curiously, since the linkage relation (unlike that of physical adjacency) is not symmetrical, neither is cyberspace neighborliness. Your site may point to others that do not point back, or the converse may be true, or there may be a roughly even balance.

So being in the right cyberspace neighborhood matters. And thus, for example, providers of search engines are willing to pay for clickable locations near the top of the Netscape browser's home page; they want potential users to be just one mouse-click away from that heavily visited location. And they are acutely aware that their major competitors are adjacent in cyberspace, like competing shops along a street.

And, just as narrow, congested streets can reduce the accessibility of a neighborhood, so insufficient bandwidth or server capacity can reduce the accessibility of a virtual place. Telephone networks respond to these conditions by giving busy signals. On the World Wide Web (commonly known to disgruntled users of popular sites as the World Wide Wait), they produce response delays or, worse, "connection was refused by the server" messages. In any case, builders of virtual places—particularly ones that expect numerous visitors—must take care to provide sufficient capacity.

Logical Landmarks

It is not enough for a virtual place to be accessible. To pull in visitors, it must also be visible, attention-getting, and attractive.

Traditionally, buildings have accomplished this by being landmarks. Thus churches have steeples for visual prominence, and bells to attract attention acoustically. Important public buildings are architecturally imposing and prominently sited. Headquarters of large corporations are in logolike high-rise towers. Alternatively, instead of serving as a landmark itself, a building might separate out the functions of shelter and signification, becoming a relatively simple "shed" with a highly visible sign out front—the strategy of Las Vegas, the commercial strip, and Robert Venturi.[17]

There are counterparts to these strategies in cyberspace. One way to attract attention, for example, is to erect logical "landmarks" for the increasingly numerous search engines and agents that now constantly roam the on-line landscape. Many of these relentless software snoops create indexes to on-line sites by searching for occurrences of keywords, so the designer of a virtual place can respond by including words that function as descriptors and identifiers—much as steeples function as identifiers of churches.

Another useful strategy is to create a buzz, like that of a crowded, successful restaurant or club.[18] Some Web sites attempt to do this, in a rudimentary way, by prominently displaying access counters (like the mileage counters on automobiles); when you surf in, you see that many others have been there before you.[19] "Cool Site of the Day" lists generate traffic by drawing attention to selected sites. If a site does get large numbers of hits, it will be noticed by directory systems, like 100hot,[20] that monitor Web traffic and produce directories listing the most popular sites—then appearance in such directories usually attracts still more hits.

And, like fast-food restaurants on a commercial strip, virtual places can have attention-grabbing electronic "signs" "out front." But where in cyberspace is the front? And what corresponds to being in a prominent location beside the road? On the Web, and in similar hyperlinked structures, the equivalent of having a sign to drag in the customers is having a clickable graphic at a highly visible location on a frequently accessed site, such as the home page for a search engine or a major entertainment site. Space here is scarce and usually expensive, of course, as it is for billboards in Times Square. Like ad-space buyers working with more traditional media, then, designers of Web sites may choose to put their resources into expensive representation at a few very prominent locations or into more, less expensive, but less trafficked spots.

Since there is no necessary physical relationship between a Web advertisement and a site, and since electronic content can be changed much more quickly and easily than the content of traditional billboards, a site can be represented by a fluid, constantly changing set of linked advertisements. It is as if a building could have facades and entry points on many different streets in a city, and could rearrange these at will to respond to changing needs and conditions.

Staying Around

If you are like me, you never return to most of the virtual places that you encounter. Why should this be so? Conversely, what might motivate people to return to virtual places? What generates loyalty to virtual communities?

Often, in fact, there is very little such loyalty. Many virtual places are more like the legendary Woodstock music festival than the nearby village of the same name. Inhabitants appear briefly, interact for a while, then leave. Nobody except the promoters has much of a stake in the place or an incentive to invest in it—particularly for the long term. In the actual village of Woodstock, New York, by contrast, there *are* long-term residents, there is a system of land tenure, people invest in buildings and businesses, and there is a dense web of ongoing social relationships.

The difference, clearly, is largely one of persistence. If you know that your environment will be there, as you left it, the next time you log in, then you have some motivation to invest time and resources in improving it. If you have a persistent, recognizable avatar instead of a temporary mask and costume, you will be careful about your (its?) reputation. If you realize that you will have to live with your fellow inhabitants for a long time, and that you will need them to respect and trust you, then you will be less tempted by role-playing and momentarily amusing deceptions. If there is some social capital in the associations that you have formed with fellow inhabitants, then you will think twice about ditching them and moving on.

Your personal computer's desktop is a simple and familiar example of a persistent virtual place; when you start up, you find the icons and folders exactly where you left them. Technically, this is achieved straightforwardly by preserving the values of variables that describe the locations of these objects rather than resetting them at the start of each new session. In large, shared virtual places, the issue becomes more complicated; if anyone could change anything, there would soon be utter chaos. So, as pioneering MUDs and MOOs quickly discovered, there have to be some concepts of property and ownership,[21] some conventions governing who has control of what, and some ways of enforcing the conventions. In the MUD/MOO tradition of virtual placemaking, this has commonly been accomplished by creating different classes of inhabitants with different privileges and powers. And on the World Wide Web, you basically have complete control of your own site and very little capacity to alter the sites of others. But these are crude expedients in comparison with the sophisticated rules and customs that have evolved to cover the growth and transformation of our jointly constructed and inhabited physical cities, and they will certainly need to be elaborated as virtual places grow in scale, complexity, and importance.

Ken Goldberg's project, The Telegarden, poetically suggests some of the ways in which this goal might be accomplished. It is a telerobotically tended garden accessed through the Web. You can join the community that jointly maintains it by providing your E-mail address to the project organizers and to the other gardeners. Membership of this community allows you remotely to maneuver a robotic arm via a Web interface, to plant and water seeds, and to monitor all actions and view the state of the garden. This all creates a sense of accountability for one's actions, and people keep returning because they want to see how *their* garden is growing and changing, and because they feel they have a personal stake in it. *Gardening Design* magazine—not usually noted for its attention to the digital world—commented, "Sowing a single, unseen and untouched seed thousands of miles away might seem mechanical, but it engenders a Zen-like appreciation for the fundamental act of growing. Though drained of sensory cues, planting that distant seed still stirs anticipation, protectiveness, and nurturing. The unmistakable vibration of the garden pulses and pulls, even through a modem."[22]

Persistent 3D virtual environments like Diamond Park, and hybrids like the Telegarden, have many of the characteristics of successful bricks-and-mortar architecture. They become increasingly familiar with repeated visits. They do seem to possess the power to evoke memories of previous events that took place there. As they grow and change over time, they become—like cities—records of an unfolding history. And they can sustain communities by providing something of cultural and emotional value to hold in common.

Where Are We Now?

Little more than a decade after the invention of the term, cyberspace is taking definite shape. At the lowest level of abstraction, it is nothing but countless billions of bits stored at the nodes of a worldwide computer network. At an intermediate level—that of the programmer—it resolves itself into a vast, complex structure of sites, addresses, and linkages. And at the highest level—that of the user interface—it reinvents the body, architecture, and the complex relationship of the two that we call inhabitation.[23] In doing so, it appropriates promiscuously from textual narrative, the encyclopedia, the comic strip, animated cartoons, the arts of the ventriloquist and the puppeteer, stage drama, film, dance, architecture, and urban design. With increasing subtlety and expressive power, and on a rapidly growing scale, virtual places now do much of real estate's traditional job.

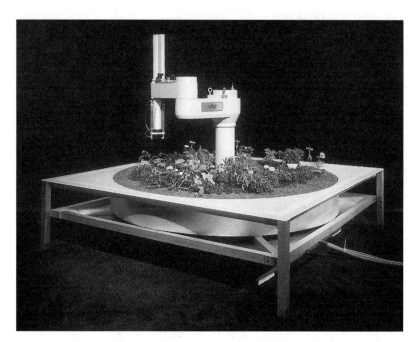

Installation view of the Telegarden.
Photo by Robert Wedemeyer. Courtesy of Ken Goldberg.

Part III

The Medium and the Message

"The medium is the message": Marshall McLuhan's wonderfully compact phrase has gone from provocation to axiom in three decades. For years, communication theory had been structured by the distinction between the how and the what: how information is transmitted on the one hand, and what constitutes that information on the other. In his 1964 book, *Understanding Media: The Extensions of Man,* McLuhan cut through that dialectic like Alexander cleaving the Gordian knot. After languishing in intellectual exile since his blazingly original (and hype-driven) ascendancy crashed in the 1970s, McLuhan is now so thoroughly "back" as to have been anointed the patron saint of *Wired.*

But what does McLuhan's signature phrase mean? McLuhan insists that the content of communication (the message) is determined more by the way it is sent (the medium) than by the intentions of the sender; and that rather than being two strictly separated functions, the medium *is* the message. This kind of hyperbole is typical of McLuhan's best work, which functions as much as mystical incantation as literal explication. Thus the very axiomatic status of "the medium is the message" actually limits its utility. In mathematics, the axiom is a statement that does not need a proof because its truth is completely obvious, like Euclid's axiom that an element is equal to itself. Yet very few, if any, statements about media, much less about messages, rise to that level of self-evidence. Not to be retrograde, but a medium is only as interesting as the messages it manages to transmit. In the vocabulary of the market, this is an issue of content as well as of tech. The three essays in this section offer the closest readings of discrete media and individual projects with an eye toward their intent. They come the nearest to defining what is actually "new" about new media, while at the same time situating them in their historical, aesthetic, and technological contexts.

Throughout a career that has included stints as a linguist, a librarian, the director of the Expanded Books project at the Voyager Company, and a producer/designer of Web sites, Florian Brody has been obsessed with the importance of memory to the development of media forms. In "The Medium Is the Memory," he plumbs the history of print and those strategies of storage and retrieval that predated print to determine how different cultures have used media to create memory systems.

As is evident to any user—whether novice or experienced—certain structures work in new media and others do not. Brody reintroduces the *mnemnoteche* of the classical era, for "in the cybernetic age, textual memory representation returns to the mind, where it resided before the technology of the book became ubiquitous." He argues that reading will move away from the page and onto the screen, just as writing began to do over a decade ago, and that in the coming decades, we have much work to do in designing not simply the content but also the delivery systems for text. As Brody notes, attention to memory is all the more important because new media culture is still at the point where calling something "new" has to substitute for the kind of substantive naming that adds meaning and sets structures in memory.

George P. Landow is ideally suited to extend this skeptical inquiry into the new. The author of seminal works on hypertext's relationship to critical theory, Landow wears many hats: he is both an art historian and a literary critic, and for more than a decade he has pioneered scholarly webs and electronic pedagogies. "Hypertext as Collage-Writing" explores that part of hypertext that fits the "medium is the message" approach: how the ability to link documents makes them "open-ended, a kind of Velcro-text," affecting both creative and critical writing. But Landow also takes into account the specifics of collage as a distinct historical practice within the history of art, segueing from the influence of photographic montage to the function of the cut-up within cubism to discussions of specific hypertexts. His overarching message is that new media by necessity bring into being new kinds of writers and species of readers, who generate new messages that often confound the very media they employ.

Digital artist and theorist Lev Manovich looks to a different set of formative histories and theories in his essay, "What Is Digital Cinema?" In this, he transforms our understanding of film as it becomes digital. For Manovich, the issue is neither the branching tree structures of interactive narratives nor the commercial success of special effects-driven spectaculars, but rather the relationship between the cinema and the real. The impact of electronic imaging technologies shifts the focus of the cinema from photographing motion to animating motion. Linking *Forrest Gump* to the protocinematic Zootropes of the nineteenth century, "What Is Digital Cinema?" offers a unexpected answer: the movies are moving back to their earliest roots, and becoming animation. The magic lantern show of 150 years ago returns, but this time with animatronic dinosaurs and inverse kinematic software systems (which set limits as to how high an animated ball can bounce or an animated elbow can bend). Like Brody and Landow, Manovich cycles between the specificities of the medium and the meaning of its messages.

The Medium Is the Memory

Florian Brody

Media Fetishes

For a long time I would go to bed early. Sometimes, the candle barely out, my eyes closed so quickly that I did not have time to tell myself: "I'm falling asleep." And half an hour later the thought that it was time to look for sleep would awaken me; I would make as if to put away the book which I imagined was still in my hands, and to blow out the light; I had gone on thinking, while I was asleep, about what I had just been reading, but these thoughts had taken a rather peculiar turn; it seemed to me that I myself was the immediate subject of my book: a church, a quartet, the rivalry between François I and Charles V.
— MARCEL PROUST[1]

Books have been on the way out for most of the twentieth century. Our dreams are no longer located between their covers; first movies, then television, and now the computer have offered more involving fantasies. For those in search of narrative rapture, technological media are indeed seductive: Why take the trouble to dream when you can so easily consume that which has already been visualized? While the relation between the story and the apparatus has been much discussed in relation to film and television, we are only now at a point where we can develop a theoretical discourse that ties the consumption of narrative to the media that have been spawned in the computer's wake. And yet, I contend that digital media—unlike film and video—have the potential to emerge as a new type of book.[2]

We "know" what books are. We can define them in terms of type: they are novels, collections of poetry and short stories, reference works, technical manuals, and so forth. A book has a typical topology: a bound set of pages with a cover, rectangular in shape, containing text and images, printed on pages of uniform size. Though we would be hard pressed to offer an all-inclusive definition of "the book," we know one when we see one. Books are more than repositories of text; they are icons of knowledge and are therefore praised, ignored, or burned, depending on the meaning they have for the user. Books stand in metonymic relation to human archetypes and ideas. This is why a book-burning is a terroristic act.

The book has always been used in personal ways, as an extension of memory. Changes in printing affect the availability, portability, and longevity of the book, as well as its position within the reader's life. Paperback editions are available worldwide at reasonable prices—a dramatic change from the last century, when the average household was unlikely to possess any volume other than the Bible; much less the medieval monastery, with its sacred manuscripts chained to shelves.

In this age of textual ubiquity, a bibliophilic culture has flourished. Collectors are happy to buy books without reading them, valuing them as commodities independent of their position within the intellectual culture.[3] Other bibliomaniacs cannot resist the temptation of a bookstore for different reasons. Their obsessions bind them to printed matter not as a commodity, nor simply because of the information it contains, but because the book has the quality of captured memory. Between the covers lies a promise: the possession of a book will mystically extend the mind of the owner.

Thoughout this essay, I will return to this key point: the book is a personal item, an extension of an individual's memory. Medieval books of hours were intimate objects, the only book carried on the person: read, reread, and contemplated. The contemporary equivalent of book as extension of self is the Filofax (and those palm-size machines that ape it) as a compendium of blank pages to be filled and then discarded with each passing year. Changes in printing have affected the availability, portability, and longevity of the book, and its position within the reader's life. It strikes me that we are in the midst of returning to a medieval model: deaccessioning our large-scale personal libraries, unifying all our texts in one place: the computer.

Window on TomorrowLand

> The equipment-free aspect of reality . . . has become the height of artifice; the sight of immediate reality has become an orchid in the land of technology.
> — WALTER BENJAMIN[4]

I must acknowledge certain factors that militate against my basic thesis that digital media will mutate into the new book. At first glance, the realm of digital media is clearly the Tomorrowland of the information society. As much as the world still needs Disneyland and its colonies, the culture of the information age demands its own colorful and interactive environment to offer up a cornucopia of possibilities and prospects.[5] All the hopes and

A page from the Simon Marmion book of hours.
Courtesy of the Henry E. Huntington Library and Art Gallery.

The Medium is the Memory

desires that theme parks can fulfill for only a short period are now available, in the words of an old Microsoft campaign slogan, "at your fingertip."[6] While television continues to fulfill its McLuhanist expectation to be a "window on the world," digital media—especially as they are linked and webbed via the Internet—actually connect the user to the world. Yet for all the hype, the Internet as we find it remains a remarkable concoction of sentimental snippets. As much as the private home page on the Internet is put forward (and put down) as the worst possible use of Web resources, the home page is nevertheless the ultimate form of personal publishing—a memory machine in and of itself.

Before engaging these issues any further, we would do well to remember Ludwig Wittgenstein's observation that paradigmatic differences lie in the rules that define meaning in terms of usage.[7] So we need to define our terms more fully, to determine the distinguishing features and unifying elements among interactive multimedia, academic hypertexts, Web-based infotainment, computer effects-driven cinema, broadcast graphics, and all the other variants of that multiheaded beast called "new media."

Buzzwords and Hyphenates

> To read text
> is to make
> your own text of it
> — GERALD UNGER[8]

How are we to theorize that which does not even have a fully accepted, much less acceptable, name? In the transitional stage between extant and emerging media we are left without an adequate taxonomy to describe the qualitative assets of these media. We have either no words or too many words to describe what they are and what we do with them. The computer industry fills this void with buzzwords and marketing campaigns: words to describe boxes that can be purchased and softwares that will run on them. Though I use the terms "multimedia," "hypermedia," and "new media" thoughout this essay, I do so not out of choice but out of neccesity.

A hyphenate like multi-media always augurs a preliminary stage of a new medium. A multimedia structure need not necessarily become a new medium, but it has the potential to do so. The film projector connected to the gramophone by a rotating wire was as much multimedia as the multiple-slide projection with sound so ubiquitous in the 1960s. The former turned into the talkies; the latter died of overcomplexity. As much as the television was the *Wunschmaschine* of the 1950s, the multimedia PC is today's wishing machine—the new apparatus of desire.[9] Yet these desires are still somewhat inchoate, and the imprecision of the nomenclature extends to the complexities of conceptualizing digital information on screen: text, graphics, motion, and sounds in an interactive environment.

The transition from the computer as a computational device to a multimedia communication machine happened in distinct steps: the move from punch cards to VDUs (visual display units); the transitions from uppercase, light-green-on-dark-green monitors to white-page multifont representation, and then to full-color displays; from straight text to the incorporation of graphics to the recent onslaught of sound and video. Looked at historically, it becomes hard to set the point where multimedia begin.

A new medium is new only until it is established and no longer new; but since any usage of a medium is based upon communicative conventions, a new medium is somewhat of a contradiction. By defining the medium as "new," we acknowledge the transitory stage of the integration of our current analysis, limited though this may be by its temporal frame. While it is still unclear if all the areas encompassed by "new media"—the wide range from Internet to CD-ROM-based edutainment/ infotainment titles to art pieces to interactive TV and kiosk information systems—can pass as one medium, we need to define basic structural parameters through the following question: How do they modulate time and space?

Time is as much a human convention as it is a condition of existence. Every "user" of time perceives it on an individual level that is in turn informed by social and cultural conditioning. The way we define the concepts of past, present, and future (and even the unidirectionality of time) are reflected in all media and, furthermore, are actually enforced by the way we use media. It is precisely because time and space are the cornerstones by which we define our environments that they are central categories within any discourse about media. If, following McLuhan, the medium is the message, and if the message is inextricably bound to space and time, what we are truly dealing with is not message so much as memory: the technology, the message, and the memory ultimately conflate. True multimediality is therefore not defined by the concoction of different media types but by the integration of spatial, temporal, and interactional media. New places for our images allow for new explanations as well as new forms of contextualization.

Models and Content

> Vive la jeune muse cinéma, car elle possède le mystère du rêve et
> rends l'irréalité réaliste.
> —JEAN COCTEAU[10]

One of the best models for conceptualizing a multimediality structural analysis I have ever run across is the diagrammatic "score" Sergei M. Eisenstein developed for his 1938 sound film, *Alexander Nevsky.* This preproduction diagram of the construction of the underlying structure of a story line shows the initial phase of the battle on the ice between the Russians and the German knights, one of the fiercest battles in film history. The layout of the images is highly structured and follows exact graphical concepts. By actively constructing every single scene, Eisenstein generated a different type of memory system than that developed for and by the silent cinema. While he constructed every single frame as an entity, he also carefully choreographed the temporal flow of the images. The clear concept, the spatial and temporal composition of both the image and the development of the story, together with the sound, are evident in these diagrams.

Eisenstein's diagrams for *Alexander Nevsky* remind me of nothing so much as the scores for interactive multimedia programs like Macromedia Director. While digital media offer themselves to rigorous preplanning, too many multimedia pieces lack the sophistication of an underlying structure, and become sprawling messes. Contrast them with *Alexander Nevsky,* which is built on a rigorous theoretical base and a superlative understanding of structure. Eisenstein constructs an artificial memory of places and images within his chosen medium. In looking at his model, we gain an understanding of how he intended to deploy visual and aural elements. He offers a model of how an emergent medium finds its parameters. In new media we are not yet at the point where the conceptual interdependence of time and space is being fully exploited. The lack of such specificity in the new media speaks to the need to get beyond the obsession with placing buttons on the screen. The task of the designer is not to create a better button, but to determine if buttons are required in the first place.

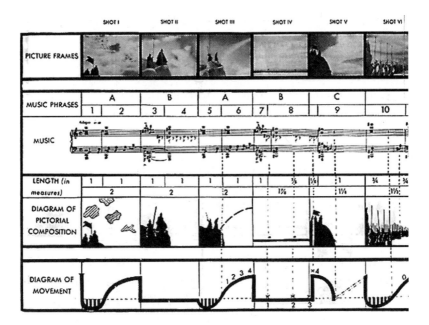

Sergei Eisenstein's visual score for *Alexander Nevsky*.
© Harcourt, Brace & Company.

At first sight, the emergent digital media offer a structured access to information, linked pathways that allow readers to define their own paths and thus gain a better and deeper understanding of the content. But despite these "tools" the reader finds herself in a maze of mirrors. Which types of content are best represented in these emergent media? Encyclopedias, dictionaries, and other reference works seem to work best, while novels are often problematic. This is to say that regardless of the hype about hypertext, there are still very few examples that fully demonstrate the power of storytelling, and thus of authorship, in the new medium.[11]

Memory and the Limits of the Library

The universe (which others call the Library) is composed of an indefinite and perhaps infinite number of hexagonal galleries, with vast air shafts between, surrounded by very low railings.
— JORGE LUIS BORGES, "THE LIBRARY OF BABEL"[12]

Babel's library is a metaphor for the limits, or infinities, of the world and the knowledge it encompasses. The computer, however, has occasioned a shift in the world, complicating the relation of text to books on the one hand, and to memory on the other. In preliterate societies, that which we now refer to as the "text" existed solely within the realm of memory, inside people's heads. With the invention of writing, the text moved to the manuscript but, like the discrete work of art, was a rare and precious object. The technology of printing transformed the text into an exchangeable commodity, ever more plentiful over the centuries. And today we live in vast libraries, yet have almost no access to the text we need.

The computer spawns the electronic text, a volatile form that paradoxically returns the text to our heads while at the same time enmeshing it in an even more sophisticated apparatus. The rampant confusion, and even revolt, that such a blurring of boundaries brings in its wake can be minimized by applying those rules for places and for images defined for the art of memory, making them hold for books as well as for new media systems. Users of hypertext systems build imaginary houses in their minds to understand where they are in the story. When they become lost, it is because the system's designers have violated the traditional structures of the *mnemotechne.*

Electronic texts have no body, only mind—they close the circle to the *mnemotechne* of the Classical era. In Western culture, books contain knowledge that can be shared, sold, or bought. Information is a commodity and, as such, independent from man—a radical shift from the antique model that posited memory as the primary container of knowledge, inseparable from the human mind. The *ars memorativa* were a major part of rhetorical training for any educated Roman, and the rules for the *mnemotechne* were of such importance that the later textual tradition still bears their imprint. Francis Yates points out the linkages between the two forms: "The art of memory is like an inner writing. Those who know the letters of the alphabet can write down what is indicated to them and read out what they have written."[13]

When we see books as spaces that we are able to enter and explore, much like a house, we find ourselves in memory spaces similar to the theaters used in the classical *ars memorativa.* The Memory Theater, a concept used by Giulio Camillo, Giordano Bruno, and later by the English hermetic philosopher Robert Fludd, was a theater that would contain the concepts and the knowledge of the world. By entering the theater, one would gain access to that knowledge and be able to grasp the concepts contained. The theater was seen reversed—the information was set up in the auditorium and the user/reader was set on the stage, where he observed from this central position all the aspects presented to him: everything in the world, everything above, and everything below.

Later, the book became the stage of our memory theater, and we hit our marks by means of the technology of text. Interestingly, as text becomes more easily manipulable in electronic form, the differences between primary and secondary text vanish—the marks of memory become blurred. While handwritten marginalia in a printed book are clearly distinguishable from the printed text, they appear on the same structural level with the primary text in a manuscript—even down to the same font.

If a medium is a conveyor of memory rather than of messages, this offers us some insight into how to design for new media. This starts at the level where our memory technologies tend to define the very way we metaphorize our lives. Three generations ago, I would likely have categorized every evocative scent as inextricably linked to Proust's madeleine. In my youth, I saw the road to work on an average morning as one long tracking shot in a *nouvelle vague* film. Today I find it difficult to think of my life as anything but an interactive network. The connection has become more important than the here and now of the situation.

Print and the People of the Book

Constat igitur artificiosa memoria ex locis et imaginibus.
— AD HERENNIUM III[14]

As noted, books and technological media have always served as memory technologies. To write a text is to save the ideas, thoughts, and stories of the text. But every external memory technology bears the risks of diminishing the individual's ability to develop her own "internal" memory systems. Plato describes the dangers of writing in *Phaedrus;* hermeneutic circles like the Druids were not allowed to write down their knowledge, but had to pass it on orally from one generation to the next. The Judeo–Christian tradition is different. The Jews refer to themselves as the People of the Book, and their laws define precise interfaces to this memory technology: the Torah is to be read and handled according to special rules and to be buried once it is no longer usable. From the Reformation on, the Christian West has seen posses-sion of the Bible as a prerequisite of faith.

This West is, of course, eschatological, and for the past few centuries its utopian hopes have had a distinctly technological flavor. These last few years before the next millennium have proven to be no exception. First interactive multimedia, then virtual reality, and now the World Wide Web have been put forward as a means to salvation. But what is it that we hope to save? I think that the hope for these technologies is that at base, they will serve as the ultimate memory machines that will help us to store everything forever: all knowledge, every story, the punch lines to the totality of human humor, all questions, the sum total of the answers. In short, we will create an eter-nity out of our collective memories.

The underlying message of hardware producers has always been one of ultimate salvation. And the problems that were supposed to disappear have always been memory problems: tokens you want to remember but cannot, and tokens you cannot forget. Today, we have a wide range of machines to help us remember, but only a few contraptions that help us forget. Perhaps we need to focus on forgetting.[15]

S   C   CS   B

My working title for this essay was "Sip Here With Cover On." This is the gnosticism of the European expatriate in that most and least American city, Los Angeles. I am Viennese no matter where I am, and for me, coffee lives in a café. Yet in Los Angeles, coffee is a part of car culture—the cup of lukewarm java to go is a convenient technology for the autobound. So I learn the secret code—revealing the memory of a lost experience. In Vienna the coffee arrives in a cup—black, of course—and we know how to activate its interface, as has every human since the discovery of the hollow gourd. Yet in LA, the coffee arrives covered and of an indeterminate hue. We no longer have access to it, and we need someone to tell us what to do. We no longer smell the aroma and feel the heat, and cannot rely on human history as a guide. Just as CDs will be harder to decode than the stone of Rosetta, who will be able to make sense of

S   C   CS   B

in the future's excavations of our present? The smell and the taste lie below the lid, and there is a door, a gateway that gives access to small quantities.

Like the computer screen, it gives way to a hyperreal perception of something that has been perfectly ordinary. Like much of the excitement effect of the movies, this wears off, too:

Sugar   Cream   Cream&Sugar   and   Black.

Trompe l'oeil is nothing but an inquiry into reality, and the painted windows in eighteenth-century houses are no more an illusion than Windows NT. They have a different functionality and serve different primary purposes. It is in their functions as memory spaces that they are of similar importance. Computers are less windows to the mind than memory spaces where users deposit icons for later use. Yet the paradox is that present systems work too much like the coffee lid—establishing a literal interface that bars the smell, the taste, and the experience of the coffee.

Seeing the interface as a lid makes us think about it in a new form. The screen of the computer loses a lot of the magic it currently holds when we understand that new media experiences cannot be shared with the machine. Interactivity is never to be seen as interactivity with the computer. The machine is the container of the memory, and thus an important part in our memory chain but nothing more. By understanding the computer as a memory machine, the question of its tool character becomes obsolete.

Materialist histories and theories interest the writer Bohumil Hrabal less than the consumption of books, the way the reader ravenously restructures fact, knowledge, and myth.

For thirty-five years now I've been in wastepaper and it's my love story. For thirty-five years I've been compacting wastepaper and books, smearing myself with letters until I've come to look like my encyclopedias—and a good three tons of them I've compacted over the years. I am a jug filled with water both magic and plain; I have only to lean over and a stream of beautiful thoughts flows out of me. My education has been so unwittingly I can't quite tell which of my thoughts come from me and which from my books, but that's how I stayed tuned to myself and the world around me for the past thirty-five years. Because when I read, I don't really read; I pop a beautiful sentence in my mouth and suck it like a fruit drop, or I sip it like a liqueur until the thought dissolves in me like alcohol, infusing brain and heart and coursing on through the veins to the root of each blood vessel. In an average month I compact two tons of books.[16]

The tons of books that Hrabal's protagonist processes eventually crush him, yet he never gains the knowledge he seeks. He tries to eat the books, to inhale them whole, rather than to analyze their contents. His totemistic approach to the text as book as food stands in contrast to the analytical, even deconstructive spirit of the computer-based hypertext.

The New Book

> We still read *according to* print technology, and we still direct almost all of what we write toward print modes of publication.
> — GEORGE LANDOW, *Hypertext*: *The Convergence of Contemporary Critical Theory and Technology*[17]

To develop the new book, we will have to analyze what it is we want from text, memory, and technologies of knowledge. Our conceptions of text and textuality are so closely linked to the physical object of the book that any paradigmatic change in its form seems to threaten the stability of representations of knowledge. Previously, the fetish character of the bound volume offered the reader a sense that memory was secure between the book's covers. The recent dynamization of text and the book as they move into the electronic matrix unhinges the dependency between reading, the printed word, and truth-value.

Take the very physicality of text, for example. Text and type have often existed in more than two dimensions. Scribes scratched hieroglyphs into papyrus; stonesmiths carved Latin inscriptions into stele; and printers from Gutenberg on have pressed type and ink, modifying the very surface of the paper. Yet new printing and reproduction technologies have all but abandoned the third dimension. Laser printing lays two-dimensional text on the page, an effect closer to stenciling than to engraving. Computer displays eliminate traditional notions of dimensionality entirely—leaving text to float in an electronic matrix.

A linear text, with specified start and end points, is a stable text. The matrix in which electronic text floats is quite different—a flexible environment that allows multiple layers and n-dimensional reading variants. It is this polyvalent ability to enter, amend, and exit the text in a nonlinear fashion that defines hypertextuality.[18]

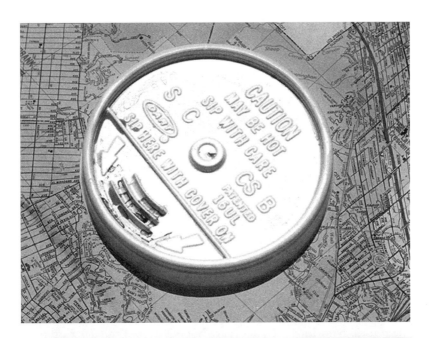

The coffee cup lid code: S C CS B.
Photo by Florian Brody.

Virtual reflections.
Photo by Florian Brody.

The Medium is the Memory

Just as the technologies of text production have changed, so have the functions of reading. Reading as a mental adventure is a relatively young concept. General access to the written word was until fairly recently restricted to the holy books. The special quality assigned to these books—the word of *G'D*—not only restricted their usage but also assigned a quality beyond its primary semiotic character as a sign. In western civilization, the written word gained a truth-value previously held by the spoken word. The arrival of electronic text forces a similar reevaluation of the pagebound text. Although text in a computer is far less stable than the written or printed word, we assign it a very high truth-value. Early computer pioneer Joseph Weizenbaum of MIT remarked, "My father used to say, 'It is written in the holy books.' Today we say, 'The computer tells us.'"[19]

In the cybernetic age, textual memory representation returns to the mind, where it resided before the technology of the book became ubiquitous. Reading will move away from paper, much as writing started to do ten years ago. This augurs a new era of design, for although machines have long been used for writing, very few have been developed through history for reading. To this point, text processors have been developed as write-only devices, conceptualized as highly sophisticated typewriters rather than as reading machines.

The new book will demand dramatic changes in reading habits, though I am unsure how willingly we will all switch to the new forms. Meanwhile, we will read conventional books on screens, experiment with hypertext applications, and explore the potentials of new media for the author as well as for the reader. Eventually, a new memory culture will emerge that will generate its own rules and its own books. Our task is ultimately to overcome the limitations of an old medium by means of a new medium—by changing not the technology but the concepts. The medium conveys memory as much as messages.

The Augustinius book.
Photo by Florian Brody.

Hypertext as Collage-Writing

George P. Landow

From this Derridian emphasis upon discontinuity comes the conception of hypertext as a vast assemblage, what I have elsewhere termed the metatext and what Nelson calls the "docuverse." Derrida in fact employs the word assemblage for cinema, which he perceives as a rival, an alternative, to print. Ulmer points out that "the gram or trace provides the 'linguistics' for collage/montage" (267), and he quotes Derrida's use of assemblage in *Speech and Phenomena:* "The word 'assemblage' seems more apt for suggesting that the kind of bringing-together proposed here has the structure of an interlacing, a weaving, or a web, which would allow the different threads and different lines of sense or force to separate again, as well as being ready to bind others together." To carry Derrida's instinctive theorizing of hypertext further, one may also point to his recognition that such a montagelike textuality marks or foregrounds the writing process and therefore rejects a deceptive transparency.

— GEORGE P. LANDOW, *Hypertext: The Convergence of Contemporary Critical Theory and Technology*

Hypertext as Collage-Writing: The Paper

Frankenstein the Movie, perhaps, but why "Hypertext as Collage-Writing: the Paper"? The answer lies in the somewhat unusual history of this essay, which began existence as series of translations of electronic documents. Most current examples of hypertext take the form of texts originally produced by the hypertext author in and for another medium, generally that of print. In contrast, this essay derives from a hypertext, though it incorporates materials ultimately derived from printed books, too.[1]

On Tuesday, June 7, 1994, at 17:01:54 Eastern Standard Time, Pierre Joris, a faculty member at the State University of New York, posted some materials about collage on a electronic discussion group called Technoculture.[2] Joris wished to share with readers of this e-conference a gathering of texts on the subject he had delivered as a combination of an academic paper and performance art while in graduate school. His materials seemed to cry out for a hypertext presentation, and so after moving them from my mailbox to a file on the Brown University IBM mainframe, I transferred them—in the jargon, "downloaded them"—in a single document via a phone line to a Macintosh whirring away in my study at home. Next, I opened them in Microsoft Word and, passage by passage, copied the individual elements of *Collage Between Writing and Painting,* pasting each into a separate writing space or lexia in a new Storyspace web and then linking them together. Along the way, I created the following opening screen (or analogue to a book's title page):

COLLAGE BETWEEN WRITING AND PAINTING

Pierre Joris

George P. Landow

b e i n g   a n   a s s e m b l a g e   s t a r r i n g
Kurt Schwitters & Tristan Tzara
with special guest appearances by
Georges Braque &
Pablo Picasso
and also featuring
dedicated to . . .

This opening screen, which also serves as a combination overview, information map, contents page, and index, contains links from the obvious places—such as, for example, all the proper names it lists. Clicking upon "COLLAGE" takes one either to one possible terminal point of the web or to the following definition of the term from *Le Petit Robert:*

COLLAGE. 1. The action of gluing. Collage d'une affiche. State of what is glued. — Arts. Papiers collés, a composition made of elements glued on canvas (possibly integrated in the paint). Les collages de Braque, de Picasso. — Techn. Assemblage through adhesion.

2. Addition of glue. Collage of paper, of cloth, in industry. See. Appr t. — Collage of wines: operation aiming at clarifying the wine by precipitating the solids in suspension it contains.

3. Fig. and Fam. Situation of a man and woman who live together without being married. See Concubinage. ANT. Decollage.

Since this dictionary definition, which mentions Picasso and Braque, serves as a another ready-made overview or crossroads document, I linked various words in it to permit readers to traverse Joris's materials in multiple ways. "COLLAGE," for example, leads to a dozen and a half mentions of the term, and the names of the artists link to works of theirs. Because I created this web largely as an experiment and not for publication, I did not have to worry at the moment about copyright issues, and therefore scanned monochrome images of Braque's *Le Courrier* and Picasso's *Still Life with Chair Caning,* and linked them to the names of the artists. At the same time I added H. W. Janson's discussions of collage, linking them as well. Finally, I created a list of thirty authors whose statements Joris included in "Collage Between Writing and Painting," linking this list to the phrase "also featuring" on the title screen.

At this point, some of the similarities between hypertext and collage will have become obvious. Having first appropriated Joris's materials by placing them in a web, and then adding materials that they seemed to demand, I found that, like all hypertexts, it had become open-ended, a kind of Velcro-text to which various kinds of materials began attaching themselves. First, I included the discussion of Derrida and appropriation from the electronic version of my book, *Hypertext: The Convergence of Contemporary Critical Theory and Technology* (1992), that I used as an epigraph to this essay. I also added definitions of hypertext and a list of qualities that it shares with collage. Next, I added several dozen screenshots, or pictures of how the screen appears while reading, of various hypertext webs; these came from a since-published web that served as an introduction to the 1995 hypertext anthology *Writing at the Edge.* Then I added a dozen photographs, each involving issues of representation, illusion, simulation, or subject and ground. Finally, I added a new title page for *Hypertext and Collage: Being in Part, an Appropriation of "Collage Between Writing and Painting."*

After using this web to deliver my contribution to the Digital Dialectic conference at Art Center College of Design, I discovered I would have to transform it into a more or less traditional essay if it were to be part of this collection. These pages thus represent a translation of the *Hypertext and Collage Web.* When I write "translation," I cannot help thinking of the Italian maxim *traduttore = traditore* (translator = traitor). Converting the essay from one information technology to another, I continually encountered the kind of reduction that one encounters when translating—or representing—

something in three (or more) dimensions within a two-dimensional medium. An examination of the differences between the two versions will take us a way into understanding the reasons for describing hypertext as collage-writing.

Hypertext

The term "hypertext" embraces both a utopian vision of writerly artistic possibilities and dramatic cultural change, and much lesser embodiments of that vision in limited technology characterized by discrete, islanded computers and hard-to-read monitors whose flickerings and unbalanced color make reading difficult and aesthetic pleasure hard to come by. Even so, much of the vision of hypertext comes through, however hindered, in these first stumbling, stammering instantiations. Drawing upon the work of Vannevar Bush, Theodor Nelson, Douglas Englebart, Andries van Dam, and other pioneering theorists and practitioners of hypertext systems, I define this new information technology as text composed of lexias (blocks of words, moving or static images, or sounds) linked electronically by multiple paths, chains, or trails in an open-ended web. Since readers can take different paths through such bodies of information, hypertext is therefore properly described as multisequential or multilinear rather than as nonlinear writing. Let me emphasize the obvious—that hypertext is an information technology in which a new element, the link, plays the defining role, for all the chief practical, cultural, and educational characteristics of this medium derive from the fact that linking creates new kinds of connectivity and reader choice.[3]

Although linking thus defines this new medium, a full hypertext environment requires other features to enact the link's full potential. Because readers can chose their own paths through bodies of information, in some circumstances they find themselves with more power than might readers of similar materials in print. Nonetheless, the full Nelsonian vision of hypertext shared by most theorists requires several additional qualities or factors, some of which might at first appear unimportant or matters of technical trivia. For example, if multiple reading paths provide one of the fundamental characteristics of this form of textuality, one-to-many links become essential, and systems must make this form of creating connections easy and indeed inevitable. By "one-to-many" I mean the form of linking in which an anchor (or hypertext point of departure) connects electronically to two or more destinations.

To make such electronic writing easy and convenient for both author and reader, a hypertext system requires certain features, among them the ability to label individual links or link paths and a means of automatically providing the reader with a list of links from a particular anchor. Clicking upon a link site produces a menu of link destinations that overlays a portion of the text one is currently reading. Systems like Microcosm, Intermedia, and Storyspace provide these features, but many, such as Hypercard and World Wide Web viewers, do not, and as a consequence they produce a kind of flattened, often disorienting experience of hypertext.

Of course, although manually creating documents that serve as link menus partially provides one way around this problem, this approach places enormous burdens on the writer, with the expected result that writers tend to avoid the extra effort. Even when one expends the time and energy to create such additional documents, one does not always fully solve the problem, since in single-window systems in which one follows a link by replacing the departure lexia with the arrival lexia, one faces two difficulties: first, someone reading a normal textual or other document finds it replaced by a menu, and second, one receives the impression of having to expend more time and energy on mouse clicks because one has to go through the retrieval of separate documents.[4]

A second, far more essential matter involves matters of size, scale, or quantity. Simply put, to appear fully hypertextual, a web must be large. Unless one encounters a large number of lexias from which to choose, one cannot take many paths through the virtual reading space of the web. In Ted Nelson's vision of hypertextuality, all documents, images, and information exist electronically joined in an all-encompassing docuverse; a link or sequence of them can carry one between lexias spread across the farthest reaches of information space. This vision derives from the recognition that quantity, particularly quantity of choices, produces radical differences in quality. Even if we cannot hope to encounter an all-embracing docuverse in the immediate future (though the World Wide Web has begun to tantalize us with its promise and threat), we can recognize that some of the promised effects of hypertext, such as the empowerment of the reader, cannot develop within small, limited webs.

Size in turn requires networked computing. Of course, one obviously can create rudimentary decentered webs on individual machines that have substantial amounts of memory. Nonetheless, local, wide-area, or even universal networks and hypertext environments capable of using them are needed to realize a full participatory, multiauthored hypertext. If one takes the library, a congeries of books, and not the individual volume in that library, as the most useful analogue for hypertext, one quickly realizes that linking texts stored between pairs of covers to other such texts produces far richer possibilities than simply linking the portions of the separately stored text to themselves. Among other things, such a conception of hypertext brings with it the fact of multiple authorship so necessarily suppressed by print technology. By crossing, and hence blurring, the borders of (what had in print been) the individual text, the electronic link reshapes our experiences of genre, mode, text, intellectual property, and even self.

In fact, it might well be that the intrinsic multivocality—read potential anarchy or decentered authority—of hypertext can arise only in materials created by a multiplicity of authors. In other words, if hypertext redefines the function of the author in ways so radical as to fulfill the much-vaunted poststructuralist death of the author, then that major redefinition of our relations to our texts arises not in the absence of an individual author authoring but in the presence of a plethora of them; not in dearth but in plenitude. So it is, perhaps, not the absence of someone writing, contributing, or changing a text that we encounter, but rather the absence of someone with full control or ownership of any particular text. We find no one, in other words, who can enforce the desire "Leave my text alone!" Linking, the electronic, virtual connection between and among lexias, changes relations and status.

The third required quality or feature of a fully hypertextual system involves another adjustment or reallocation of power from author to reader. It involves, in other words, the ability of the reader to add links, lexias, or both to texts that he or she reads.

Collage Defined

The on-line version of the *Oxford English Dictionary* (*OED*) defines collage, which it traces to the French words for pasting and gluing, as an "abstract form of art in which photographs, pieces of paper, newspaper cuttings, string, etc., are placed in juxtaposition and glued to the pictorial surface; such a work of art." *Britannica Online* more amply describes it as the artistic technique of applying manufactured, printed, or "found" materials, such as bits of newspaper, fabric, wallpaper, etc., to a panel or canvas, frequently in combination with painting. In the 19th century, *papiers collés* were created from papers cut out and put together to form decorative compositions. In about 1912–13 Pablo Picasso and Georges Braque extended this technique, combining fragments of paper, wood, linoleum, and newspapers with oil paint on canvas to form subtle and interesting abstract or semiabstract compositions. The development of the collage by Picasso and Braque contributed largely to the transition from Analytical to Synthetic Cubism.

This reference work, which adds that the term was first used to refer to Dada and Surrealist works, lists Max Ernst, Kurt Schwitters, Henri Matisse, Joseph Cornell, and Robert Rauschenberg as artists who have employed the medium.

In *The History of World Art,* H. W. Janson, who explains the importance of collage by locating it within the history of Cubism, begins by describing Picasso's *Still Life* of 1911–1912: "Beneath the still life emerges a piece of imitation chair caning, which has been pasted onto the canvas, and the picture is 'framed' by a piece of rope. This intrusion of alien materials has a most remarkable effect: the abstract still life appears to rest on a real surface (the chair caning) as on a tray, and the substantiality of this tray is further emphasized by the rope." According to Janson, Picasso and Braque turned from brush and paint to "contents of the wastepaper basket" because collage permitted them to explore representation and signification by contrasting what we in the digital age would call the real and the virtual. They did so because they discovered that the items that make up a collage, "'outsiders' in the world of art," work in two manners, or produce two contrary effects. First, "they have been shaped and combined, then drawn or painted upon to give them a representational meaning, but they do not lose their original identity as scraps of material, 'outsiders' in the world of art. Thus their function is both to represent (to be part of an image) and to present (to be themselves)."[5]

Hypertext as Digital Collage

Hypertext writing shares many key characteristics with the works of Picasso, Braque, and other Cubists. In particular, both work by means of the following:

juxtaposition
appropriation
assemblage
concatenation
blurring limits, edges, borders
blurring distinctions between border and ground.

Some of these qualities appear when one compares the hypertext and print versions of my discussion. First of all, despite my division of this essay into several sections and the use of plates that a reader might inspect in different orders, this essay really allows only one efficient way through it. In contrast, the original hypertext version permits different readers to traverse it according to their needs and interests. Thus, someone well versed in twentieth-century art history might wish to glance only briefly at the materials on collage before concentrating on the materials about hypertext. Someone more interested in hypertext could concentrate upon that portion of the web. Others might wish to begin with one portion of the discussion and then, using available links, return repeatedly to the same examples, which often gather meaning according to the contexts in which they appear.

Another difference between the two forms of "my" discussion of this subject involves the length of quoted material and the way the surrounding texts relate it to the argument as a whole. Take, for example, the material I quoted above from Janson's *History of World Art.* In the Storyspace version it is several times longer than in the print one, and it appears without any introduction. The object here is to let the quoted, appropriated author speak for himself or, rather, to permit his text to speak for itself without being summarized, translated, distorted by an intermediary voice. To write in this manner—that is to say, to copy, to appropriate—seems suited to an electronic environment, an environment in which text can be reproduced, reconfigured, and moved with very little expenditure of effort. In this environment, furthermore, such a manner of proceeding also seems more honest: the text of the Other may butt up against that by someone else; it may even crash against it. But it does seem to retain more of its own voice. In print, on the other hand, one feels constrained to summarize large portions of another's text, if only to demonstrate one's command (understanding) of it and to avoid giving the appearance that one has infringed copyright.

These two differences suggest some of the ways in which even a rudimentary form of hypertext reveals the qualities of collage. By permitting one to make connections between texts and text and images so easily, the electronic link encourages one to think in terms of connections. To state the obvious: one cannot make connections without having things to connect. Those linkable items not only must have some qualities that make the writer want to connect them, they also must exist in separation, apart, divided. As Terence Harpold has pointed out, most writers on hypertext concentrate on the link, but all links simultaneously both bridge and maintain separation. This double effect of linking appears in the way it inevitably produces juxtaposition, concatenation, and assemblage. If part of the pleasure of linking arises in the act of joining two different things, then this aesthetic of juxaposition inevitably tends toward catachresis and difference for their own end, for the effect of surprise, and sometimes suprised pleasure, they produce.

On this level, then, all hypertext webs, no matter how simple, how limited, inevitably take the form of textual collage, for they inevitably work by juxtaposing different texts and often appropriate them as well. Such effects appear frequently in hypertext fiction. Joshua Rappaport's *The Hero's Face* uses links, for example, to replace what in earlier literary writing would have been an element internal to the text; that is, the link establishes a symbolic as well as a literal relationship between two elements in a document. In *The Hero's Face,* after making one's way through a series of lexias about the members of a rock band, their experiences on tour, and their musical rivalry—all of which might seem little more than matters of contemporary banality—the reader follows a link from a discussion of the narrator's seizing the lead during one performance and finds her- or himself in what at first appears to be a different literary world, that of the Finnish epic the *Kalevala.*

Following Rappaport's link has several effects. First, readers find themselves in a different, more heroic age of gods and myth, and then, as they realize that the gods are engaged in a musical contest that parallels the rock group's, they also see that the contemporary action resonates with the ancient one, thereby acquiring greater significance as it appears epic and archetypal. This single link in *Hero's Face,* in other words, functions as a new form of both allusion and recontextualization. Juxtaposing two apparently unconnected and unconnectable texts produces the pleasure of recognition.

first leads	Singing match
The first time I climbed serious lead was after it all went sour and my partner was one of his ex-girlfriends, a leggy blond named Megan who took to the sport with unbridled enthusiasm and a god-given natural ability that left everybody stunned. Climbing lead for the first time is kind of like losing your virginity—there comes a moment when all of a sudden you look behind you and you're	Vainamoinen grew angry at that, angry and ashamed. He himself started singing himself began reciting: the songs are not children's songs, children's songs, women's cackle but for a bearded fellow which not all the children sing nor do half the boys nor a third of the suitors in this evil age with time running out. The old Vainamoinen sang: the lakes rippled, the earth shook the copper mountains trembled the sturdy boulders rumbled the cliffs flew in two the rocks cracked upon the shores.

Symbolic and literal juxtaposion of texts from *The Hero's Face*.

Such combinations of literary homage to a predecessor text and claims to rival it have been a part of literature in the West at least since the ancient Greeks. But the physical separation of texts characteristic of earlier, non-electronic information technologies required that their forms of linking—allusion and contextualization—employ indicators within the text, such as verbal echoing or the elaborate use of parallel structural patterns (such as invocations or catalogs).

Hypertext, which permits authors to use traditional methods, also permits them to create these effects simply by connecting texts with links. Hypertext here appears as textual collage—"textual" referring to alphanumeric information—but more sophisticated forms of this medium produce visual collage as well. Any hypertext system (or, for that matter, any computer program or environment) that displays multiple windows produces such collage effects. Multiple-window systems, such as Microcosm, Storyspace, Intermedia, Sepia, and the like, have the capacity to save the size and position of individual windows.

This capacity leads to the discovery of what seems to be a universal rule at this early stage of E-writing: authors will employ any feature or capacity that can be varied and controlled to convey meaning. All elements in a hypertext system that can be manipulated are potentially signifying elements. Controlled variation inevitably becomes semiosis. Hypertext authors like Stuart Moulthrop have thus far written poems in the interstices of their writing environments, creating sonnets in link menus and sentences in the arrangements of titles. Inevitably, therefore, authors make use of screen layout, tiled windows, and other factors to . . . write. For example, in an informational hypertext, such as *The "In Memoriam" Web,* tiling of documents constructs a kinetic collage whose juxtaposition and assembling of different elements permits easy reference to large amounts of information without becoming intrusive. In addition to employing the set placement of the windows, readers can also move windows to compare two, three, or more poems that refer back and forth among themselves in this protohypertextual poem.

Turning now to another work of hypertext fiction, one sees that in Nathan Marsh's *Breath of Sighs and Falling Forever,* lexias place themselves around the surface of the computer monitor, making the screen layout support the narrative as one crosses and recrosses the tale at several points. In *The "In Memoriam" Web* the collage effect of tiling, separate windows, and juxtaposed text arises in an attempt to use hypertext technology to shed light on qualities of a work created for the world of print.

Here this story arises out of the medium itself. In making their way through this fiction, readers encounter multiple narrative lines and corollary narrative worlds both joined and separated by ambiguous events or phenomena. At certain points readers cannot tell, for example, if one of the characters has experienced an earthquake tremor, a drug reaction, or a powerful illumination. Has the floor actually fallen, or are we supposed to take a character's experience as figurative? Certainly one of the first lexias that readers encounter could suggest any and all of these possibilities: "Andy paused for a second and let his senses adjust to the shock. The floor had been dropping all week now. As he sat by the open window and the frozen night air embraced the room, he realized that it was all part of the long slide down." Clicking upon this brief lexia leads one to "Clang!," which opens with the sound of an explosion and displays its single word in eighty-point type. As one reads one's way through *Breath of Sighs,* one repeatedly returns to "Clang!" but finds that it changes its meaning according to the lexia that one has read immediately before encountering it.

Marsh has arranged each of the texts that make up his web so that they arrange themselves across the screen, permitting some lexias to show in their

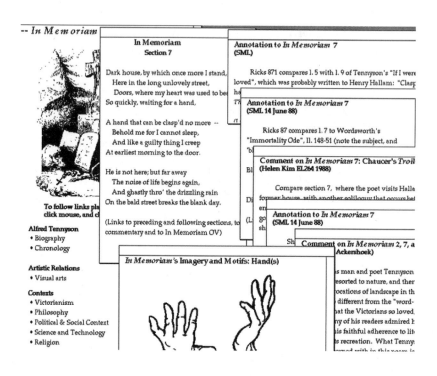

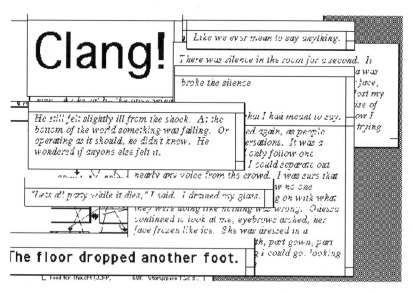

The kinetic collage of the *"In Memoriam"* Web.

The interwoven narrative lexias of *Breath of Sighs and Falling Forever.*

entirety, others only in part. As one reads through this web, one encounters a continually changing collage of juxtaposed texts. Two points about hypertext writing appear in Marsh's web. First, we realize that such collage-writing produces a new kind of reading in which we must take into account not only the main text but also those that surround it. Second, this emphasis upon the increasing importance of the spatial arrangement of individual lexias leads to the recognition that writing has become visual as well as alphanumeric; or since visual layout has always had a major impact on the way we read printed texts, perhaps it would be more accurate to say that in hypertext (where the author controls more of the layout), writing requires visual as well as alphanumeric writing.

Marsh's web exemplifies a form of hypertext fiction that draws upon the collage qualities of a multiple-window system to generate much of its effect. *Patchwork Girl,* Shelley Jackson's brilliant hypertext parable of writing and identity, carries hypertext collage much farther, for it generates both its themes and its techniques from this art form. Jackson, a published book illustrator as well as an author, creates a digital collage out of her own words and images that tells about the female companion to Frankenstein's monster whose "birth takes place more than once. In the plea of a bygone monster; from a muddy hole by corpse-light; under the needle, and under the pen." *Patchwork Girl* makes us all into Frankenstein-readers stitching together narrative, gender, and identity, for, as it reminds us: "You could say all bodies are written bodies, all lives pieces of writing."

This digital collage-narrative assembles Shelley Jackson's (and Mary Shelley's and Victor Frankenstein's) female monster, forming a hypertext Everywoman who embodies assemblage, concatenation, juxtapositions, and blurred, re-created identities—one of the many digital fulfillments of twentieth-century literary and pictorial collages. As the monster slyly informs us in a lexia one encounters early on, "I am buried here. You can resurrect me, but only piecemeal. If you want to see the whole, you will have to sew me together yourself. (In time you may find appended a pattern and instructions—for now, you will have to put it together any which way, as the scientist Frankenstein was forced to do.) Like him, you will make use of a machine of mysterious complexity to animate these parts."

Traveling within Jackson's multisequential narrative, one of the finest hypertext novels to have appeared, we first wander along many paths, finding ourselves in the graveyard, in Mary Shelley's journal, in scholarly texts, and in the life histories of the beings—largely women but also an occasional man and a cow—who provided the monster's parts. As we read, we increasingly come to realize an assemblage of points, one of the most insistent of which appears in the way we use our information technologies, our prosthetic memories, to conceive ourselves. Jackson's 175-year-old protagonist embodies the effects of the written, printed, and digital word. "I am like you in most ways," she tells us.

My introductory paragraph comes at the beginning and I have a good head on my shoulders. I have muscle, fat, and a skeleton that keeps me from collapsing into suet. But my real skeleton is made of scars: a web that traverses me in three-dimensions. What holds me together is what marks my dispersal. I am most myself in the gaps between my parts, though if they sailed away in all directions in a grisly regatta there would be nothing left here in my place.

For that reason, though, I am hard to do in. The links can stretch very far before they break, and if I am the queen of dispersal then however far you take my separate parts (wrapped in burlap and greasy fish-wrappers, in wooden carts and wherries, burying and burning me and returning me to the families from which I sprung unloved and bastard) you only confirm my reign.

Hypertext, Jackson permits us to see, enables us to recognize the degree to which the qualities of collage—particularly those of appropriation, assemblage, concatenation, and the blurring of limits, edges, and borders—characterize a good deal of the way we conceive of gender and identity. Sooner or later, all information technologies, we recall, have always convinced those who use them both that these technologies are natural and that they provide ways to describe the human mind and self. At the early stage of a digital information regime, *Patchwork Girl* permits us to use hypertext as a powerful speculative tool that reveals new things about ourselves while retaining the sense of strangeness, of novelty.[6]

Virtual Collage

Joris explained that he finds most compelling the question not whether collage arose first in painting or in poetry, but whether it functions the same way in each art. He finally suggests that collage

as such belongs to the arena of painting, which is a spatial medium, and that the application of that term to textual procedures is misleading, given that texts have

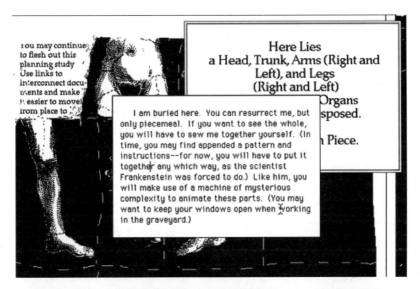

rou may continue
to flesh out this
planning study
Use links to
interconnect docu-
ments and make
it easier to move
from place to

Here Lies
a Head, Trunk, Arms (Right and
Left), and Legs
(Right and Left)

Organs
sposed.

Piece.

I am buried here. You can resurrect me, but only piecemeal. If you want to see the whole, you will have to sew me together yourself. (In time, you may find appended a pattern and instructions--for now, you will have to put it together any which way, as the scientist Frankenstein was forced to do.) Like him, you will make use of a machine of mysterious complexity to animate these parts. (You may want to keep your windows open when working in the graveyard.)

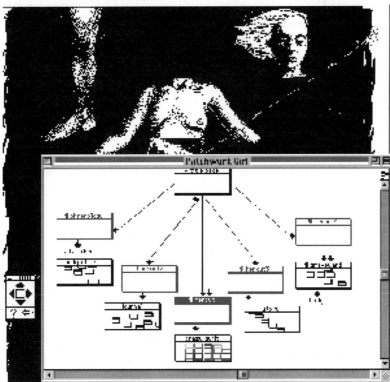

The digital collage-narrative of *Patchwork Girl*.
® Eastgate Systems.

Hypertext as Collage-Writing

essentially a temporal dimension; you take in a painting in one glance, but you read a text over time; film in that sense is closer to text than painting, and the filmic term "montage" would be better for what happens when a text makes use of disparate, found, randomly combined elements. The only true "collage" effects in literature, i.e. the presentation in the same moment of perception of disparate materials would be certain "simultaneities," such as Dada and Merz and other, later sound-poets presented.

Hypertext, as we have seen, presents us with an exception or variation, but collage clearly exists in this new writerly medium almost certainly because it so fundamentally combines the visual and the verbal. Noneless, despite interesting, even compelling, similarities, hypertext collage obviously differs crucially from that created by Picasso and Braque. Hypertext and hypermedia always exist as virtual, rather than physical, texts. Until digital computing, all writing consisted of making physical marks on physical surfaces. Digital words and images, in contrast, take the form of semiotic codes, and this fundamental fact about them leads to the characteristic, defining qualities of digital infotech: (1) virtuality, (2) fluidity, (3) adaptability, (4) openness (or existing without borders), (5) processability, (6) infinite duplicablity, (7) capacity for being moved about rapidly, and (8) networkability.

Digital text is virtual because we always encounter a virtual image, the simulacrum, of something stored in memory rather than any so-called text "itself" or a physical instantiation of it. Digital text is fluid because, taking the form of codes, it can always be reconfigured, reformatted, rewritten. Digital text hence is infinitely adaptable to different needs and uses, and since it consists of codes that other codes can search, rearrange, and otherwise manipulate, digital text is always open, unbordered, unfinished, and unfinishable, capable of infinite extension. Furthermore, since it takes the form of digital coding, it can be easily replicated without in any way disturbing the original code or otherwise affecting it. Such replicability in turn permits it to be moved rapidly across great spaces, and in being moved creates both other versions of old communication, such as the bulletin board, and entirely new forms of communication. Finally—at least for now—all these qualities of digital textuality enable different texts (or lexias) to join together by means of electronic linking. Digitality, in other words, permits hypertextuality.

The connection of the fundamental virtuality of hypertext to the issue of collage becomes clear as soon as one recalls the history of collage and the reasons for its importance to Picasso, Braque, Schwitters, and other painters. As Janson explains, collage arose within the context of Cubism and had powerful effects because it offered a new approach to picture space. Facet Cubism, its first form, still retained "a certain kind of depth," and hence continued Renaissance perspectival picture space. "In Collage Cubism, on the contrary, the picture space lies in front of the plane of the "tray"; space is not created by illusionistic devices, such as modeling and foreshortening, but by the actual overlapping of layers of pasted materials." The effect of Collage Cubism comes from the way it denies much of the recent history of Western painting, particularly that concerned with creating the effect of three-dimensional space on a two-dimensional surface. It does so by inserting some physically existing object, such as Picasso's chair caning and newspaper cuttings, onto and into a painted surface. Although that act of inclusion certainly redefines the function and effect of the three-dimensional object, the object nonetheless resists becoming a purely semiotic code and abrasively insists upon its own physicality.

The collage of Collage Cubism therefore depends for its effect upon a kind of juxtaposition not possible (or relevant) in the digital world—that between physical and semiotic. Both hypertext and painterly collage make use of appropriation and juxtaposition, but for better or worse, one cannot directly invoke the physical within the digital information regime, for everything is mediated, represented, coded.

The manner in which the hypertext version of this essay raised the issues related to oppositions between the physical and the virtual raises further questions about the nature of hypertext. In the web version, after encountering discussions of collage, hypertext, and hypertext as both pictorial and verbal collage, the reader comes upon a series of ten photographic images, many of them manipulated. Each in its way concerns oppositions of the physical and the virtual, and each takes the general form of a picture of a surface on which appear images and other forms of semiotic codes. One first encounters a lexia entitled "Providence Illusions," a photograph whose lower half reveals a slightly posterized image of a six-story brick building with a peaked roof; in the upper portion of the picture a cloudy sky appears. Nothing seems exceptionable about this image until, looking at the lower right corner, one perceives that the brick and windows are peeled back, as if on the corner of a giant paper or canvas, from the identically colored brick beneath, thus revealing that the windows are painted on a blank wall. The illusion works so well that both in the photograph of the building and at the original site, one finds it difficult to discern which windows, if any, are real (only those at the top of the building turn out to be windows and not images of them).

Clicking on this lexia brings one next to a lexia that contains a photograph of what appear to be two windows in a brick wall, the one on the left pretty clearly a trompe d'oeil rendering of a flat window within an oval convexity. To its right, four or so feet away, an ordinary window above what appears to be a granite sill pierces the brick surface. Only a single clue, one not easily noticed, suggests that all is not as it seems: a brick cornice runs through the convex oval and across the wall surface. But, one realizes, if it runs *through* the illusory convexity, then it, too, has to be an illusion, a matter of paint and not of brick. In fact, as I discovered when I approached the wall from a distance of a yard or so, after having seen it many times from a greater distance, *everything* other than the window is painted cinder block. The entire project layers illusory representations one upon another and makes one illusion acceptable or accepted as reality by juxtaposing it with another —the convexity—more obviously trompe d'oeil.

Clicking upon this lexia produces a menu offering two choices—one to graffiti in Victoria, British Columbia, and the second to a lexia entitled "This Is Not a Window." Following the link to the second, one arrives at the same photograph of the Providence wall of illusions upon which, using the graphics software Photoshop, I have overlaid a series of texts in bright red Helvetica type:

This is not a window.
This is a picture of a picture of a window.
But this [window at right] is a picture of a window.
[and on the bricks at upper right]
This is not a picture of a brick wall.
These are not bricks.
This is not a window sill.

Continuing on one's way, one can choose various paths through lexias containing graffiti and reflections of buildings on the surfaces of glass buildings, all of which raise issues of the way we differentiate—when we can—between illusory surface images and the true physical surface they cover.

The final lexia in this grouping, however, moves this more traditional form of virtuality to that found in the world of digital information technology, for it both repeats sections of all the images one may have seen (in whatever order), blending them with multiply repeated portions of a photograph of a Donegal, Ireland, sunset, and it also insists on the absence of any solid, physical ground: not only do different-sized versions of the same image appear to overlay one another, but in the upper center a square panel has moved aside, thus revealing a what the eye reads as colored background or empty space. In this photographic collage or montage, appropriation and juxtaposition rule, but since all the elements and images consist of virtual images, this lexia, like the entire web to which it contributes, does not permit us to distinguish (in the manner of Collage Cubism) between virtual and real, illusion and reality.

This last-mentioned lexia bears the title "Sunset Montage," drawing upon the secondary meaning of "montage" as photographic assemblage, pastiche, or, as the *OED* puts it, "the act or process of producing a composite picture by combining several different pictures or pictorial elements so that they blend with or into one another; a picture so produced." I titled this lexia "Sunset Montage" to distinguish the effect of photographic juxtaposition and assemblage from the painterly one, for in photography, as in computing, the contrast of physical surface and overlaying image does not appear.

Upon hearing my assertion that hypertext should be thought of as collage-writing, Lars Hubrich, a student in my hypertext and literary theory course, remarked that he thought "montage" might be a better term than "collage." He had in mind something like the first *OED* definition of montage as the "selection and arrangement of separate cinematographic shots as a consecutive whole; the blending (by superimposition) of separate shots to form a single picture; the sequence or picture resulting from such a process." Hubrich is correct in that whereas collage emphasizes the stage effect of a multiple-windowed hypertext system on a computer screen at any particular moment, montage, at least in its original cinematic meaning, places important emphasis upon sequence, and in hypertext one has to take into account the fact that one reads—one constructs—one's reading of a hypertext in time. Even though one can backtrack, take different routes through a web, and come upon the same lexia multiple times and in different orders, one nonetheless always experiences a hypertext as a changeable montage.

Hypertext writing, of course, does not coincide fully with either montage or collage. I draw upon them chiefly not to extend their history to digital realms and, similarly, I am not much concerned to allay potential fears of this new form of writing by deriving it from earlier avant-garde work, though in another time and place either goal might provide the axis for a potentially interesting essay. Here I am more interested in helping us understand this new kind of hypertext writing as a mode that both emphasizes and bridges gaps, and that thereby inevitably becomes an art of assemblage in which appropriation and catachresis rule. This is a new writing that brings with it implications for our conceptions of text as well as of reader and author. It is a text in which new kinds of connections have become possible.

What Is Digital Cinema?

Lev Manovich

Cinema, the Art of the Index

Thus far, most discussions of cinema in the digital age have focused on the possibilities of interactive narrative. It is not hard to understand why: since the majority of viewers and critics equate cinema with storytelling, digital media are understood as something that will let cinema tell its stories in a new way. Yet as exciting as the ideas of a viewer participating in a story, choosing different paths through the narrative space, and interacting with characters may be, they address only one aspect of cinema that is neither unique nor, as many will argue, essential to it: narrative.

The challenge that digital media pose to cinema extends far beyond the issue of narrative. Digital media redefine the very identity of cinema. In a Hollywood symposium on the digitization of the cinema, one of the participants provocatively referred to movies as "flatties" and to human actors as "organics" and "soft fuzzies."[1] As these terms accurately suggest, what used to be cinema's defining characteristics have become just the default options, with many others available. When one can "enter" a virtual three-dimensional space, viewing flat images projected on the screen is hardly the only option. When, given enough time and money, almost everything can be simulated in a computer, filming physical reality is just one possibility.

This "crisis" of cinema's identity also affects the terms and the categories used to theorize about cinema's past. French film theorist Christian Metz wrote in the 1970s that "Most films shot today, good or bad, original or not, 'commercial' or not, have as a common characteristic that they tell a story; in this measure they all belong to one and the same genre, which is, rather, a sort of 'super-genre.'"[2] In identifying fictional films as a "supergenre" of twentieth-century cinema, Metz did not bother to mention another characteristic of this genre because at that time it was too obvious: fictional films are *live action* films. These films consist largely of unmodified photographic recordings of real events that took place in real physical space. Today, in the age of computer simulation and digital compositing, invoking this live-action characteristic becomes crucial in defining the specificity of twentieth-century cinema. From the perspective of a future historian of visual culture, the differences between classical Hollywood films, European art films, and avant-garde films (apart from abstract ones) may appear to be less significant than this common feature: they relied on lens-based recordings of reality.

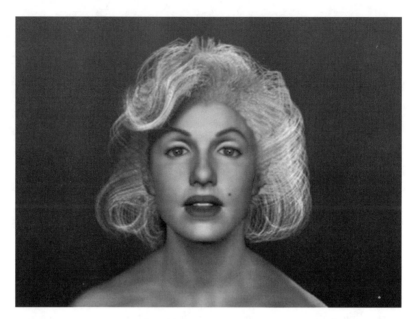

Virtual Marilyn, the digital synthespian.
Courtesy of Scott Billups.

This essay is concerned with the effect of the so-called digital revolution on cinema, as defined by its "supergenre" as fictional live-action film.[3]

During cinema's history, a whole repertoire of techniques (lighting, art direction, the use of different film stocks and lenses, etc.) was developed to modify the basic record obtained by a film apparatus. And yet behind even the most stylized cinematic images we can discern the bluntness, the sterility, the banality of early nineteenth-century photographs. No matter how complex its stylistic innovations, the cinema has found its base in these deposits of reality, these samples obtained by a methodical and prosaic process. Cinema emerged out of the same impulse that engendered naturalism, court stenography, and wax museums. Cinema is the art of the index; it is an attempt to make art out of a footprint.

Even for Andrey Tarkovsky, film-painter par excellence, cinema's identity lay in its ability to record reality. Once, during a public discussion in Moscow sometime in the 1970s, he was asked whether he was interested in making abstract films. He replied that there can be no such thing. Cinema's most basic gesture is to open the shutter and to start the film rolling, recording whatever happens to be in front of the lens. For Tarkovsky, an abstract cinema was thus impossible.

But what happens to cinema's indexical identity if it is now possible to generate photorealistic scenes entirely in a computer by using 3D computer animation; to modify individual frames or whole scenes with the help of a digital paint program; to cut, bend, stretch and stitch digitized film images into something that has perfect photographic credibility, although it was never actually filmed?

This essay will address the meaning of these changes in the filmmaking process from the point of view of the larger cultural history of the moving image. Seen in this context, the manual construction of images in digital cinema represents a return to nineteenth-century precinematic practices, when images were hand-painted and hand-animated. At the turn of the twentieth century, cinema was to delegate these manual techniques to animation and define itself as a recording medium. As cinema enters the digital age, these techniques are again becoming commonplace in the filmmaking process. Consequently, cinema can no longer be clearly distinguished from animation. It is no longer an indexical media technology but, rather, a subgenre of painting.

This argument will be developed in three stages. I will first follow a historical trajectory from nineteenth-century techniques for creating moving images to twentieth-century cinema and animation. Next I will arrive at a definition of digital cinema by abstracting the common features and interface metaphors of a variety of computer softwares and hardwares that are currently replacing traditional film technology. Seen together, these features and metaphors suggest a distinct logic of a digital moving image. This logic subordinates the photographic and the cinematic to the painterly and the graphic, destroying cinema's identity as a media art. Finally, I will examine different production contexts that already use digital moving images— Hollywood films, music videos, CD-ROM games and artworks—in order to see if and how this logic has begun to manifest itself.

A Brief Archaeology of Moving Pictures

As testified by its original names (kinetoscope, cinematograph, moving pictures), cinema was understood, from its birth, as the art of motion, the art that finally succeeded in creating a convincing illusion of dynamic reality.

If we approach cinema in this way (rather than as the art of audiovisual narrative, or the art of a projected image, or the art of collective spectatorship, etc.), we can see it superseding previous techniques for creating and displaying moving images.

These earlier techniques shared a number of common characteristics. First, they all relied on hand-painted or hand-drawn images. The magic lantern slides were painted at least until the 1850s; so were the images used in the Phenakistiscope, the Thaumatrope, the Zootrope, the Praxinoscope, the Choreutoscope, and numerous other nineteenth-century procinematic devices. Even Muybridge's celebrated Zoopraxiscope lectures of the 1880s featured not actual photographs but colored drawings painted after the photographs.[4]

Not only were the images created manually, they were manually animated. In Robertson's Phantasmagoria, which premiered in 1799, magic lantern operators moved behind the screen in order to make projected images appear to advance and withdraw.[5] More often, an exhibitor used only his hands, rather than his whole body, to put the images into motion. One animation technique involved using mechanical slides consisting of a number of layers. An exhibitor would slide the layers to animate the image.[6] Another technique was to move a long slide containing separate images slowly in front of a magic lantern lens. Nineteenth-century optical toys enjoyed in private homes also required manual action to create movement: twirling the strings of the Thaumatrope, rotating the Zootrope's cylinder, turning the Viviscope's handle.

It was not until the last decade of the nineteenth century that the automatic generation of images and their automatic projection were finally combined. A mechanical eye became coupled with a mechanical heart; photography met the motor. As a result, cinema—a very particular regime of the visible—was born. Irregularity, nonuniformity, the accident, and other traces of the human body, which previously had inevitably accompanied moving image exhibitions, were replaced by the uniformity of machine vision.[7] A machine that, like a conveyer belt, was now spitting out images, all having the same appearance, all the same size, all moving at the same speed, like a line of marching soldiers.

Cinema also eliminated the discrete character of both space and movement in moving images. Before cinema, the moving element was visually separated from the static background, as in a mechanical slide show or Reynaud's Praxinoscope Theater (1892).[8] The movement itself was limited in range and affected only a clearly defined figure rather than the whole image. Thus, typical actions would include a bouncing ball, a raised hand or eyes, a butterfly moving back and forth over the heads of fascinated children—simple vectors charted across still fields.

Cinema's most immediate predecessors share something else. As the nineteenth-century obsession with movement intensified, devices that could animate more than just a few images became increasingly popular. All of them—the Zootrope, the Phonoscope, the Tachyscope, the Kinetoscope—were based on loops, sequences of images featuring complete actions that could be played repeatedly. The Thaumatrope (1825), in which a disk with two different images painted on each face was rapidly rotated by twirling a strings attached to it, was in its essence a loop in its simplest form: two elements replacing one another in succession. In the Zootrope (1867) and its numerous variations, approximately a dozen images were arranged around the perimeter of a circle.[9] The Mutoscope, popular in America throughout the 1890s, increased the duration of the loop by placing a larger number of images radially on an axle.[10] Even Edison's Kinetoscope (1892–1896), the first modern cinematic machine to employ film, continued to arrange images in a loop.[11] Fifty feet of film translated to an approximately twenty-second-long presentation. The genre's potential development was cut short when cinema adopted a much longer narrative form.

From Animation to Cinema

Once the cinema was stabilized as a technology, it cut all references to its origins in artifice. Everything that characterized moving pictures before the twentieth century—the manual construction of images, loop actions, the discrete nature of space and movement—was delegated to cinema's bastard relative, its supplement, its shadow: animation. Twentieth-century animation became a depository for nineteenth-century moving-image techniques left behind by cinema.

The opposition between the styles of animation and cinema defined the culture of the moving image in the twentieth century. Animation foregrounds its artificial character, openly admitting that its images are mere representations. Its visual language is more aligned to the graphic than to the photographic. It is discrete and self-consciously discontinuous: crudely rendered characters moving against a stationary and detailed background;

sparsely and irregularly sampled motion (in contrast to the uniform sampling of motion by a film camera—recall Jean-Luc Godard's definition of cinema as "truth 24 frames per second"); and space constructed from separate image layers.

In contrast, cinema works hard to erase any traces of its own production process, including any indication that the images we see could have been constructed rather than recorded. It denies that the reality it shows often does not exist outside of the film image, the image that was arrived at by photographing an already impossible space, which itself was put together through the use of models, mirrors, and matte paintings, and which was then combined with other images through optical printing. It pretends to be a simple recording of an already existing reality—both to a viewer and to itself.[12] Cinema's public image stressed the aura of reality "captured" on film, thus implying that cinema was about photographing what existed before the camera, rather than about "creating the 'never-was'" of special effects.[13] Rear projection and blue screen photography, matte paintings and glass shots, mirrors and miniatures, push development, optical effects, and other techniques that allowed filmmakers to construct and alter the moving images, and thus could reveal that cinema was not really different from animation, were pushed to cinema's periphery by its practitioners, historians, and critics.[14]

Today, with the shift to digital media, these marginalized techniques move to the center.

What Is Digital Cinema?

A visible sign of this shift is the new role that computer-generated special effects have come to play in Hollywood industry in the last few years. Many recent blockbusters have been driven by special effects; feeding on their popularity. Hollywood has even created a new minigenre, "The Making of . . ." videos and books that reveal how special effects are created.

To illustrate some of the possibilities of digital filmmaking, I will make reference to the use of special effects in a few recent, key Hollywood films. Until recently, Hollywood studios were the only places that had the money to pay for digital tools and for the labor involved in producing digital effects. However, the shift to digital media affects not just Hollywood but filmmaking as a whole. As traditional film technology is universally being replaced by digital technology, the logic of the filmmaking process is being redefined. What I describe below are the new principles of digital filmmaking that are equally valid for individual or collective film productions, regardless of whether they are using the most expensive professional hardware/software packages or their consumer equivalents.

Consider, then, the following principles of digital filmmaking:

1. Rather than filming physical reality, it is now possible to generate film-like scenes directly in a computer with the help of 3D computer animation. Therefore, live-action footage is displaced from its role as the only possible material from which the finished film is constructed.

2. Once live-action footage is digitized (or directly recorded in a digital format), it loses its privileged indexical relationship to pro-filmic reality. The computer does not distinguish between an image obtained through the photographic lens, an image created in a paint program, and an image synthesized in a 3D graphics package, since they are made from the same material: pixels. And pixels, regardless of their origin, can be easily altered, substituted one for another, and so on. Live-action footage is reduced to just another graphic, no different from images that were created manually.[15]

3. If live-action footage was left intact in traditional filmmaking, now it functions as raw material for further compositing, animating, and morphing. As a result, while retaining visual realism unique to the photographic process, film obtains the plasticity that previously was possible only in painting or animation. To use the suggestive title of a popular morphing software, digital filmmakers work with "elastic reality." For example, the opening shot of *Forrest Gump* (Robert Zemeckis, Paramount Pictures, 1994; special effects by Industrial Light and Magic) tracks an unusually long and extremely intricate flight of a feather. To create the shot, the real feather was filmed against a blue background in different positions; this material was then animated and composited against shots of a landscape.[16] The result: a new kind of realism, that can be described as "something which is intended to look exactly as if it could have happened, although it really could not."

4. Previously, editing and special effects were strictly separate activities. An editor worked on ordering sequences of images together; any intervention within an image was handled by special-effects specialists. The computer collapses this distinction. The manipulation of individual images via a paint program or algorithmic image processing becomes as easy as arranging sequences of images in time. Both simply involve "cut and paste." As this basic computer command exemplifies, modification of digital images (or other digitized data) is not sensitive to distinctions of time and space or of differences of scale. Thus, reordering sequences of images in time, compositing them together in space, modifying parts of an individual image, and changing individual pixels become the same operation, conceptually and practically.

5. Given the preceding principles, we can define digital film in this way:

digital film = live-action material + painting + image processing + compositing + 2D computer animation + 3D computer animation.

Live-action material can be recorded either on film or video or directly in a digital format.[17] Painting, image processing, and computer animation are the processes of modifying already existent images as well as of creating new ones. In fact, the very distinction between creation and modification, so clear in film-based media (shooting versus darkroom processes in photography, production versus postproduction in cinema), no longer applies to digital cinema, since each image, regardless of its origin, goes through a number of programs before making it to the final film.[18]

Let us summarize the principles discussed thus far. Live-action footage is now only raw material to be manipulated by hand: animated, combined with 3D computer-generated scenes, and painted over. The final images are constructed manually from different elements; and all the elements are either created entirely from scratch or modified by hand.

We can finally answer the question "What is digital cinema?" Digital cinema is a particular case of animation that uses live-action footage as one of its many elements.

This can be reread in view of the history of the moving image sketched earlier. Manual construction and animation of images gave birth to cinema and slipped into the margins . . . only to reappear as the foundation of digital cinema. The history of the moving image thus makes a full circle. *Born from animation, cinema pushed animation to its boundary, only to become one particular case of animation in the end.*

The relationship between "normal" filmmaking and special effects is similarly reversed. Special effects, which involved human intervention into machine-recorded footage and which were therefore delegated to cinema's periphery throughout its history, become the norm of digital filmmaking.

The same applies to the relationship between production and postproduction. Cinema traditionally involved arranging physical reality to be filmed through the use of sets, models, art direction, cinematography, and so on. Occasional manipulation of recorded film (for instance, through optical printing) was negligible compared with the extensive manipulation of reality in front of a camera. In digital filmmaking, shot footage is no longer the final point but just raw material to be manipulated in a computer, where the real construction of a scene will take place. In short, the production becomes just the first stage of postproduction.

The following examples illustrate this shift from rearranging reality to rearranging its images. From the analog era: for a scene in *Zabriskie Point* (1970), Michelangelo Antonioni, trying to achieve a particularly saturated color, ordered a field of grass to be painted. From the digital era: to create the launch sequence in *Apollo 13* (Universal, 1995; special effects by Digital Domain), the crew shot footage at the original location of the launch at Cape Canaveral. The artists at Digital Domain scanned the film and altered it on computer workstations, removing recent buildings, adding grass to the launch pad, and painting the skies to make them more dramatic. This altered film was then mapped onto 3D planes to create a virtual set that was animated to match a 180-degree dolly movement of a camera following a rising rocket.[19]

The last example brings us to yet another conceptualization of digital cinema—as painting. In his book-length study of digital photography, William J. Mitchell focuses our attention on what he calls the inherent mutability of a digital image:

The essential characteristic of digital information is that it can be manipulated easily and very rapidly by computer. It is simply a matter of substituting new digits for old. . . . Computational tools for transforming, combining, altering, and analyzing images are as essential to the digital artist as brushes and pigments to a painter.[20]

As Mitchell points out, this inherent mutability erases the difference between a photograph and a painting. Since a film is a series of photographs, it is appropriate to extend Mitchell's argument to digital film. With an

Composited launch sequence from *Apollo 13*.
Publicity photo from Universal Studios.

artist being able to easily manipulate digitized footage either as a whole or frame by frame, a film in a general sense becomes a series of paintings.[21]

Hand-painting digitized film frames, made possible by a computer, is probably the most dramatic example of the new status of cinema. No longer strictly locked in the photographic, it opens itself toward the painterly. It is also the most obvious example of the return of cinema to its nineteenth-century origins—in this case, to hand-crafted images of magic lantern slides, the Phenakistiscope, the Zootrope.

We usually think of computerization as automation, but here the result is the reverse: what previously was automatically recorded by a camera now has to be painted one frame at a time. But not just a dozen images, as in the nineteenth century, but thousands and thousands. We can draw another parallel with the practice, common in the early days of silent cinema, of manually tinting film frames in different colors according to a scene's mood.[22] Today, some of the most visually sophisticated digital effects are often achieved by using the same simple method: painstakingly altering thousands of frames by hand. The frames are painted over either to create mattes (hand-drawn matte extraction) or to change the images directly, as in *Forrest Gump,* where President Kennedy was made to speak new sentences by altering the shape of his lips, one frame at a time.[23] In principle, given enough time and money, one can create what will be the ultimate digital film: ninety minutes of 129,600 frames completely painted by hand from scratch, but indistinguishable in appearance from live photography.[24]

Multimedia as "Primitive" Digital Cinema

3D animation, compositing, mapping, paint retouching: in commercial cinema, these radical new techniques are mostly used to solve technical problems while traditional cinematic language is preserved unchanged. Frames are hand-painted to remove wires that supported an actor during shooting; a flock of birds is added to a landscape; a city street is filled with crowds of simulated extras. Although most Hollywood releases now involve digitally manipulated scenes, the use of computers is always carefully hidden.[25]

Commercial narrative cinema continues to hold on to the classical realist style where images function as unretouched photographic records of some events that took place in front of the camera.[26] Cinema refuses to give up its unique cinema effect, an effect that, according to Christian Metz's penetrating analysis made in the 1970s, depends upon narrative form, the reality effect, and cinema's architectural arrangement all working together.[27]

Toward the end of his essay, Metz wonders whether in the future nonnarrative films may become more numerous; if this happens, he suggests that cinema will no longer need to manufacture its reality effect. Electronic and digital media have already brought about this transformation. Since the 1980s, new cinematic forms have emerged that are not linear narratives, that are exhibited on a television or a computer screen rather than in a movie theater—and that simultaneously give up cinematic realism.

What are these forms? First of all, there is the music video. Probably not by accident, the genre of music video came into existence at exactly the time when electronic video effects devices were entering editing studios. Importantly, just as music videos often incorporate narratives within them, but are not linear narratives from start to finish, so they rely on film (or video) images, but change them beyond the norms of traditional cinematic realism. The manipulation of images through hand-painting and image processing, hidden in Hollywood cinema, is brought into the open on a television screen. Similarly, the construction of an image from heterogeneous sources is not subordinated to the goal of photorealism but functions as an aesthetic strategy. The genre of music video has been a laboratory for exploring numerous new possibilities of manipulating photographic images made possible by computers—the numerous points that exist in the space between the 2D and the 3D, cinematography and painting, photographic realism and collage. In short, it is a living and constantly expanding textbook for digital cinema.

A detailed analysis of the evolution of music video imagery (or, more generally, broadcast graphics in the electronic age) deserves a separate treatment, and I will not try to take it up here. Instead, I will discuss another new cinematic nonnarrative form, CD-ROM games, which, in contrast to music videos, relied on the computer for storage and distribution from the very beginning. And, unlike music video designers who were consciously pushing traditional film or video images into something new, the designers of CD-ROMs arrived at a new visual language unintentionally, while attempting to emulate traditional cinema.

In the late 1980s, Apple began to promote the concept of computer multimedia; and in 1991 it released QuickTime software to enable an ordinary personal computer to play movies. However, for the next few years the computer did not perform its new role very well. First, CD-ROMs could not hold anything close to the length of a standard theatrical film. Second, the computer would not smoothly play a movie larger than the size of a stamp. Finally, the movies had to be compressed, which degraded their visual appearance. Only in the case of still images was the computer able to display photographic-type detail at full screen size.

Because of these particular hardware limitations, the designers of CD-ROMs had to invent a different kind of cinematic language in which a range of strategies, such as discrete motion, loops, and superimposition, previously used in nineteenth-century moving-image presentations, in twentieth-century animation, and in the avant-garde tradition of graphic cinema, were applied to photographic or synthetic images. This language synthesized cinematic illusionism and the aesthetics of graphic collage, with its characteristic heterogeneity and discontinuity. The photographic and the graphic, divorced when cinema and animation went their separate ways, met again on a computer screen.

The graphic also met the cinematic. The designers of CD-ROMs were aware of the techniques of twentieth-century cinematography and film editing, but they had to adapt these techniques both to an interactive format and to hardware limitations. As a result, the techniques of modern cinema and of nineteenth-century moving image have merged in a new hybrid language.

We can trace the development of this language by analyzing a few well-known CD-ROM titles. The best-selling game *Myst* (Broderbund, 1993) unfolds its narrative strictly through still images, a practice that takes us back to magic lantern shows (and to Chris Marker's *La Jetée*).[28] But in other ways *Myst* relies on the techniques of twentieth-century cinema. For instance, the CD-ROM uses simulated camera turns to switch from one image to the next. It also employs the basic technique of film editing to subjectively speed up or slow down time. In the course of the game, the user moves around a fictional island by clicking on a mouse. Each click advances a virtual camera forward, revealing a new view of a 3D environment. When the user begins to descend into the underground chambers, the spatial distance between the points of view of each two consecutive views decreases sharply. If earlier the user was able to cross a whole island with just a few clicks, now it takes a dozen clicks to get to the bottom of the stairs! In other words, just as in traditional cinema, *Myst* slows down time to create suspense and tension.

In *Myst,* miniature animations are sometimes embedded within the still images. In the next best-selling CD-ROM, *7th Guest* (Virgin Games, 1993), the user is presented with video clips of live actors superimposed over static backgrounds created with 3D computer graphics. The clips are looped, and the moving human figures clearly stand out against the backgrounds. Both of these features connect the visual language of *7th Guest* to nineteenth-century procinematic devices and twentieth-century cartoons rather than to cinematic verisimilitude. But like *Myst, 7th Guest* also evokes distinctly modern cinematic codes. The environment where all action takes place (an interior of a house) is rendered by using a wide-angle lens; to move from one view to the next, a camera follows a complex curve, as though mounted on a virtual dolly.

Next, consider the CD-ROM *Johnny Mnemonic* (Sony Imagesoft, 1995). Produced to complement the fiction film of the same title, marketed not as a "game" but as an "interactive movie," and featuring full-screen video throughout, it comes closer to cinematic realism than the previous CD-ROMs—yet it is still quite distinct from it. With all action shot against a green screen and then composited with graphic backgrounds, its visual style exists within a space between cinema and collage.

It would not be entirely inappropriate to read this short history of the digital moving image as a teleological development that replays the emergence of cinema a century earlier. Indeed, as computers' speed keeps increasing, the CD-ROM designers have been able to go from a slide show format to the superimposition of small moving elements over static backgrounds, and finally to full-frame moving images. This evolution repeats the nineteenth-century progression: from sequences of still images (magic lantern slide presentations) to characters moving over static backgrounds (for instance, in Reynaud's Praxinoscope Theater) to full motion (the Lumières' cinematograph). Moreover, the introduction of QuickTime in 1991 can be compared with the introduction of the Kinetoscope in 1892: both were used to present short loops, both featured images approximately two by three inches in size, both called for private viewing rather than collective exhibition. Finally, the Lumières' first film screenings of 1895, which shocked their audiences with huge moving images, found their parallel in recent titles in which the moving image—here full-screen, full-motion video—

finally fills the entire computer screen. Thus, exactly a century after cinema was officially "born," it was reinvented on a computer screen.

But this is only one reading. We no longer think of the history of cinema as a linear march toward only one possible language, or as a progression toward more and more accurate verisimilitude. Rather, we have come to see its history as a succession of distinct and equally expressive languages, each with its own aesthetic variables, each new language closing off some of the possibilities of the previous one—a cultural logic not dissimilar to Thomas Kuhn's analysis of scientific paradigms.[29] Similarly, instead of dismissing visual strategies of early multimedia titles as a result of technological limitations, we may want to think of them as an alternative to traditional cinematic illusionism, as a beginning of digital cinema's new language.

For the computer/entertainment industry, these strategies represent only a temporary limitation, an annoying drawback that needs to be overcome. This is one important difference between the situation at the end of the nineteenth and the end of the twentieth centuries: if cinema was developing toward the still open horizon of many possibilities, the development of commercial multimedia, and of corresponding computer hardware (compression boards, storage formats such as Digital Video Disc), is driven by a clearly defined goal: the exact duplication of cinematic realism. So if a computer screen more and more emulates the cinema screen, this is not an accident but a result of conscious planning.

The Loop

A number of artists, however, have approached these strategies not as limitations but as a source of new cinematic possibilities. As an example, I will discuss the use of the loop in Jean-Louis Boissier's *Flora petrinsularis* (1993) and Natalie Bookchin's *The Databank of the Everyday* (1996).[30]

As already mentioned, all nineteenth-century procinematic devices, up to Edison's Kinetoscope, were based on short loops. As "the seventh art" began to mature, it banished the loop to the low-art realms of the instructional film, the pornographic peepshow, and the animated cartoon. In contrast, narrative cinema has avoided repetitions; like modern Western fictional forms in general, it put forward a notion of human existence as a linear progression through numerous unique events.

Cinema's birth from a loop form was reenacted at least once during its history. In one of the sequences of the revolutionary Soviet montage film, *A*

Man with a Movie Camera (1929), Dziga Vertov shows us a cameraman standing in the back of a moving automobile. As he is being carried forward by the automobile, he cranks the handle of his camera. A loop, a repetition created by the circular movement of the handle, gives birth to a progression of events—a very basic narrative that is also quintessentially modern: a camera moving through space recording whatever is in its path. In what seems to be a reference to cinema's primal scene, these shots are intercut with the shots of a moving train. Vertov even restages the terror that the Lumières' film supposedly provoked in its audience; he positions his camera right along the train track so the train runs over our point of view a number of times, crushing us again and again.

Early digital movies share the same limitations of storage as nineteenth-century procinematic devices. This is probably why the loop playback function was built into the QuickTime interface, thus giving it the same weight as the VCR-style "play forward" function. So, in contrast to films and videotapes, QuickTime movies are supposed to be played forward, backward, or looped. *Flora petrinsularis* realizes some of the possibilities contained in the loop form, suggesting a new temporal aesthetics for digital cinema.

The CD-ROM, which is based on Rousseau's *Confessions,* opens with a white screen containing a numbered list. Clicking on each item leads us to a screen containing two frames, positioned side by side. Both frames show the same video loop but are slightly offset from each other in time. Thus, the images appearing in the left frame reappear in a moment on the right and vice versa, as though an invisible wave is running through the screen. This wave soon becomes materialized: when we click on one of the frames, we are taken to a new screen showing a loop of a rhythmically vibrating water surface. As each mouse click reveals another loop, the viewer becomes an editor, but not in a traditional sense. Rather than constructing a singular narrative sequence and discarding material that is not used, here the viewer brings to the forefront, one by one, numerous layers of looped actions that seem to be taking place all at once, a multitude of separate but coexisting temporalities. The viewer is not cutting but reshuffling. In a reversal of Vertov's sequence where a loop generated a narrative, the viewer's attempt to create a story in *Flora petrinsularis* leads to a loop.

The loop that structures *Flora petrinsularis* on a number of levels becomes a metaphor for human desire that can never achieve resolution. It can be also read as a comment on cinematic realism. What are the minimum conditions necessary to create the impression of reality? As Boissier demonstrates, in the case of a field of grass, or a close-up of a plant or a stream, just a few looped frames become sufficient to produce the illusion of life and of linear time.

Steven Neale describes how early film demonstrated its authenticity by representing moving nature: "What was lacking [in photographs] was the wind, the very index of real, natural movement. Hence the obsessive contemporary fascination, not just with movement, not just with scale, but also with waves and sea spray, with smoke and spray."[31] What for early cinema was its biggest pride and achievement—a faithful documentation of nature's movement—becomes for Boissier a subject of ironic and melancholic simulation. As the few frames are looped over and over, we see blades of grass shifting slightly back and forth, rhythmically responding to the blowing of nonexistent wind that is almost approximated by the noise of a computer reading data from a CD-ROM.

Something else is being simulated here as well, perhaps unintentionally. As you watch the CD-ROM, the computer periodically staggers, unable to maintain a consistent data rate. As a result, the images on the screen move in uneven bursts, slowing and speeding up with humanlike irregularity. It is as though they are brought to life not by a digital machine but by a human operator cranking the handle of the Zootrope a century and a half ago. . . .

If *Flora petrinsularis* uses the loop to comment on cinema's visual realism, *The Databank of the Everyday* suggests that the loop can be a new narrative form appropriate for the computer age. In an ironic manifesto that parodies their avant-garde precursors from the earlier part of the century, Bookchin reminds us that the loop gave birth not only to cinema but also to computer programming. Programming involves altering the linear flow of data through control structures, such as "if/then" and "repeat/while"; the loop is the most elementary of these control structures. Bookchin writes:

As digital media replaces [*sic*] film and photography, it is only logical that the computer program's loop should replace photography's frozen moment and cinema's linear narrative. The Databank champions the loop as a new form of digital storytelling; there is no true beginning or end, only a series of the loops with their endless repetitions, halted by a user's selection or a power shortage.[32]

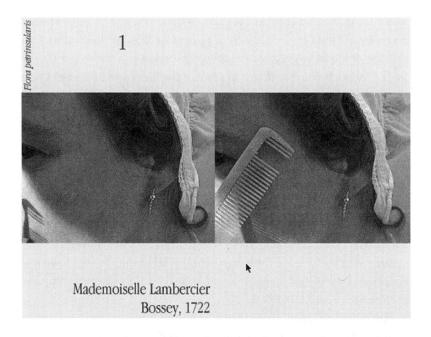

1

Mademoiselle Lambercier
Bossey, 1722

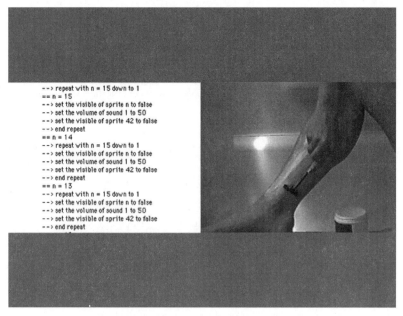

```
--> repeat with n = 15 down to 1
== n = 15
--> set the visible of sprite n to false
--> set the volume of sound 1 to 50
--> set the visible of sprite 42 to false
--> end repeat
== n = 14
--> repeat with n = 15 down to 1
--> set the visible of sprite n to false
--> set the volume of sound 1 to 50
--> set the visible of sprite 42 to false
--> end repeat
== n = 13
--> repeat with n = 15 down to 1
--> set the visible of sprite n to false
--> set the volume of sound 1 to 50
--> set the visible of sprite 42 to false
--> end repeat
```

Flora petrinsularis: the repetitive image.
Jean-Louis Boissier and the ZKM.

The Databank of the Everyday: the loop as action and as code.
Courtesy of Natalie Bookchin.

Lev Manovich

The computer program's loop makes its first "screen debut" in one particularly effective image from *The Databank of the Everyday*. The screen is divided into two frames, one showing a video loop of a woman shaving her leg, the other a loop of a computer program in execution. Program statements repeating over and over mirror the woman's arm methodically moving back and forth. This image represents one of the first attempts in computer art to apply a Brechtian strategy; that is, to show the mechanisms by which the computer produces its illusions as a part of the artwork. Stripped of its usual interface, the computer turns out to be another version of Ford's factory, with a loop as its conveyer belt.

Like Boissier, Bookchin explores alternatives to cinematic montage, in her case replacing its traditional sequential mode with a spatial one. Ford's assembly line relied on the separation of the production process into a set of repetitive, sequential, and simple activities. The same principle made computer programming possible: a computer program breaks a task into a series of elemental operations to be executed one at a time. Cinema followed this principle as well: it replaced all other modes of narration with a sequential narrative, an assembly line of shots that appear on the screen one at a time. A sequential narrative turned out to be particularly incompatible with a spatialized narrative that played a prominent role in European visual culture for centuries. From Giotto's fresco cycle at the Scrovegni Chapel (1305–1306) in Padua to Gustave Courbet's *Burial at Ornans* (1850), artists presented a multitude of separate events (which sometimes were even separated by time) within a single composition. In contrast to cinema's narrative, here all the "shots" were accessible to a viewer at once.

Cinema has elaborated complex techniques of montage between different images replacing each other in time, but the possibility of what can be called "spatial montage" between simultaneously coexisting images was not explored. *The Databank of the Everyday* begins to explore this direction, thus opening up again the tradition of spatialized narrative suppressed by cinema. In one section we are presented with a sequence of pairs of short clips of everyday actions that function as antonyms—for instance, opening and closing a door, or pressing Up and Down buttons in an elevator. In another section the user can choreograph a number of miniature actions appearing in small windows positioned throughout the screen.

Conclusion: From Kino-Eye to Kino-Brush

In the twentieth century, cinema has played two roles at once. As a media technology, its role was to capture and to store visible reality. The difficulty of modifying images once they were recorded was exactly what gave cinema its value as a document, assuring its authenticity. The rigidity of the film image has defined the limits of cinema as I defined it earlier—that is to say, the super-genre of live-action narrative. Although it includes within itself a variety of styles—the result of the efforts of many directors, designers, and cinematographers—these styles share a strong family resemblance. They are all children of the recording process that uses lenses, regular sampling of time, and photographic media. They are all children of a machine vision.

The mutability of digital data impairs the value of cinema recordings as documents of reality. In retrospect, we can see that twentieth-century cinema's regime of visual realism, the result of automatically recording visual reality, was only an exception, an isolated accident in the history of visual representation, which has always involved, and now again involves, the manual construction of images. Cinema becomes a particular branch of painting—painting in time. No longer a kino-eye, but a kino-brush.[33]

The privileged role of the manual construction of images in digital cinema is one example of a larger trend: the return of pre-cinematic moving-images techniques. Marginalized by the twentieth-century institution of live-action narrative cinema that relegated them to the realms of animation and special effects, these techniques reemerge as the foundation of digital filmmaking. What was supplemental to cinema becomes its norm; what was at its boundaries comes into the center. Digital media return to us the repressed of the cinema.

As the examples discussed in this essay suggest, the directions that were closed off at the turn of the century, when cinema came to dominate the modern moving-image culture, are again beginning to be explored. Moving-image culture is being redefined once more; cinematic realism is being displaced from its dominant mode to become only one option among many.[34]

Part IV

The World and the Screen

The twentieth century was one of technical prowess and relentless violence, of shortening distances and expanding diasporas, of increased communication and mounting alienation. It was also the century when the screen became an integral part of the industrialized world. The nineteenth century pointed the way with magic lanterns, illuminated slide tours, and the birth of the cinema. For the next century, screens expanded to fill movie palaces, and then shrank to fit inside domestic appliances known as televisions. Personal computers moved screens back out of the den, scattering them wherever information of any kind was created, recorded, or accessed. From the writer's desk to the medical office, from the designer's studio to the factory floor, from the library kiosk to the fast-food sales counter, the screen became ubiquitous.

The screen engendered by the convergence of digital media with telecommunications is one where people interact and form communities, activities formerly thought to be restricted to the world. In the wake of this kind of boundary blurring, the easy denunciation of the screen as pallid simulation of "reality" ignores the validity of the pleasures and experiences people derive therein. Yet the screen is not the world, and, technofabulism to the contrary, never will be. How to discuss the gap?

Some authors in this collection use the language of theory: the vocabulary of semiotics, deconstruction, and poststructuralism. Others employ the apparatus of history: tracing the developments of technologies and their use. There are many other strategies, however, including the personal account that leads to something like visceral journalism. The final two essays of this collection are by far the most personal in nature, and the least overtly "academic." There is a reason for the shift in both tone and method: the digital dialectic, as noted in the introduction, grounds the discussion of new media in the constraints of its production. Yet the constraints of production exist in a wider arena than the purely technical. Very explicitly, these two essays take on the gaps between new media and the very experiences, places, people, and things they mediate. These are ruminations on the world by two people who know the screen all too well.

Founder of the Voyager Company, and for some time the most influential publisher in new media, Bob Stein chose time and again to take an interventionist role in the dialectical development of digital media. The idea of publisher as intellectual and moral force has taken a drubbing in this era of media conglomerates and supersized chain book dealers. Independent publishers still contribute to the debate in Europe, but in America their role has essentially been abandoned to the editors at academic presses. One of the things that stands out about Bob Stein is that he countered these forces. Not only did he strive to prove that people are keenly interested in interesting material, he did so while pushing the technical and aesthetic boundaries of emerging media.

"'We Could Be Better Ancestors Than This': Ethics and First Principles for the Art of the Digital Age" poses a series of important questions. What is art for? Whom does it serve? What kind of a society do we want to live in? It grounds these questions in a discussion of what it was actually like to run a new media publishing company—the daily negotiations between technology, content, sales, and intent. In the end, Stein the publisher stakes out a position in regard to the dialectic: he is not nearly as driven to telling both sides of the story as he is to "having one side . . . present their side of the story as best they can."

From her work developing video games specifically for girls, to creating complex virtual reality environments, to writing on the convergence of computers and the theater, Brenda Laurel has been passionate about telling her side of the story. Laurel is an expert in human–computer interaction and game design, but at the same time possesses a conviction that life is not meant to be lived entirely in any kind of box. Her "Musings on Amusements in America, or What I Did on My Summer Vacation" is a travelogue that moves from a new media trade show to Walt Disney World, and then on to the Iowa State Fair.

Her musings leaven the dialectics that structure this collection with family stories, mucking up the sterile perfection of mathematical worlds. Not for her either black or white; Laurel writes about a world filled with the brilliant green of a cornfield, the azure of the sky, and (to acknowledge that we are our culture as much as our culture is us) the hot pink of Barbie's stretch limousine at Epcot.

"We Could Be Better Ancestors Than This": Ethics and First Principles for the Art of the Digital Age

Bob Stein

When I heard the phrase "the digital dialectic," I got pretty excited. For most of this century the word "dialectic" has been linked to the "M" word—not multimedia, but Marxism. The thing about Karl Marx was that he asked very big questions, the kind of questions that nobody ever asks these days, particularly in the electronic publishing or "multimedia" industry that I've been in for the last fifteen years. Usually the biggest questions people ask are about another "M" word: marketing. People just don't spend much time thinking or talking about the historical or ideological implications of the new communication technologies.

Where there is this kind of reflection, there is the almost automatic assumption that the new technologies will work for the *benefit* of humankind. It's really an extension of Adam Smith's old notion of the hidden hand of capital automatically working the most good for the most people through the unrestrained market.

I'd like to examine and draw out some of the implications for one extremely important area being impacted by the new digital technology: the creation of art. The purpose of art is to enrich our lives. But is that always its function? You always have to ask these questions about art: Whom does it serve? What's it for?

Whom does it serve? is a big question because most art that we see in our culture comes to us packaged in various forms that in various ways serve the interests of the capitalist class. I realize that using the word "capitalist" to indicate an economic and social class may cause some of the people reading this (especially those under thirty) to immediately glaze over. I suppose I could use "bourgeoisie," or "the rich people," or "the powers that be." But we do live in a class society—whether we like to admit it or not—and in one way or another most of the art that we see ends up serving the tastes, interests, and agendas of the people who paid for it. And overwhelmingly the people who have paid for art in this century have been members of the capitalist class. That's an entry point for this discussion of what is happening with art in the digital age.

A few summers back, I read an article in *Time* magazine by their art critic, Robert Hughes.[1] He made a strong defense of federal funding for the National Endowments for the Arts and Humanities and Public Broadcasting. Hughes took the position that the culture needs the government to fund art, and came out swinging against the plans of Speaker of the House Newt Gingrich et al. to gut federal funding. I contrasted this to an issue of

Wired that featured Gingrich that same summer. The cover read "Friend and Foe," indicating a mix of the good and the bad. But in the interview it became mostly good. Esther Dyson, a well-respected media writer, actually referred to Gingrich as a "revolutionary" She justified this label, in part, because he was supposed to be a politician who understood something about bits and bytes.[2]

More to the point, Gingrich led the "revolutionary" charge to eliminate government regulation or oversight of capitalist corporations and eradicate government support for institutions and activities that can't survive in the "free market" or live on through private philanthropy (except for corporate welfare and perks for politicians at the trough).

Wired is supposed to be a hip, on-the-edge magazine. What it really is, in a fundamental way, is an ideological opinion maker for new capitalists rising in the digital industries. *Time* magazine is a venerable and no less enthusiastic defender of capitalism. So, I wondered, what's the core difference between the Gingrich types and *Time* on this issue?

One way to look at it is that *Time* represents analog culture and *Wired* is the mouthpiece for digital culture being born. I think that *Time,* to some extent, still holds in its collective mind the notion that the means of making art should be much more widely distributed than they are likely to be in the digital world, particularly in a world without government support. I don't think this flows so much from *Time*'s democratic sentiments as it does from recognition that government patronage keeps more artists within the pale of establishment acceptability while providing some monitored outlet for dissident voices.

Wired and Gingrich, it seems to me, are very clearly putting forward an all-accepting enthusiasm for these new digital tools that are coming into being and are being used by artists. We're seeing incredible tools being developed to make art, but—and here's the dialectical way of looking at it—it puts these tools in the hands of a smaller number of artists than ever before. So, great tools, but many fewer artists will be using them. Because they are more expensive, they are even more directly in the service of capital than ever before.

If it costs U.S.$500,000 for companies to put out the average CD-ROM, then it's pretty clear that the new media industry is already modeling itself on the Hollywood cinema: lots of trained technicians working for others on large-scale, investment-driven productions rather than independent artists, individuals working with affordable materials on personal projects.

It's a question about allocation of resources and the basis on which we make those decisions. There are many other ways to organize our lives. Even in a field like new media, it's a mistake to restrict our reading to the trade magazines and popular sources like *Wired*. Their thinking is so narrow, so limited. We need to burst out of the straitjacket we're in about what the possibilities are. Instead of spending half a million dollars on a CD-ROM, maybe it would be more beneficial to spend some of this money for storytellers in the community. For example, fund people in their seventies and eighties from different cultures to tell stories to kids. Or maybe it would be better to pay for ten yoga instructors who could go out and give lessons to people. We are so alienated from our bodies at this point that before we get to the cyborg state (in the Hollywood sense), it might be much better to get used to our bodies again.

Another way of looking at this is that we have remarkable methods of distributing works of art. Digital technology offers a tremendously powerful method of connecting us and distributing artworks. We can ship bits all around the world, almost instantaneously. It's a tremendously powerful method of connecting us and distributing the work of our minds and hands.

But the main way it's being used is to transport culture from the haves (principally the United States, secondarily Europe) to the rest of the world. The new digital means and media of transmission are being used principally to develop a flattened world culture, a monoculture that is basically coming out of Hollywood, New York, and a few other centers. The idea that we are going to have a cornucopia, a cacophony of cultural works coming from around the world isn't the case now, nor is it likely to be, in the current climate.

People talk about how clearly these new technologies are being used to develop a world culture that's coming into being. But there's a difference between what is actually coming into being and a truly world culture where somebody making music in Africa has as much currency as somebody signed to a contract with Warner Brothers in the United States, or where writers from Afghanistan have access to these global markets. But that's not what's happening. We're not getting that. We're getting one culture, and it's basically one that comes out of U.S. culture corporations.

We have to be careful of the whole concept of "globalism," because the same economic and political forces in the world that have used the concepts of nationalism for their benefit the past couple of hundred years, as they become transnational companies, are talking about globalism and "global markets." But they will be developing a globalism that serves rather narrow interests, as nationalism and "free trade" did previously. "Globalization" in this sense is just another word for "homogenization."

Many people see the Internet as an interesting and hope-inspiring counterphenomenon. You can talk to people all over the world. People with fairly basic technology can send images and music from their cultures, we have the potential to be broadcasters as well as spectators. Well, that may be a current of what's happening now, but what will happen with these technologies in the future? Already the Internet seems to be dominated by the same mass culture we have on television and in movies. Read the trades and you'll see that the top ten sites are *Time* Magazine, ESPN, and so on. The content doesn't look very different from the *New York Times* top ten list of anything: movies, TV, even books.

The Internet is rapidly becoming basically another method for the transmission of the dominant culture's ideas. Yes, they will let us all have a little bit of bandwidth, but we won't have enough of a bandwidth, and increasingly it will look more and more like a broadcast medium than a common carrier. There are, and will be, important battles about this. And we should fight hard. But we shouldn't think of the Internet so much as "our thing" as something that increasingly models itself on the rest of the culture. How could it really be any different?

One of the mistakes people make is to think that a technology itself is so revolutionary that it will transform the underlying social relationships that determine how and for whose benefit a technology gets used.

For fifteen years I've resisted saying that machines or software are revolutionary. People make revolutions, machines don't. But the technological level of the society does set the basis for the kind of society that can be created. And these machines and their users provide *the basis* for a new kind of social structure. When Marx wrote in 1849 that the working class was going to have a successful revolution, he wasn't right in terms of the timing, but it seems to me that the process of profound changes in the way that humans communicate with each other that we are going through will accelerate the need and possibility for a new social structure. Whether that will happen in the next ten, fifty, or two hundred years, I don't know. But I do think that it is up to us to take the technological base of our society and to build on top of it the structures we want to build. I'm pretty sure that what we do right now will have a massive impact on what we become.

The issue is not really about our relationship to the machines we create. It's about our relationships to each other in class and personal terms, and how we decide to use these machines, and who is involved in those decisions.

If you look at all the Hollywood movies about machines in the past few years, they all end up making us feel powerless. I think that the message out there, in many ways, is that the machines are inevitable, the machines are taking over, you're a cipher, give up. And we get the message from *Wired* and other apostles of the digital revolution that we should sit back and enjoy. It will all be for our own good.

We all hear a lot of comments that "it's the content that counts." People take a certain comfort that the "geeks" are not so evidently in control, that the technology is becoming more invisible and user-friendly. I don't think it's enough to say that the machines are secondary to the content that's transmitted over them. It's true that the technologists are less evident and the content developers, including the artists, seem increasingly at center stage.

But this doesn't necessarily mean that artists are going to be addressing the needs of the broadest range of people. If anything, because of the cost of and accessibility to the technology, artists are in greater thrall than ever to capital. The only thing that is really inevitable is that capital will seek every advantage it can. Big companies are going to use all the ways they can to deliver consumers to advertisers, to sell you their products and ideas; they're going to use new technologies every way they can, to do what they need to do, which is to create more capital. And the artist can be yoked to that task quite easily through criteria for access to markets and the means to create.

Again, it's not primarily about the technology or the machines. The Luddites, the early nineteenth-century movement in England, are often misrepresented as a bunch of hooligans who hated technology. But on closer inspection, it turns out that the Luddites did not hate technology per se, but rather the way in which the new technologies were being used. Though famous as machine-breakers in the early period of industrial capitalism, they were surprisingly selective in terms of their targets. They would go after looms and shops that were being used in particularly oppressive ways for child labor, that were operated by those who showed no concern, and even some glee, about the wrenching effects on the people who were being displaced. The Luddites did not win, of course, and probably could not have won. In the early 1800s there was no way to overcome the budding capitalist system and its attendant ideology. While I am in no way a technophobe, I do manage to admire their position, for I don't think that in liking technology, you have to admire every variant it comes in or how it is deployed.

I used to do a thought experiment when speaking in front of large audiences: "If you had the opportunity to invent the automobile, knowing what it did to society in the century following its introduction, would you do it?" I was talking not simply about the environmental issues but also about the broader questions of how this particular technology helped to shape society: about what it did to the development of the inner cities, about the development of the suburbs, and, at least in my opinion, about the way the automobile contributed to the alienation of people from various aspects of their lives. What shocked me about the answers I received was not so much the one I already expected—"Yes, because it would have happened anyway, by somebody else"—but rather the deep antagonism from the audience that this question engendered in the first place. They were angry because they didn't want the responsibility. They didn't want to have to take on their own shoulders the problem of thinking about something as deep as whether society should have gone in the direction it did.

I raised this question publicly, because if there are any qualms at all about what the automobile did, they will be nothing compared with the global digital culture that's going to be brought to us by Disney and Microsoft. Media critic Neil Postman wrote an homage to Aldous Huxley in his introduction to the Voyager electronic book that paired Postman's *Amusing Ourselves to Death* with Huxley's *Brave New World.* When 1984 came and went, Americans congratulated themselves on the fact that George Orwell's Big Brother had not materialized in the West. But what people missed, of course, was that Huxley's infinitely darker vision had come true. As Postman put it, in *Brave New World,* Huxley saw a time coming when "people will come to love their oppression, to adore the technologies that undo their capacities to think." In Huxley's fiction it's the drug soma; in Postman's analysis of our society, it's television.[3]

Given the fact that I generally address my remarks to audiences composed precisely of those involved in the development of new digital techno-

AMUSING OURSELVES TO DEATH

NEIL POSTMAN

VOYAGER
EXPANDED
B · O · O · K

"Cover" of the electronic book version of *Amusing Ourselves to Death*.
© The Voyager Company.

logies, they understand this reference to soma's addictive powers. They understand, at least subliminally, that when immersive games, interactive television, and on-line entertainment come into their own, they will be incredibly powerful. (And in the service of those who don't mind having people controlled.) Anyone with eight- or nine-year-old children at home who watches them play in front of a game screen for half the day can attest to the attractions that even our still quite primitive machines offer. For that matter, this applies to any adult who has been sucked into playing Marathon or Tetris for seven hours and then wondered—whoosh—where did that time go? If the name of the game is control, then these technologies are really good for it.

My theme boils down to two questions: What are we going to use these technologies for? What kind of society do we want to live in? I think it behooves us to start asking ourselves these questions in every way we can— by ourselves, in groups, in public forums—because if we do not ask the questions, there is no doubt in my mind that we are going to end up in a bad place. The only way we are ever going to take control of these technologies and make them serve the desire of a broad mass of people for a better life is if we can really start to get at the questions. What's it for? What kind of life we want to have?

I think that everything about these new technologies as they've been developed so far militates against really asking these questions. The whole structure of this business, the moneys involved, the temporal compression—eighteen-hour workdays, rushing products to market—force us to rush ahead when we should be stepping back and reevaluating our purpose. I'm not calling for us to join Kirkpatrick Sale on stage when he smashes computers.[4] I am in favor of stopping significantly for major periods of time. An hour, a day, a week, or a month, some span of time to talk to each other, because what we are doing now will absolutely determine the shape of human culture for the next millennium.

John Perry Barlow once remarked that "we could be better ancestors than this." When the world looks back five hundred years from now, how will it view our development and deployment of these new communication and information technologies?

These are ethical and ideological issues, and their importance is such that every unit in every company in this industry should go off and have two-hour study groups where they read philosophical works and think about these things in bigger terms. Is that going to happen? Probably not, unless it's pushed from the bottom. It isn't, and won't be, easy. But it's probably one of the most important things we need to do. In America it's even harder than in Europe and Japan to get people to grapple with these kinds of ideological issues. The apparent global triumph of capitalism has left even those who deal with these kinds of questions professionally at a loss for context and alternatives, almost unwilling to discuss alternative worldviews.

I was invited to participate in a conference in Israel called "The Future of History." I think I was expected to be the techno guy who was going to say that the future of history was digital or something else equally banal. I didn't want to play that role, so instead I sat there for two days, listening to a group of historians—all in their forties, all coming out of the 1960s, many from a basically Marxist perspective (if not explicitly, at least close to it)—and tried to determine exactly what they had learned from the last twenty years. The Soviet Union had gone down the tubes, China had gone Confucian capitalist, and everywhere in the world where socialism had had even the slightest possibility, it had died. In most public discourse, Marxism was beyond dead, and ideology had disappeared as a category for discussion. And there in Israel, these historians were rootless. They sat there for two days, looking for something that could give them a foundation and they couldn't find anything.[5]

As a publisher, one of the things I've tried to do is encourage and give voice to artists and writers who are willing to dig into these issues, from a lot of different angles and experiences. I am proud of the products we developed at the Voyager Company, yet I am less interested in the products than in the processes that brought them into being. Let me give a few examples.

When we put out *Who Built America?,* a disc created by the American Social History Project, Apple decided to bundle it with the CD-ROM pack it was giving away to all the schools that bought multimedia-equipped Macintosh computers.[6] Someone with a far-right agenda somewhere called Apple because the disc mentioned homosexuality and abortion. Apple asked us if we would edit it or take those parts out so it wouldn't offend anyone. Naturally, we declined, and Apple said they would stop selling it. We decided as a company to write something publicly about Apple's passing on this, to take them to task for it. We made a public statement, the first time in this industry I've ever encountered a corporation (albeit a small one) taking on the actions of another corporation purely on political terms. We got a fair amount of publicity, and we actually ended up winning: Apple backed down and continued to distribute the title. We could not have done that in the 1980s; the climate was not such that we could do that and, to be honest, inside the company the climate was not there either.

The conflict with Apple, and the issues it raised, were widely debated among the employees at Voyager. I think this helped prepare the company to discuss and decide to publish a very controversial CD-ROM in 1995. Voyager's *First Person* series pairs an author's writings with audio and video of the author talking. The first three discs featured white scientists—Marvin Minsky, Stephen J. Gould, and Don Norman—good pieces all, but we were trying to figure out where to go with them. We were making lists, thinking about whom to do next, and the list was becoming very eclectic, very broad. Somebody mentioned doing something on an African-American journalist named Mumia Abu-Jamal, who was on death row in Pennsylvania.

Abu-Jamal is a long-time political activist and radical journalist who was convicted of killing a police officer in 1982, despite evidence of his innocence and misconduct by police and prosecutors. He has since become the

Multimedia resources from *Who Built America?*
© The Voyager Company.

fulcrum for discussions of institutionalized racism in the American criminal justice system, the ethics of capital punishment, and the targeting of political dissidents in the United States. We had a big discussion at the company. All eighty of us in the New York offices got together for several hours, discussing what it meant to include this person's work in the *First Person* context. A unanimity developed about the importance of doing this, and the feelings generated in that discussion indicated to us that there would be a market for this title.

Abu-Jamal was already a flash point: he had been contracted to do a series of radio reports from prison for National Public Radio (NPR). When the Fraternal Order of Police found out about this, they enlisted the aid of then senator Bob Dole to get the show stopped, at the pain of cutting PBS and

Bob Stein

NPR still further. One day before Abu-Jamal's scheduled debut, NPR caved in to the pressure and canceled the project before airing the first tapes; all of the materials Abu-Jamal had generated for them were impounded. On June 2, 1995, his death warrant was signed and the date of execution was set for later that year. Though we had already decided to do *First Person: Mumia Abu-Jamal,* this was the moment that catalyzed the company. We put the disc together in five weeks—an incredibly fast turnaround for the medium. This experience gave us tremendous freedom: we put together a strong product and could apply the production experience to other titles.

First Person: Mumia Abu-Jamal showcases a man with an extremely eloquent voice who speaks from a place that Americans don't get much of a chance to hear from.[7] When Abu-Jamal was fourteen years old, George Wallace, the race-baiting governor of Alabama, and sometime presidential candidate, gave a public speech in Philadelphia. Abu-Jamal went with friends to bear witness against Wallace, and as he recounts, a crowd of Wallace supporters suddenly began to attack him. Abu-Jamal called out to the police, and they came over to help the Wallace people beat him. That is when Abu-Jamal started to form his own worldview. He went on to become one of the founding members of the Black Panther party in Philadelphia, and committed himself to radical journalism. The circumstances of his arrest, trial, conviction, and subsequent death sentence were controversial and, for many, troubling.

Voyager had really wanted to do this on the strength of the material alone, but after the death warrant was signed, it seemed even more timely. We felt that we might have some effect on the case just by the act of publishing it. One thing about a medium like the CD-ROM is that it allows for the accumulation of lots of different sources, from a variety of media, to create an interlaced argument. Thus the disc's user can move from photocopies of the COINTELPRO documents that show how Abu-Jamal was tracked by various governmental bodies for years, to a video interview recorded in 1989 while his sentence was under appeal, to the entire text of his book *Live from Death Row,* to audio clips of Abu-Jamal in prison, discussing the statistics that although African Americans make up less than 10 percent of the population of the state of Pennsylvania, they constitute over 40 percent of its death row population, and then to digital video interviews with his supporters from around the world: E. L. Doctorow, John Edgar Wideman, Cornel West, Derrick Bell, and Ramona Africa.

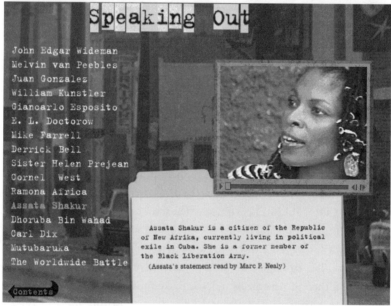

The title screen of *First Person: Mumia Abdu-Jamal.*
© The Voyager Company.

Text, audio, and digital video combine in *First Person: Mumia Abdu-Jamal.*
© The Voyager Company.

Bob Stein

As a publishing company, Voyager was always involved with social issues. We published *Dead Man Walking* by Sister Helen Prejean as an electronic book years before the movie by Tim Robbins, for example. When I started Voyager, my model was André Schiffren's Vintage/Knopf/ Pantheon, a company that would publish across a very broad range of fiction and nonfiction but would consistently publish books that were important to raising big, important questions.

What excited me most about *First Person: Mumia Abu-Jamal* is that it is the first CD-ROM to be published that was actually about a current event and not simply a derivative work or a piece of historical scholarship. This was a new media work about a man fighting for his life. At the time of its release, large distributors and chains, who never committed in great numbers to other Voyager products, were asking to buy thirty to forty copies for their shelves. It said quite a bit about the maturation of both the market for new media and that market's hunger for meaningful content. The front page of *USA Today*'s Style section ran a story the day the CD-ROM was released, which was part of building public awareness of the case.[8] Simply by being published, *First Person: Mumia Abu-Jamal* had the effect we wanted it to have. It was one of many factors that created more awareness of the man and his case, and sparked a large outpouring of protest demanding a new trial. It also contributed to the public pressure that influenced the judge to temporarily void the death warrant. Abu-Jamal remains on death row, fighting for a new trial and writing.

When Martin Nisenholtz was brought in to head interactive media at the *New York Times*, he called many people in the industry for input. He asked what I would do if I were in his position. I have the same problem with that question as I did when my son asked me what I would do if I had a billion dollars. I tried to explain that if I had a billion dollars, I wouldn't be me. The reality is, if I were sitting at the *New York Times*, I wouldn't be me. As a publisher I am involved in a continuous process of evaluating new media to determine how well they communicate, as well as trying to influence what messages they actually do communicate.

The *New York Times* would never put me in charge of their new media initiatives. There is no way that particular company is going to let me come in and figure out how they should present the news. So the question should never be how I would present the news in their shoes, but rather what their goals are in presenting the news in the first place. I could then give them my opinion on how these new technologies might be used to further their goals, but it's not necessarily going to be the same as my goals. Once their goals are identified and out on the table, there is a whole technological and service apparatus that exists to work toward those goals. But here the issue of ethics and first principles returns: What kind of world do you want to live in? I don't want to do the 6 o'clock news or the daily paper better; I want to do them completely differently.

Some final words in regard to the dialectic and digital media: I'm not so much interested in presenting both sides of the story, the classic thesis and antithesis of dialectical reasoning, as I am in having one side (generally the one I'm most interested in) present their side of the story as best they can. Alternatively, I'm interested in having the person who is producing a piece say, "Well, I looked at this one, I looked at that one, here are the questions that came up in my mind, here is the research I did, and here's the conclusion I made." I raise all of this because there is an issue about how to mollify the dialectic, to render discourse less rancorous, and perhaps in academia this is an important issue. But in the world where I work, there are not enough people taking passionate stands, not enough people working contentiously through an issue, coming to opinions and defending them. That's why I'm interested in these digital technologies to the extent that they can help people make up their minds and then take a position with some passion. One of the things I've always liked from Mao is his line that "truth emerges in the course of struggle." Contention by itself is not a bad thing if it's in the right spirit.

When the world looks back five hundred years from now on the development of hypertext, nonlinear modes of thinking, the infrastructure of worldwide networking, and our nascent virtual environments, all of these will perhaps be seen as the most important things that humans did during this period.

Digital technology is accelerating and intensifying the impact of the tools we make and use on our lives, even our own biology, and shapes the way we understand what's going on and what our choices are. But I think that all of us and future generations will be better served if we are associated not just with the development of the technologies, but also with questioning and debating how they should be used, whom they should serve. We could be better ancestors.

Musings on Amusements in America, or What I Did on My Summer Vacation

Brenda Laurel

Prelude: SIGGRAPH '94

It was a dark and steamy night when I arrived in Orlando, traveling alone to attend the SIGGRAPH conference and give a couple of talks. It would be two days before the Little Kid, my official excuse for cruising Walt Disney World, would arrive on her first solo flight. In the meantime I would have to content myself with the amazing flight-sim-motion-platform-big-vehicles-making-loud-noises VR demos on the SIGGRAPH exhibit floor. Terence McKenna and I, feeling like aliens for different reasons and thrown together by virtue of speaking on the same panel, set out to make a fifteen-minute tour. With his invariably apt cynicism and unerring sense of the bizarre, Terence is the best imaginable tour guide for this sort of expedition.

The first thing we stumble on is a kind of marine mammal combat game. Intended to break the gender barrier in location-based entertainment, Iwerks has concocted a weird undersea adventure with something for everyone. For the girls, a nurturing goal of saving the eggs of the Loch Ness monster ("Nessie"), earnestly narrated by a thirty-something blond "biologist." For the boys, a great big metal submarine with grappling claws and guns and very loud mechanical noises. For the girls again, the guide character of a cute little dolphin whose enthusiasm is dimmed not one whit by the staggering load of military equipment strapped to his lithe little body. Once you get underwater, things get really mixed up—the guns shoot paint balls and the grappling claws latch onto Nessie's eggs with the satisfying clang of big metal. The bad guys are also zipping around in a nasty metal submarine but are immediately rendered irrelevant by their paint-ball-only weaponry. Iwerks has come up with a bad recipe for gender-encompassing entertainment—like Tiny Tim, a gender blend that makes everyone a little queasy.

Disney is presenting its premiere VR demo—a magic carpet ride through the movie world of *Aladdin.* The contrast between the virtual world and the exterior of the installation is extreme—inside, you slide slick as celluloid on a path through Aladdin's cartoon world, complete with gratuitous one-way conversations with those adorable Arab characters, all at 60 Hz, since no body parts are being tracked; outside, a shiny black HMD elongated to resemble the face of one of James Cameron's aliens clamps onto your head, and you straddle the vehicle-sim interface like a big black Harley. Little girls look really, uh, funny doing this.

The trade show floor at SIGGRAPH.
Photo by Oscar & Associates, courtesy of ACM-SIGGRAPH.

Seaching for "Nessie's" eggs in Virtual Adventures.
© Evans & Sutherland and Iwerks Entertainment.

Meanwhile, in the backwaters of SigKids and the Edge, where only wandering breeders seem to go, there is a little dolphin exhibit. Young men talk to you earnestly about the puzzling evidence: swimming with dolphins leads to dramatic medical reversals in some cancer patients. "We don't think we can simulate it because we don't know what it is," they say, and add apologetically that "it seems to be volitional on the part of the dolphins." Nevertheless, they offer you a therapeutic dolphin experience. You lie on a water bed with your head under a curtain, wearing polarizing 3D glasses, little pads with obscure functionality on your temples, and earphones. Presently, New Age music heavy with low frequencies and mixed with dolphin sounds begins to vibrate through the water bed and into your marrow. Turquoise velvet art deco flowers start blooming out of your sternum. The empty video screen above you fills with a 3D first-person POV film of dolphins with whom you are evidently swimming. They glide by circumspectly at first, then nose your midsection, and finally, as the image fades, they grin right in your face. Two minutes later you float out of the installation, moving very slowly, wondering what happened to the tension between your shoulder blades.[1]

Although the SIGGRAPH big-VR crowd doesn't seem too keen on tracking bodies, the SIGGRAPH animation crowd is ever more adept at mutilating, exploding, stabbing, and amputating. The video show vacillates between images of utter despair and meaningless abstraction, one notable exception being a brilliant Smirnoff commercial in which a bottle of vodka carried on a tray by a waiter, as it passes between the viewer and various everyday objects, transforms what is seen through it into fantastical objects of desire. Even the effects reel from the movie *The Mask* features only moderately disturbing demonstrations of technology without content. This is the art of the nineties—worse, the mid-nineties—smack in the middle of a decade of anesthesia—too early for the millennium, and nothing goes over threshold. But what can we expect from an era in which a superhighway is supposed to be an interesting metaphor?

Eventually the conference powers down. I leave Terence sorting things out with a pal from Costa Rica and head for the airport to pick up my six-year-old daughter, Brooke, a nineties kid par excellence—recovering from a divorce, seriously attached to Dad, and ready to be bored, hard-boiled, or pissed—anything but the kid, or the family, that Walt had in mind.

Cracks in the Kingdom

The air is viscous with humidity when we catch the bus to the Magic Kingdom on Saturday morning. By the time we reach the monorail port, we are both dripping wet. The overabundance of green plants, bugs, and slithery things that normally accompanies such a junglelike atmosphere has been removed, presumably to bring this landscape into line with its all-but-obliterated dual in the LA desert.

Upon arriving at Main Street, we know exactly where we are by virtue of our previous visit to Disneyland in California. Streetwise Disneyworlders both, the first thing we do is make reservations for dinner in Cinderella Castle. While we watch a troupe of effusive young actors battle dripping makeup and limp crinolines in a musical revue, I ask Brooke which ride she would like to go to first. She chooses the Submarine because Daddy had taken her there once, and it brings back fond memories. We hike to the upper left corner of the map, where a courteous sign informs us that the wait in line will be forty-five minutes. Since this is our first line of the day, Brooke feels this is an acceptable interval.

Several surprising things happen in this line—things that would not have happened twenty-five or ten or even five years ago, at least not with the same flagrancy and frequency—things that reveal some cracks in the Kingdom. For example, the idea of an entire family actually standing in line behind the people in front of them—a rule that was followed without question by nearly everyone a decade ago—is now observed only by a slim majority of sluggish suburban types. Three different extended families— two groups of African Americans dressed in matching T-shirts proclaiming family reunions and an enthusiastic bunch of Italian Americans from New York—put proxies in the line, one or two patient elders. As the proxies reach the entrance to the ride, suddenly fifteen or twenty relatives of all ages come bursting through the line at open throttle—those who can, leaping over obstacles, others lifting small children and passing them across the serpentine undulations of ropes and people, and all of them piling into the next submarine in a noisy, chaotic parade of utterly insular celebration.

A few ladies in crumpled linen shorts grumble. Some, like me, give their kids a halfhearted lecture on manners and the necessity of standing in lines, which dribbles off into a reverie of what it would actually be like to have a family like that—so numerous, so unrestrained, so alive. I grip Brooke's hot, clammy hand a little harder, searching in vain for a pulse that might

Cinderella Castle.
© Disney Enterprises, Inc.

indicate the possibility of such a family. The uniformed teenagers hired by the Kingdom to manage the line do not notice these incidents. They cannot notice them; they have no category to put them in and no way to prevent or avert them without violating the Prime Directive of Disney World: Pleasantness.

Yet another assault to the Line Ordinance comes from a band of well-dressed white teens, all looking superficially serious and vaguely athletic in coordinated shorts outfits and expensive shoes. Brooke and I are within a sub's length of the head of the line when this crew parades gravely through the handicapped entrance, pushing one of their fallen friends in a rented wheelchair. He has a shoe on one foot and only a sock on the other, and wears a long-suffering look. Twelve of his closest friends have accompanied him and line up with their hands behind their backs in a paramilitary at-ease position facing the sweltering multitude in the line. There is a tense moment while the uniformed teen line managers absorb the magnitude of this effrontery, but for this breach, too, they seem to find no course of action but feigned normalcy. You don't just ask someone in a wheelchair to prove that he is crippled. The temporarily handicapped youth and his bodyguards commandeer the next sub.

When we finally get on a submarine, Brooke is critical. "It was better at Disneyland," she grumbles, careful to make the distinction between the LA park and Florida's Magic Kingdom. "We couldn't be 20,000 leagues under the sea—I can see the top of the water." "Yes, you're right—it's pretend," I reply seriously. "You were younger at Disneyland. I think the idea is that we're supposed to make believe." She harrumphs and crosses her arms, but her eyes involuntarily draw her closer to the porthole as we pass the mermaids—"I'm looking for trick wires," she says—and by the time the tentacles show up, she is genuinely startled. At the end of the ride cynicism returns—"the pilot was all the way out of the water, see? No way that was 20,000 leagues."

Seeing the day in jeopardy and thinking fast, I suggest that we shop. She drags me to the gift shop she has already cased in Cinderella Castle. Out of the fifty bucks I've given her to spend on the three-day trip, she immediately chooses a thirty-dollar plaster castle with a crystal mounted on one of the turrets. "That's a lot of your money gone," I say. This is a bad move; she feels criticized and looks for a way to strike back. "I'll take this to Daddy's house," she retorts, giving me a hard stare. "I'd like you to keep it at my house," I say, "so I can remember this swell trip, too." "Maybe I'll take it back and forth," she concedes.

So the day continues. After a fifteen-dollar hot-dog lunch, we ride the carousel—she runs on ahead and I breathlessly catch the horse next to her, fumbling with my camera to get a shot of her smiling. She catches me in the act and her face twitches as she considers the power of a frown, then graciously she grants me a photogenic grin. As the carousel turns, distant thunder begins and cheerful teenage vendors appear with five-dollar Mickey Mouse rain parkas. When we dismount, Brooke catches a few bars of "It's a Small World After All" on the wind and we dodge fat, warm raindrops to enter the forty-five-minute line to the ride I've been dreading most, because I know it will set up a music virus in my brain that will last for weeks.

There are punks in the line for It's a Small World. This baffles me—this, the most sugary and least high-tech ride in the park. Why are they here? They jostle the family-values crowd and make loud, cynical remarks, sit on the ropes, and act bored when they run out of wisecracks. Meanwhile, a weary, overweight mother carrying a baby startles me as she shouts at her toddler who is peeking through the crowd to see the boats up ahead. She grabs his hand and yanks him back to her side. "Stay with me, I said," she snarls, and brandishes a green willow switch. I have not seen a switch like this since I was a kid in Indiana. The woman closes her eyes and the toddler stands very still.

Water from the cloudburst is pouring through the line as we get into a boat. Brooke asks for a penny to throw into the water. I don't have one, so I give her a quarter. "Bigger wish," I say. The ride is just as I remember it— identical animated dolls with chubby kid faces, in different colors and native costumes. They are all singing *that song.* Sometimes I think I hear voices singing in different languages. The boat moves through large chambers that represent the continents. Somehow Disney has miraculously avoided offending any particular culture by translating each into equally innocuous sixties kitsch. There is a warm breeze in our faces as we move. My brain begins to whisper, "Full leisurely we glide. . . ." Brooke is entranced. People become quiet as the line of boats winds slowly through the singing dolls. As we arrive again at the dock, I look at the faces in our boat. Some people are smiling; all are subdued. There are tears on my face, and I see that one of the punks has been crying, too.

It's a Small World.
© Disney Enterprises, Inc.

Brenda Laurel

We determine that the line will always be too long at Space Mountain and Splash Mountain, and we proceed to other rides—Peter Pan, Mr. Toad's Wild Ride, the Haunted Mansion. Brooke is starting to get into the spirit of things. As we pass the graveyard near the entrance to the Haunted Mansion, she asks, "Mommy, are there really dead people buried there?" We make eye contact. "Oh, yes," I reply gravely. "Good," she says, and takes my hand.

After another thunderstorm and a brief shopping frenzy in Adventureland, we are ready for dinner at Cinderella Castle. Cinderella herself is there, all dolled up in her ball gown and graciously signing autographs. The waiter calls Brooke "milady" and gives her a paper crown. We are seated next to stained glass windows in the tower of the castle, and have an admirable view of the pea-green sky and sheets of rain sweeping across the carousel and courtyard. Yellow-parka-ed people scurry about below like ants whose anthill has just been kicked over. The waiter brings rolls with butter molded into a perfect three-dimensional figure of Mickey Mouse. Brooke gets really excited and grabs her knife. "I think I will cut off his ears first," she exclaims, then adds reasonably, "since that's the right amount of butter for a roll." She asks, "Will they fix him if I don't eat him all?" We imagine a hospital for little maimed butter Mickeys. I search in vain for a wine list.

As we emerge from dinner, it is clear that the rain has settled in for the night. I convince Brooke that the Electric Light Parade will be canceled; we have already learned that Tinker Bell is indisposed and will not make her traditional flight from the tower to the courtyard. My bones are aching. We slosh our way back down Main Street to the monorail station, past anxious parents and hopeful kids huddling under their regulation parkas on the curbs, waiting in the rain for the parade that won't happen. When we finally get back to the room, we order chocolate sundaes from room service. Brooke calls her daddy and we both have a good cry. The rain stops at ten, and I hope she doesn't hear the distant sound of the fireworks we are missing. She falls asleep in a puddle of chocolate. Finally, I order a glass of wine.

Epcot: Yesterday's Tomorrow

The next day, we arrive at Epcot[2] after a room-service breakfast of various sugar-based substances—I have given up on healthy food for the duration— and Brooke is consumed with curiosity about the big white geodesic dome that stands at the entrance to the park. The line is short—in fact, the place seems almost deserted. The dome houses what I judge to be the very best ride in Disney World, AT&T's "History of Communication." Walter Cronkite's narration transports me instantly to the sixties, and my pulse rate rises the way it did the night I watched the moon landing on TV. Jetson-like cars take small groups through the dome, past exhibits with Disney's finest audio-animatronics enacting great moments in communication from Lascaux to modern times—a scene from Greek theater, a Roman messenger, Gutenberg's printing press, an early American telegrapher, a twenties-style telephone operator. Things start to veer off from reality as we pass the automated office, and are seriously off course as we reach an array of computer terminals with images from outer space. The ride attempts a climax as we rise and swirl weightlessly through a starry sky. Cronkite's thrilling, fatherly voice trembles with excitement and hope as he describes a future when man finally travels to the stars.

As we reenter the daylight, I see that Brooke is bored. Perhaps the narration was over her head. But it strikes me that there is nothing in our culture now to replace the swelling hope of those times, the heyday of the space program, the age of which this ride is an artifact, a future that Brooke never knew. Those grand stirrings have been narrated into complacency by cultural myth; we no longer need the space program for excitement, we have *Star Trek* for that—and there are more important things to spend our money on. As I look up at the dome in the sunlight, I feel that the finest thing a president could do to rekindle hope in America's youth would be to revitalize the space program. I imagine how it would be to taste that hope again, and wonder if anything else could ever come close.

Seeking refuge from the bright heat (now nearly a hundred degrees), we settle in a trendy chrome espresso joint on the periphery of the fountains to survey the scene and make a plan. We are the only customers. We look out over the fountains and across the lake at the center of the park; all of the national pavilions encircle the lake, and there are elaborate fireworks launched from floating platforms at night. Brooke reads over the schedule of events. "Mom!" she says. "You are really not going to like this." There is an evil gleam in her eye. "What?" She waits a beat for dramatic effect. "*Barbie,*" she intones. "Oh, my God," I reply, "do you think I can have my picture taken with her?" She gasps; I score. "MOM!"

Spaceship Earth at Epcot®.
© Disney Enterprises, Inc.

We have twenty minutes to wait at the site where Barbie signs autographs after her live stage show at the far side of the lake. Heat rises from the all-but-deserted plaza, but suddenly we see a sizable whorl of people forming near a hot pink sign: *Barbie's Autograph. Please form one line. One photo per family.* We wait patiently with little girls from everywhere and their moms in the shade of a few palm trees. We are instantly bonded, an ad hoc community waiting for Barbie. After several minutes, a muscle-bound young man in a hot pink polo shirt materializes and reiterates the rules. "Do you know Barbie?" I ask him. "I know Ken," he replies, eyes front like a Marine.

Fifteen minutes have passed when our heat-oppressed brains are roused by a surreal vision. A hot pink limousine emerges noiselessly through curtains of heat-distorted air. As it draws close, we see that it is an eighteen-wheel limousine; it is the biggest limousine I have ever seen; it is an Andy Warhol limousine. Ken's friend's eyes narrow and he assumes a rigid pose. The limo stops and Barbie steps out. She is wearing a hot pink halter top and has very big blonde hair. Skipper bubbles out behind her, chewing gum. Everyone lines up. Barbie and Skipper saunter over into the shade, smiling.

Brenda and Brooke, Barbie and Skipper.
Courtesy of Brenda Laurel.

Ken's friend announces the rules again. Then he ceremonially draws back
the hot pink velvet cord that separates Barbie from the rest of us.

Brooke and I are third in line for pictures; since we are allowed only one
shot, I ask a mom from Oklahoma to photograph us with my camera. Barbie
smells like Chantilly. I slip my arm companionably around her waist, and
she shoots me a look meant to kill. I scowl, and the Oklahoma lady refuses
to take the photo. "Not till you smile," she chirps. I grimace, she snaps, and
Ken's buddy ushers us over to the limo for a look. There are photos of all of
Barbie's friends on her ornate dresser, along with a French provincial telephone and several gilded hand mirrors, brushes, and combs. The seats are
upholstered in hot pink velvet. Barbie has a TV, a stereo, and a VCR in her
limo, as well as a cut-glass pitcher of pink lemonade with matching glasses.
Peeking out from under the third seat is a pack of Marlboro Lights. I snicker

and hustle Brooke off to the gift shop to get out of the heat. It is truly weird, I muse, that Barbie is the main attraction at Epcot Center. She is definitely not Walt's type.

We wander off to the Canada pavilion where there is a CircleVision movie called *Oh, Canada!* Brooke is feeling nostalgic for Banff (where we lived all last summer), and she's excited about the prospect of seeing a movie about a place where she's been. The theater building is an enormous faux log lodge with lots of atmospheric stuff like antlers and old pottery. The movie, made in the early eighties, is narrated by a woman who was probably pretending to be Quebecois before it was problematic. She takes us from coast to coast, stopping at famous cities and tourist attractions like Lake Louise, presenting smatterings of history and geography woven into what is otherwise a long commercial for tourism. All of the faces in the movie are white. At the end Brooke and I look sideways at each other and enter into a silent conspiracy. "Well, sweetheart," I begin loudly, "I noticed that there were some people missing in the movie, didn't you?" Brooke looks around to see that we're getting some attention. "Yes, Mommy," she replies in her best schoolgirl voice. "There were no Japanese people, and I didn't see a single Indian." A few more people turn and look at us, blinking; we can see that we've made some of them notice the oversight.

As we leave the theater building, Brooke scolds me sotto voce. "Mom, why do you *always* have to get *upset* about that stuff?" "Because your great-grandpa was an Indian." "I know we're part Indian," she says, "but I'm *half* Scandinavian." I sigh, resolved not to argue. "Yes, that's why you usually have cold feet." She nods, and seems satisfied that her roots have been fully examined.

We spend the hot afternoon strolling around the lake and sampling—Germany, Japan, Italy. At the Chinese pavilion, we sit on the sizzling cement to watch the Red Panda acrobats. We are close enough to see where their costumes are mended, and also to marvel at their unflinching nerve and unwavering smiles. A girl on a very tall unicycle catches bowls on her toe, then kicks them up to land in a stack on her head. Another girl twists and curls her body through a series of impossible positions, moving like a slow, graceful snake. A young man juggles blocks, batons, china. A fourth man, older than the rest of the troupe and wearing a grim expression, does nothing at all except stand formally in his costume at the back of the stage. He takes a bow with the rest of the troupe. This is Brooke's favorite attraction, and the spiciest part of it is speculating about the sad, mysterious man. "Maybe they are his slaves," she speculates. "Maybe he's a spy. Maybe he used to be an acrobat but has a terrible disease now but they let him be here anyway because otherwise it would break his heart."

For dinner we visit the Coral Reef Restaurant, scoring a table for two with an excellent view of an enormous aquarium through the glass wall. We can dimly see visitors to the Living Seas exhibit at the other side of the expanse of water. The waitresses' clothing, tablecloths, napkins, china, and crystal are all various shades of sea green. With the menu Brooke gets a program for the aquarium showing the silhouette of each kind of fish with its name printed underneath. You can also order many of these types of fish to eat. Remembering Butter Mickey, I feel there may be a streak of totemism running through the collective Disney unconscious—or at least a kind of entertainment-oriented eating disorder. As we dine, we watch a scuba diver in the tank who appears to be feeding butter lettuce to the fish. He strokes the manta rays as they slide under his hands like affectionate cats.

After an excellent meal we walk about the aquarium. Brooke has always loved to watch fish. She admires the peaceful way they glide about; I can feel the calming effect that the underwater world has on both of us. But upon returning to the plaza at dusk, Brooke declares that she has HAD ENOUGH OF EPCOT and demands that we go back to the Magic Kingdom—where the action is—to watch the parade and fireworks. I tell her that the fireworks on the lake at Epcot are world famous and sure to be better than those over Cinderella Castle, but she will not be persuaded. She wants to be with fellow kids. Back on the monorail, I wonder about Epcot—this artifact of yesterday's tomorrow, more poignantly off the mark than the Jetsons or Tomorrowland, a Woodrow Wilson fairy tale of benign nationalism and Higher Values, where memories of fantasies of cultures of the world glide like fish around the lake—where adults stroll about, nostalgic and fragile, imbued with a sense of the world in which today's children cannot engage.

On our third and last day we go directly to the Magic Kingdom. Brooke has an agenda—to repeat rides she has enjoyed, and to leverage her remaining seven dollars into several more souvenirs by asking for matching funds. In late afternoon, after the obligatory thundershower and before our encore dinner at Cinderella Castle, Brooke wants to visit It's a Small World one last time. As we stand in the line, I wonder why I am not dreading it.

Perhaps the raging emotions of the last three days have exhausted my potential for anxiety. I am asking myself why this silly, annoying ride makes me cry. The ride is familiar now, and I study visual details as the continents slip by. I wonder again why the clown in the balloon has a sign that says "help"; I notice the bird that comes only halfway out of its egg in the rain forest; I enjoy the volcanic eruptions made of blowing scarves.

In the last chamber of the ride, it hits me. Everything here is more or less white. Dolls from all the different countries are here, still in national dress, but their costumes are white. They are all mixed up, all dancing and singing together. I ask Brooke, "Do you think this is supposed to be heaven?" Without turning toward me she shrugs her narrow shoulders. She is gripping the side of the boat, looking at the dolls with shining eyes, singing along in a whisper.

Meanwhile, Back in the Midwest

Two weeks later we find ourselves in Indianapolis, beginning a visit to the Midwest in August, a folly that can be explained only by the fact that relatives reside hereabouts. Brooke and I are joined by my nine-year-old daughter, Hilary; my boyfriend, Rob; and his seven-year-old daughter, Suzanne. This is something of an obligatory journey of mutual family sniffing, as well as a social experiment in long trips with little girls and the efficacy of adjoining rooms in motels. The Grand Objective and culmination of this tour, however, is to visit the world's largest state fair—the Iowa State Fair in Des Moines.

Indiana is a funny place—"funny peculiar," not "funny ha-ha." For two days in a row the local news carries the same stories about a head-on car accident in which an extended family met their deaths and a fire that claimed the lives of several small children while their mother was in a bar (peace in the Middle East and other tidbits of world news are discussed, if at all, after sports and weather). Rush Limbaugh harangues us through my mother's radio. After a three-day visit that exhausts my mother and her husband, the children—who have been assiduously deprived of these flavors of mass media in California—are beginning to exhibit an unhealthy interest in the television. We snatch them up and plant them in the back seat of a rented Lincoln Town Car before their hungry little minds disappear beneath the waves of fire, blood, and tornado warnings, and take off on a one-day gonzo road trip from Indianapolis to Des Moines. Strip malls and suburbs have overwritten the landscape I grew up in like colonies of toxic bacteria in a petri dish. As we clear the edge of the sprawl, the baroque green abundance of the Midwestern countryside causes me to make happy little noises in my throat.

The road trip passes without major ugly incident, due in large part to Rob's superb ability to engage the children in a game called Would You Rather. He has evidently played this game for years; I encountered it as a gross-out technique in college,[3] and have noticed the tendency to create horrific alternatives in both of my kids as they graduated from toddlerhood.[4] Rob's questions typically combine kid-level humor with a good dollop of sensory imagination.[5] But the genius of his approach lies in his style: he asks these questions in the persona of an intensely curious psychological theorist who feels he is on the verge of a major breakthrough in understanding the human mind, and he follows up the children's answers with a penetrating "Why?" They delight in explaining their choices to him as he nods gravely and occasionally exclaims, "Aaah! I *see*!"

About halfway across Illinois the children grow restless and it begins to rain. We stop for gas at a place that calls itself, ambiguously, "the World's Biggest Truck Stop in Illinois." This warehouse of road culture offers everything from Harley T-shirts to enormous chrome exhaust pipes to lenticular mud flaps with the silhouettes of reclining naked women on them, their gravity-defying breasts pointing skyward. The children are both intrigued and grossed out by a display of dash-mountable beer can holders, the handles of which are shaped like scantily clad, wide-eyed blonde women held up by very large breasts draped over the frame of the device. The merchandise in this establishment achieves the impossible: the girls find absolutely nothing they want to buy.

Golden late afternoon sunlight slants out from beneath flat-bottomed purple cumulonimbus clouds in visible rays. My best friend in Indiana used to call this kind of display an "advertisement for God." Rob notes that it is starting to look like Iowa—miles and miles of corn-forested swells breathing with the wind. The country is somehow bigger now, and houses, too, are bigger, more gracious, and farther apart. I feel as though I am traveling back in time, riding through a country made big by my smallness, seeing the towns and cities of my childhood without malls or convenience stores or tract houses or sodium-vapor-poisoned night skies. In the outskirts of Des Moines I see incandescent streetlights coming on at dusk. A few lightning bugs are signaling in the front yard when we pull into Rob's parents' drive-way. Everyone shows up—parents, brothers, brothers' wives and children, a new baby, two dogs, three little blonde girls, and us. We begin our acquaintances, share food, then retire for the night to adjoining rooms on the eleventh and top floor of the Fort Des Moines hotel—once the tallest building in town—where the bellman is so old I offer to help him with the suitcases. We tuck the kids in between thick white sheets.

Up bright and early in the morning, everyone gathers at the house to make a caravan to the fair. Rob's mother, Barbara, serves us all a breakfast that falls just tastefully short of enormous. We climb into two cars and a pickup, Rob's "sensible" brother in the lead. After much stopping and starting and waiting in traffic, we finally find more or less adjacent parking places in the once and future mud of the Iowa State Fairgrounds. The children, who are after all California girls and have been exposed only to Disneyland and Great America, cannot parse the scene. No well-designed, top-down theme park with coherent messages and an integrated style, the Iowa State Fair's only consistent features are neon, noise, and dirt. The girls are further frustrated by a routine that the natives take for granted: we march through the midway without stopping to find the animals.

Our first destination is a petting zoo where the children ride ponies and then make friends with a large and diverse group of goats. The smallest kids (as in young goats) are slipping in and out of the fence at will to be petted and fed by a hundred filthy little hands, whose initial coating of cotton-candy residue is now enhanced by goat slobber and bits of straw. An older goat chews urgently on the hem of Hilary's skirt. Brooke is about to split a gut in frustration—"Why are we *doing* this?"—when she spies vending machines across the way with live animals inside. The game cabinets are very old, with such labels as "Play Tic-Tac-Toe with a Chicken!" and "Watch the Duck Play a Ukulele!" She begs me for quarters; this is the most interactive entertainment she has seen in a long time.

After a suitable interval of rising suspense (including a downright cruel interlude of viewing unusually large vegetables), we begin the trek back to the midway. As we pass the public rest rooms, I snap and order the children to go inside and wash their hands; they emerge with dirt lines at the wrists, and demand corn dogs and lemonade. We wolf down our food as the kids survey the scene through slitted eyes, calculating how many rides they can go on for the number of tickets we've given them, measuring each ride for its

Wood-chopping contest at Pioneer Hall, Iowa State Fair.
Photo by Carolyn McNurlen Tenney, courtesy of Iowa State Fair.

Hilary and Suzanne at the Iowa State Fair.
Courtesy of Brenda Laurel.

Brenda Laurel

throw-up factor and rejecting those on which a number of little kids appear. After warm-ups on the bumper cars, Hilary and Suzanne choose what is without question the most seriously barfogenic ride at the fair—something called the Kamikaze, two scythe-shaped structures that violently swing their occupants upside down. Brooke puddles up because she is too short ("You must be 48 inches tall and prove it!") and cries until I offer to buy her a whistle.

The kids move on to one of many stand-up spin-around rides that now seem to be run by young black deejays who perform vocal improvisations over loud rap music, exhorting the riders to raise their hands or shout in a kind of call-and-response rhythm. This is an element of carnival culture that has changed since I was a kid; in those days men of indeterminate ethnicity operated the rides with minimal interaction with their patrons. You could imagine them sitting around together at night—the "carnies" seemed to be a pretty homogeneous lot. These young rappers are new squares in the quilt. I wonder how well everyone gets along at night, whether they drink together and tell stories, and whether I am remembering something real or just snatches of old Ray Bradbury stories. My grandma used to tell me that the gypsies would steal me if I strayed too far from the family, and I don't suppose that was true either, but it was a delicious sort of fright.

Rob and I leave the girls with an uncle and take a ride on the double Ferris wheel. Having inherited my mother's propensity for motion sickness, this is the most daring ride I am able to contemplate. The first time we are at the top of the top wheel, I start screaming; Rob looks horrified. The second time we are at the top of the top, he kisses me, presumably to avoid embarrassment. Pastel neon blurs against the pastel sky, and I am floating; it is the Midwest, it is the State Fair, I have just been kissed on the Ferris wheel, and I am surely not a middle-aged lady.

Several hours and a few hundred dollars later, we haul semicomatose children back to the hotel for a good scrubbing. Later in the evening we reconvene at Barbara's house for a meal that includes sweet corn, pasta with fresh herbs from her garden, and deep red tomatoes that are just about as good as sex. Barbara digs out a black-and-white photo of Rob and his brothers as kids, walking down the boulevard at the State Fair. Each one is carrying cotton candy on a stick. I note what a nice picture it is, how well it seems to capture the day. Barbara remarks that the boys' father made them walk down the boulevard three times before he got the picture he wanted.

This sets me to musing on all the video and photographs we have been taking on our summer vacation. If we are not careful, we reduce life with kids to a series of photo opportunities. Certainly, Disney's Empire is optimized for this worldview. We are more than our artifacts, I think, and if we are living life well, our photographs are puzzling evidence of experiences that are legible only as character and desire.

On our last day in Iowa, Rob's little brother Bill takes us all to a friend's place outside of town where there is a pond—an expanse of deep green water ringed by cattails and graceful old trees, with an old wooden dock that wiggles and creaks when you walk on it, and an old rowboat pulled up among the weeds. This is the archetypal Pond, and we are having, it seems, the archetypal Midwestern Day. Hilary complains that there is nothing to do, and wanders off to poke things with a stick. The grownups sit on coolers or fiddle with fishing equipment; Uncle Jack takes the girls (all except Hilary) swimming in borrowed life jackets. One of the dogs goes for a swim and produces squeals of dismay when she shakes her coat. Bill lets each child catch a fish—a slick, yellow-green bluegill about as long as your hand, flopping and gaping on the dock just long enough for a kid to look at it, touch it, wonder at it, and throw it back. Rob and I eat little cherry tomatoes picked warm off the vine and drink cold beer. Jack's wife produces pineapple cookies made after his grandmother's recipe; everyone nibbles them reverently while agreeing that they are surely too sweet. Rob piles all five little girls (including Jack's two) into the rowboat and paddles them noisily around the pond.

When the children have returned to fishing, I ask Rob to give me a ride in the boat. I rediscover that I cannot row; the physics of it defeats me, and I give up as the boat turns in slow circles. Rob rows close to the water's edge, and I am reminded of my turtle-hunting adventures as a child—I caught and sold dozens of them to the local drugstore until it dawned on me what their fate was likely to be. Sometimes I would find them with fragments of elaborate paint jobs spread apart like puzzle pieces on the expanded segments of their shells. We are too noisy to catch turtles today; they hear us coming. The sun is very bright; Rob and I drift for a while in and out of shadows along the bank. The children begin waving at us from the dock. "Rob, come back!" Little voices drift across the water. For a moment time has stopped; now time is past. "We need another ride, Rob!" "Mommy, there's nothing to dooooooo!"

The next morning we say our farewells over another sumptuous break-fast. Barbara and I have our heads together over old photographs until the last possible moment. Bill's baby smiles like a Buddha as the girls coo over him and kiss him good-bye. The trip to the airport is a blur; somehow the luggage is checked and we find our way onto the plane, children squabbling about seating arrangements and debating what will be served for lunch. The plane rises, weightless, through white Midwestern clouds into timeless blue. We are going home, I realize, someplace vaguely to the west. I sleep, and dream myself a turtle, slipping noiselessly from sunlight into dark green water.

Notes

Introduction: Screen Grabs

1. The contributors to this volume tend to be sympathetic to the history and the continued vitality of the dialectic. There is, however, a strong body of work critiquing digital culture from the antidialectical position promoted by Gilles Deleuze and Félix Guattari. Deleuze and Guattari regard the dialectic as a hierarchical tool, one that too easily closes off the possibilities of creative investigation. Deleuze has written that what he hated "more than anything else was Hegelianism and the Dialectic" (Gilles Deleuze, "I Have Nothing to Admit," trans. Janis Forman, *Anti-Oedipus/Semiotext(e),* Sylvère Lotringer, special editor, 2, no. 3 [1977]: 12). Deleuze and Guattari proposed a rhizomatic discourse to counter the dialectic (the peanut is a rhizome, and its root structure is nodal, rather than growing off of a central trunk). See *A Thousand Plateaus: Capitalism and Schizophrenia,* trans. Brian Massumi (Minneapolis: University of Minnesota Press, 1987 [orig. 1980]). Manuel De Landa offers some of the best applications of rhizomatic thinking to the discourses of technology in *War in the Age of Intelligent Machines* (New York: Zone Books, 1991) and *A Thousand Years of Nonlinear History* (New York: Zone Books, 1997).

2. *Hegel's Logic,* trans. William Wallace (Oxford: Oxford University Press, 1975), pp. 116–17.

3. In allotting this amount of space to Hegel and Marx, one can only cursorily introduce the parameters of battle, and expect to be damned for doctrinal failings. So be it.

4. Theodor W. Adorno, *Negative Dialectics,* trans. E. B. Ashton (New York: Continuum, 1983 [orig. 1966]), p. 6.

5.   I discuss this "vapor theory of ruminations unsupported by material underpinnings" at length in "Theorizing in Real Time: Hyperaesthetics for the Technoculture," *Afterimage* 23, no. 4 (January/February 1996): 16–18.

6.   This bit rot creates an intriguing problem for editing a collection like this. Michael Heim, for example, had to be pressed to list any addresses at all, while William Mitchell believes that the information should get out, and if the sites go down, it will at least serve as a spur for those interested to seek out other sites that could offer similar or more expansive experiences.

7.   Carl Andre and Hollis Frampton, "On Literature and Consecutive Matters, December 8, 1962," *12 Dialogues 1962–1963,* photographs by Hollis Frampton (Halifax: Press of the Nova Scotia College of Art and Design, 1980): 49.

Chapter 1: Unfinished Business

1.   Gregory Bateson, *Steps to an Ecology of Mind* (New York: Ballantine Books, 1972).

2.   Jean Starobinski sees Boullée (1728–1799) as "driven by a lyricism that was more pictorial than architectural." Jean Starobinski, *1789, The Emblems of Reason,* trans. Barbara Bray (Cambridge, MA: MIT Press, 1988), p. 79.

3.   One has only to see the scholarly reconstructions of the concluding scenes of *The Magnificent Ambersons* to understand why the word "unfinished" harbors such a strong sense of pathos.

4.   Susan Buck-Morss, *The Dialectics of Seeing: Walter Benjamin and the Arcades Project* (Cambridge, MA: MIT Press, 1989).

5.   Ted Nelson, "Hypertext Is Ready: HTML for Home and Office," *New Media* 5, no. 8 (August 1995): 17.

6.   <www.yahoo.com>.

7.   In a 1995 E-mail to the fellow members of the Cyborganic on-line community, Hall wrote about his own evolution. "For the first couple of months, my magazine consisted largely of reviews—pointers to nifty net nuggets with commentary. Engaging, sure, because I found cool stuff and I liked to talk about it. Back then, it was hard to find guides in cyberspace, and I relished that role. I had anticipated a trend—soon the net was huge, and everybody and their service provider had a list of hot links (some even using my material!). In this smattering of sites, covering everything was pointless. To alleviate self-referential on-line uselessness, I shifted gears. In addition to luscious links, I now publish stories about my life. Having been at this for over a year and a half, talking about myself keeps me going." This text can be found at <www.links.net/inc/index/yahoo.html>. Hall's continuing and evolving project can be found at *Justin's Homepage,* <www.justin.org>.

8.   Guy Debord, "Theory of the Dérive," in *Situationist International Anthology,* ed. and trans. Ken Knabb (Berkeley, CA: Bureau of Public Secrets, 1981), p. 50. One site devoted to the SI can be found at <www.nothingness.org/SI>.

9.   Marcos Novak, "Liquid Architectures in Cyberspace," in *Cyberspace: First Steps,* Michael Benedikt, ed. (Cambridge, MA: MIT Press, 1991), pp. 225–54.

10.   Coop Himmelblau, "The End of Architecture," in *The End of Architecture?: Documents and Manifestos,* Peter Noever, ed. (Munich: Prestel-Verlag, 1992), p. 18.

11.   As mentioned earlier, Etienne-Louis Boullée stands as the very model of the "paper" architect, and his work becomes a new avatar. Paper architecture is both unfinished and unfinishable, and historically has ranged from the macabre prison plans of Giovanni Battista Piranesi in eighteenth-century Italy to the impermanent wooden model of Soviet Constructivist Vladimir Tatlin's Monument to the Third International (1919–20). See Christian W. Thomsen, *Visionary Architecture : From Babylon to Virtual Reality* (Munich and New York: Prestel, 1994). Not even these unfinished architectures are left unfinished. At MIT, a research program is under way that aims at building a series of famous unbuilt projects in virtual space. These "Unbuilt Buildings Built" include Michael Webb's Drive-in House (1960) and Tatlin's monument. The project is directed by Tekehiko Nagakura and Kent Larson. See the MIT publication *PLAN* no. 47 (June 1997).

12. Bernard Tschumi, "Urban Pleasures and the Moral Good," *assemblage* 25 (December 1994): 9.

13. Stewart Brand, *How Buildings Learn: What Happens After They're Built* (New York: Viking, 1994), p. 2. I first came across photos of the Quaker Hilton on p. 105. Brand is a name to reckoned with in the digital world; he is the founder of the Bay Area electronic community known as the WELL and the author of *The Media Lab: Inventing the Future at MIT* (New York: Penguin, 1988).

14. I write about the phenomenon of the early user in "Commodity Camaraderie and the TechnoVolksgeist," *Frame-Work: The Journal of Images and Culture* 6, no. 2 (Summer 1993).

15. Vivian Sobchack, "Breadcrumbs in the Forest: Three Meditations on Being Lost in Space," in her *Carnal Thoughts: Bodies, Texts, Scenes and Screens* (Berkeley: University of California Press, forthcoming).

16. From the Baal cycle, in *Stories from Ancient Canaan,* ed. and trans. Michael David Coogan (Philadelphia: Westminster Press, 1978), p. 93.

17. Stuart Moulthrop, *Victory Garden,* intro. Michael Joyce and J. Yellowlees Douglas (Watertown, MA: Eastgate Systems, 1993)

18. Gérarde Genette, *Paratexts: Thresholds of Interpretation,* trans. Jane E. Lewin (Cambridge: Cambridge University Press, 1997).

19. Think of the contemporary Hollywood cinema. The vast mechanism of publicity that the movie industry employs today is just the most obvious source of paracinematic material. More interesting by far is the question of what actually constitutes the film, and what the parafilm, in an environment replete with "director's cuts," pan and scanned videos, colorized versions, letterboxed laserdiscs, and proliferating formats like DVD.

20. This quote comes from the no longer active site, <www.mnemonic.sony.com>.

21. *Wired* 3.06 (June 1995): 157–159, 207–208. The original short story was published in *Omni* magazine in 1981, and is collected in William Gibson, *Burning Chrome* (New York: Ace, 1987), pp. 1–22.

22. Even that which was finished as unfinished—Edith Wharton's manuscript for *The Buccaneers,* for example, was left incomplete at her death—is now "completed" by Marion Mainwaring; one expects a sequel to follow. Edith Wharton, *The Buccaneers: A Novel,* completed by Marion Mainwaring (New York: Viking, 1993 [unfinished manuscript published 1938]).

23. This process is not limited to the comic book, of course; similar dynamics run through the soap opera industry as well.

24. One of the fixed descriptions of *Waxweb* can be found in the 1995 Interactive Media Festival catalog, edited by Timothy Druckrey and Lisa Adams. It documents the show held at the Variety Arts Center in Los Angeles, June 4–7, 1995. *Waxweb* was a featured piece in the show.

25. Howard Rheingold, *The Virtual Community: Homesteading on the Electronic Frontier* (New York: HarperPerennial, 1993), p. 145. This citation is taken from the electronic text version, <www.well.com/user/hlr/vcbook/vcbook5.html>.

26. Blair and his team have designed *Waxweb* so that "visitors to the MOO were invited not just to read the ported hypertext, but to add to it using the on-line hypertext tools, and in addition to talk to one another. Traditional writing, hypertext writing, various levels of programming, as well as several types of synchronous and asynchronous text communication were all supported in this environment, a hybrid functionality resulting from the placement of a constructive hypertext in a virtual-reality environment." Taken from David Blair's 1994 article, "Waxweb: Image-Processed Narrative" <jefferson.village.virginia.edu/wax/wax.html>. The WaxwebMOO can be found at <bug.village.virginia.edu>.

27. Michael Nash, "Vision After Television: Technocultural Convergence, Hypermedia, and the New Media Arts Field," in *Resolutions: Contemporary Video Practices,* Michael Renov and Erika Suderburg, eds. (Minneapolis: University of Minnesota Press, 1996), p. 392

28. Don DeLillo, *Libra* (New York: Viking, 1988), p. 221.

29. I ran across this quote in Italo Calvino's *Six Memos for the Next Millennium,* a monument to unfinish. The essays—or memos, as he called them—were written to be delivered at Harvard in 1985, but Calvino died just before leaving for the United States. This slim volume, compiled by his wife, was published a few years later.

Carlo Levi, introduction to an Italian edition of Laurence Sterne's *Tristram Shandy*, quoted in Italo Calvino, *Six Memos for the Next Millennium* (Cambridge, MA: Harvard University Press, 1988), p. 47.

30. Rob La Frenais is the organizer of The Incident. The first, in 1995, was Fribourg, Switzerland; the second, at the Institute of Contemporary Arts in London in 1996. Speakers have included astrophysicist and UFO reseacher Jaques Vallee; artist James Turell; ethnobotonist and millennial journalist Terrence McKenna; network artist and philosopher Roy Ascott; telepath researcher Keiko Sei; and artist H. R. Geiger.

31. Marshall McLuhan, *Understanding Media: The Extensions of Man* (Cambridge, MA: MIT Press, 1994 [orig. 1964]), p. 85.

32. The following is a reprint of the Extropian Principles 2.5, dated July 1993 and written by Max More, president of the Extropy Institute. For more information see their journal, *The Extropian*.

Extropy: A measure of intelligence, information, energy, vitality, experience, diversity, opportunity, and growth. Extropianism: The philosophy that seeks to increase extropy. Extropianism is a transhumanist philosophy: Like humanism, transhumanism values reason and humanity and sees no grounds for belief in unknowable, supernatural forces externally controlling our destiny, but goes further in urging us to push beyond the merely human stage of evolution. As physicist Freeman Dyson has said: "Humanity looks to me like a magnificent beginning but not the final word." Religions traditionally have provided a sense of meaning and purpose in life, but have also suppressed intelligence and stifled progress. The Extropian philosophy provides an inspiring and uplifting meaning and direction to our lives, while remaining flexible and firmly founded in science, reason, and the boundless search for improvement.

1. Boundless Expansion: Seeking more intelligence, wisdom, and effectiveness, an unlimited lifespan, and the removal of political, cultural, biological, and psychological limits to self-actualization and self-realization. Perpetually overcoming constraints on our progress and possibilities. Expanding into the universe and advancing without end.

2. Self-Transformation: Affirming continual moral, intellectual, and physical self-improvement, through reason and critical thinking, personal responsibility, and experimentation. Seeking biological and neurological augmentation.

3. Dynamic Optimism: Fueling dynamic action with positive expectations. Adopting a rational, action-based optimism, shunning both blind faith and stagnant pessimism.

4. Intelligent Technology: Applying science and technology creatively to transcend "natural" limits imposed by our biological heritage, culture, and environment.

5. Spontaneous Order: Supporting decentralized, voluntaristic social coordination processes. Fostering tolerance, diversity, long-term thinking, personal responsibility, and individual liberty.

33. E. J. Holmyard, *Alchemy* (New York: Dover, 1990 [orig. 1957]), p. 16.

Chapter 2: The Cyberspace Dialectic

1. William Gibson, *Neuromancer* (New York: Ace Books, 1984); and Michael Benedikt, ed., *Cyberspace: First Steps* (Cambridge, MA: MIT Press, 1991).

2. Theodore J. Kaczynski, a Montana recluse who once taught mathematics at the University of California, Berkeley, has confessed to the Unabomber's crimes. The merits of my arguments are predicated on a different set of criteria than the adjudication of this particular case. To browse the many variants of the Unabomber Manifesto, the reader can begin at the Yahoo Internet site (www.yahoo.com) and look under "Society and Culture." Then click on "Crime," then "Crimes" and "Homicides," then "Serial Killers," under which are "Unabomber" and "Unabomber Manifesto." Along the way, the reader will also find many satirical and not-so-satirical Web sites devoted to the mythos of the Unabomber.

3. The Unabomber Manifesto appeared in the *Washington Post* on September 19, 1995. The name "Unabomber" came from the Federal Bureau of Investigation code for "university—airlines bomber," since the majority of the twenty-three bomb targets were people who worked at universities or traveled on the airlines.

4. Jacques Ellul, *The Technological Society,* trans. John Wilkinson (New York: Vintage, 1964).

5. Unabomber Manifesto, "Industrial Society and Its Future," para. 178. The paragraph numbering I use belongs to the CoE/Bono version, revision 2, which corrects most, if not all, of the known errors in the *Washington Post* version, including the omission of para. 116. The CoE/Bono version is on the Web in a hypertext version at <www.envirolink.org/orgs/coe/resources/fc/unabetoc.html>. A search via Yahoo will turn up several other versions.

6. See Mark Poster's perceptive treatment of Baudrillard in Poster's *The Second Media Age* (Cambridge, MA: Blackwell, 1995), pp. 95–117.

7. I am using the term "media" here as a kind of shorthand for an admittedly vast segment of society whose components are often at odds with each other, and sometimes even with themselves.

8. James Brook and Iain Boal, eds., *Resisting the Virtual Life* (San Francisco: City Lights Books, 1995); Kirkpatrick Sale, *Rebels Against the Future: The Luddites and Their War on the Industrial Revolution* (Reading, MA: Addison-Wesley, 1995); Clifford Stoll, *Silicon Snake Oil: Second Thoughts on the Information Highway* (New York: Doubleday, 1995); Bill McKibben, *The Age of Missing Information* (New York: Plume, 1992); Sven Birkerts, *The Gutenberg Elegies* (Boston: Faber & Faber, 1994); Mark Slouka, *War of the Worlds: Cyberspace and the High-Tech Assault on Reality* (New York: Basic Books, 1995); Stephen L. Talbott, *The Future Does Not Compute: Transcending the Machines in Our Midst* (Sebastopol, CA: O'Reilly & Associates, 1995).

9. Thoreau spent two years on the shore of Walden Pond (1845–1847). His essays on the topic appear in his book *Walden* (1854).

10. See Wendell Berry, *A Continuous Harmony: Essays Cultural and Agricultural* (New York: Harcourt Brace Jovanovich, 1970).

11. See Alvin Toffler, *Powershift: Knowledge, Wealth, and Violence in the 21st Century* (New York: Bantam Books, 1990).

12. See F. H. Bradley, *Ethical Studies* (Oxford: Oxford University Press, 1926 [orig. 1876]).

13. This line actually comes from the libretto to Leonard Bernstein's musical version of Voltaire's *Candide*. The libretto was put into lyric verse by the poet Richard Wilbur.

14. Ferdinand de Saussure, *Course on General Linguistics,* trans. Wade Baskin (New York: McGraw-Hill, 1966 [orig. 1915]).

15. See Pierre Teilhard de Chardin, *The Future of Man,* trans. Norman Denny (New York: Harper & Row, 1964), and *The Phenomenon of Man,* trans. Bernard Wall (New York: Harper & Row, 1959).

16. William Torrey Harris (1835–1909) was the American philosopher and Hegel translator who in 1873 established the first public-school kindergarten in the United States; he later served as U.S. commissioner of education from 1889 to 1906. Hegelians in St. Louis and in Ohio took seriously Hegel's view that the Absolute Spirit (citizenship under a free constitution) had emigrated from Europe to America. These social reformers rejected Marx's revolutionary violence while promoting public-spirited projects like national parks, public libraries, and the 1904 International Exhibition that invoked "the Spirit of St. Louis." See William H. Goetzmann, ed., *The American Hegelians: An Intellectual Episode in the History of Western America* (New York: Knopf, 1973); Loyd David Easton, ed., *Hegel's First American Followers: The Ohio Hegelians* (Athens: Ohio University Press, 1966); and Paul Russell Anderson, *Platonism in the Midwest* (New York: Columbia University Press, 1963). To understand the break between the Hegelians and Karl Marx, see Harold Mah, *The End of Philosophy and the Origin of "Ideology": Karl Marx and the Crisis of the Young Hegelians,* (Berkeley: University of California Press, 1987). Classic Hegelian idealism differs in its historical depth and breadth from the network idealism described in this paper. But that is another story in itself.

17. See Carolyn Marvin, *When Old Technologies Were New: Thinking About Electric Communication in the Late Nineteenth Century* (New York: Oxford University Press, 1988).

18. The Electronic Frontier Foundation, founded in 1990, is a civil liberties advocacy group for the Internet at <www.eff.org>. It offers legal counsel for members of the on-line community regarding issues of privacy, intellectual property, and telecommunications legislation. The EFF sometimes joins with the American Civil Liberties Union in representing "netizens" involved in litigation.

19. See Max Horkheimer and Theodor W. Adorno, *Dialectic of Enlightenment,* trans. John Cumming (New York: Continuum Books, 1987, © 1972). See also Theodor W. Adorno, *Negative Dialectics,* trans. E. B. Ashton (New York: Seabury Press, 1973).

20. See Jürgen Habermas, *The Theory of Communicative Action,* trans. Thomas McCarthy (Boston: Beacon Press, 1984).

21. See especially Herbert Marcuse, *The Aesthetic Dimension: Toward a Critique of Marxist Aesthetics* (Boston: Beacon Press, 1978). See also Marcuse's *Negations: Essays in Critical Theory,* trans. Jeremy J. Shapiro (Boston: Beacon Press, 1968). For Marcuse's treatment of his roots in Marxian and Hegelian dialectic, see his *Reason and*

Revolution: Hegel and the Rise of Social Theory (London and New York: Oxford University Press, 1941).

22. See Mark Poster's three studies: *Critical Theory and Poststructuralism: In Search of a Context* (Ithaca, NY: Cornell University Press, 1989); *Existential Marxism in Postwar France: From Sartre to Althusser* (Princeton: Princeton University Press, 1975); and *Foucault, Marxism, and History: Mode of Production Versus Mode of Information* (Cambridge and New York: Blackwell, 1984).

23. Michael Heim, *Virtual Realism* (New York: Oxford University Press, 1997). Chapter 2 takes up the idea of dialectic from another angle.

24. I make the argument for virtual entities in cyberspace in ibid. Here I want to emphasize the pragmatic nature of virtuality and of the status of virtual entities, because I base virtual realism on pragmatism as the middle between naïve realism and network idealism.

25. *Electric Language: A Philosophical Study of Word Processing* (New Haven: Yale University Press, 1987; rev. ed. 1999); for more on the notion of balance, see my *The Metaphysics of Virtual Reality* (New York: Oxford University Press, 1993).

26. This essay is not the place to go further into these notions, and in the first three chapters of *Electric Language* the reader can find one approach to that larger history with its ontological shifts.

Chapter 3: The Ethical Life of the Digital Aesthetic
Thank you to Peter Lunenfeld and my fellow panelists for the wonderful environment created at the Digital Dialectic Conference, where I had the chance to think this essay through in public.

1. See Carol Adams and Josephine Donovan, eds., *Animals and Women* (Durham, N.C.: Duke University Press, 1995).

2. See Morris Berman, *Coming to Our Senses: Body and Spirit in the Hidden History of the West* (New York: Simon & Schuster, 1989).

3. Jon Katz, "The Rights of Kids in the Digital Age," *Wired* 4.07 (July 1996): 170.

4. Terry Eagleton, *The Ideology of the Aesthetic* (Cambridge, MA: Basil Blackwell, 1990), p. 4.

5.   See especially the excellent review by Henry A. Giroux, "Hollywood, Race and the Demonization of Youth: The 'Kids' Are Not 'Alright,'" *Educational Researcher* 25, no. 2 (March 1996): 31–35.

6.   I am indebted to Cornel West's phrasing of this question, as well as to his brilliant insights on cultural politics. Cornel West, "The New Cultural Politics of Difference," in Russell Ferguson, Martha Gever, Trinh T. Minh-ha, and Cornel West, eds., *Out There: Marginalization and Contemporary Cultures* (Cambridge, MA: MIT Press, 1990), pp. 19–38.

7.   Ludwig Wittgenstein, *Culture and Value,* G. H. Wright, ed., and P. Winch, trans. (Chicago: University of Chicago Press, 1980 [first published as *Vermischte Bermerkungen,* 1977]), p. 24e.

8.   Eagleton, *The Ideology of the Aesthetic,* p. 414.

9.   Newt Gingrich, "Only America Can Lead," *New Perspectives Quarterly* 12, no. 2 (Spring 1995): 6.

10. Ibid.

11. Andrew Feenberg, "Subversive Rationalization: Technology, Power, and Democracy," in Andrew Feenberg and Alastair Hannay, eds., *Technology and the Politics of Knowledge* (Bloomington: Indiana University Press, 1995), p. 12.

12. Michel Foucault, "Two Lectures," trans. Kate Sober, in Colin Gordon, ed., *Power/Knowledge: Selected Interviews and Other Writings 1972–1977* (New York: Pantheon Books, 1980), pp. 78–108.

13. "A Cyborg Manifesto: Science, Technology and Techno-Feminism in the Late Twentieth Century," in Donna Haraway, *Simians, Cyborgs, and Women: The Reinvention of Nature* (New York: Routledge, 1991), p. 181.

14. Carol Gigliotti, "Aesthetics of a Virtual World," *Leonardo* 28, no. 4 (1995): 289–295.

15. Mary Midgley, *Can't We Make Moral Judgments?* (New York: St. Martin's Press, 1991), p. 23.

16. Eagleton, *The Ideology of the Aesthetic.*

17. Gigliotti, "Aesthetics of a Virtual World."

18. Barbara Pollack, "Lost in Cyber-space: The Commercial Art World On-line," in the second issue of the online journal, *Talk Back! A Forum for Critical Discourse* (1996). Available from <math240.lehman.cuny.edu/talkback>.

19. Personal communication, Markus Kruse, president of World Wide Arts Resources, September 4, 1996.

20. Douglas Crimp, "The Postmodern Museum," in *On the Museum's Ruins* (Cambridge: MIT Press, 1993), p. 302.

21. I am thinking specifically of Owen Flanagan, "Situations and Dispositions," in Alvin I. Goldman, ed., *Readings in Philosophy and Cognitive Science* (Cambridge, MA: MIT Press, 1993), pp. 681–695; Mark Johnson, *Moral Imagination: Implications of Cognitive Science for Ethics* (Chicago: University of Chicago Press, 1993); Martha C. Nussbaum, *Love's Knowledge: Essays on Philosophy and Literature* (Oxford: Oxford University Press, 1990).

22. Johnson, *Moral Imagination,* p. 242.

Chapter 4: The Condition of Virtuality

This essay has also appeared in *Language Machines: Technologies of Literary and Cultural Production,* Jeffrey Masten, Peter Stallybrass, and Nancy Vickers, eds. (New York: Routledge, 1997).

1. For an important collection of essays arguing convincingly that how people understand and use technology is crucial to directing technological change, see *Does Technology Drive History? The Dilemma of Technological Determinism,* Merritt Roe Smith and Leo Marx, eds. (Cambridge, MA: MIT Press, 1994).

2. Erwin Schrödinger, *What Is Life: The Physical Aspect of the Living Cell* (Cambridge: Cambridge University Press; New York: Macmillan, 1945).

3. Richard Doyle, *On Beyond Living: Rhetorical Transformations of the Life Sciences* (Stanford: Stanford University Press, 1997).

4. George Gamow, *Mr. Tompkins Inside Himself: Adventures in the New Biology* (New York: Viking Press, 1967).

5.   Richard Dawkins, *The Selfish Gene* (New York: Oxford University Press, 1976).

6.   N. Katherine Hayles, "Narratives of Evolution and the Evolution of Narratives," in *Cooperation and Conflict in General Evolutionary Processes,* John L. Casti and Anders Karlqvist, eds. (New York: John Wiley and Sons, 1994), pp. 113–132.

7.   Hans Moravec, *Mind Children: The Future of Robot and Human Intelligence* (Cambridge, MA: Harvard University Press, 1988).

8.   Claude Shannon, *The Mathematical Theory of Communication* (Urbana: University of Illinois Press, 1949).

9.   *Cybernetics: Circular Causal and Feedback Mechanisms in Biological and Social Systems,* Heinz von Foerster, ed., 5 vols. (New York: Josiah Macy, Jr., Foundation, 1950–55). [Transcripts of the sixth–tenth Conferences on Cybernetics, sponsored by the Josiah Macy Foundation.]

10.   Donald M. MacKay, "In Search of Basic Symbols," in *Cybernetics: Circular Causal and Feedback Mechanisms in Biological and Social Systems* (eighth Conference), Heinz von Foerster, Margaret Mead, and Hans Lukas Teuber, eds. (New York: Josiah Macy, Jr., Foundation, 1952), pp. 181–221. A fuller account is in Donald M. MacKay, *Information, Mechanism and Meaning* (Cambridge, MA: MIT Press, 1969).

11.   Norbert Wiener, *Cybernetics: Or Control and Communication in the Animal and the Machine* (Cambridge, MA: MIT Press, 1948) and *The Human Use of Human Beings: Cybernetics and Society* (Boston: Houghton Mifflin, 1950).

12.   Jay Clayton, in "The Voice in the Machine," presented at the English Institute at Cambridge, MA, in August 1995, argued that the telegraph could have been interpreted in the 1880s as a disembodying technology. Significantly, however, his research indicates that during the late nineteenth century it was perceived as an odd or different kind of embodiment, but not as a disembodiment. Wiener's proposal, coming seventy years later, occurred in a different cultural context that was much more inclined to construct the telegraph and many other technologies as disembodying media. The comparison is further evidence for Clayton's (and my) point that perceptions of how the body related to technologies are historical constructions, *not* biological inevitabilities.

13. The tendency to ignore the material realities of communication technologies has been forcefully rebutted in two important works by Friedrich A. Kittler: *Discourse Networks 1800–1900,* Michael Metteer, trans. (Stanford: Stanford University Press, 1990) and *Materialities of Communication,* Hans Ulrich Gumbrecht and K. Ludwig Pfeiffer, eds., and William Whobrey, trans. (Stanford: Stanford University Press, 1994).

14. Michel Serres, *The Parasite,* Lawrence R. Schehr, trans. (Baltimore: Johns Hopkins University Press, 1982).

15. John Arthur Wilson, "Entropy, Not Negentropy," *Nature* 219 (1968): 535–536.

16. *The Maximum Entropy Formalism: A Conference Held at the Massachusetts Institute of Technology on May 2–4, 1978,* Raphael D. Levine and Myron Tribus, eds. (Cambridge, MA: MIT Press, 1979).

17. William J. Mitchell, *City of Bits: Space, Place, and the Infobahn* (Cambridge, MA: MIT Press, 1995). See his "Replacing Place" in this volume.

18. The Universal Turing Machine is conveniently described by Roger Penrose in *The Emperor's New Mind: Concerning Computers, Minds, and the Laws of Physics* (New York: Oxford University Press, 1989). Verostko drew on this description specifically in creating his work. Artist's Note at the Art Show, SIGGRAPH '95.

19. Artist's Note, Art Show, SIGGRAPH '95.

20. Andre Kopra, private communication.

21. Michael Joyce, *Of Two Minds: Hypertext Pedagogy and Poetics* (Ann Arbor: University of Michigan Press, 1995).

22. Paul Connerton makes this point about ritual in *How Societies Remember* (Cambridge and New York: Cambridge University Press, 1989).

23. I am indebted to Nicholas Gessler for suggesting this metaphor to me and for pointing out the significance of the CPU's non-Cartesian operation.

24. Eric Havelock, *Preface to Plato* (Cambridge, MA: Harvard University Press, 1963).

25. Walter Ong, *Orality and Literacy: The Technologizing of the Word* (New York: Routledge, 1982); Elizabeth Eisenstein, *The Printing Press as an Agent of Change: Communications and Cultural Transformations in Early Modern Europe* (Cambridge: Cambridge University Press, 1979); and Marshall McLuhan, *Understanding Media: The Extensions of Man* (New York: McGraw-Hill, 1964).

26. Marsha Kinder, "The Dialectics of Transmedia Screens: From Joseph Andrews to Carmen Sandiego," paper presented at the English Institute, Cambridge, MA, August 1995.

27. The simulation is documented in a video of the same name. A discussion of how the simulation was produced and what its goals are can be found in Brenda Laurel and Rachel Strickland's essay "Placeholder," in *Immersed in Technology,* Mary Anne Moser and Douglas MacLeod, eds., (Cambridge, MA: MIT Press, 1995).

28. Allucquère Rosanne Stone, *The War Between Technology and Desire at the Close of the Mechanical Age* (Cambridge, MA: MIT Press, 1995).

29. Catherine Richards's virtual reality video, *Spectral Bodies,* illustrates how proprioceptive coherence can be disrupted by even such low-tech methods as massaging a blindfolded subject's arms at certain key points with a electrical vibrator. Don Idhe also discusses proprioceptive coherence in *Technology and the Lifeworld: From Garden to Earth* (Bloomington: Indiana University Press, 1990).

30. Joyce, *Of Two Minds;* Jay David Bolter, *Writing Space: The Computer, Hypertext, and the History of Writing* (Hillsdale, NJ: Lawrence Erlbaum Associates, 1991); George P. Landow, *Hypertext: The Convergence of Contemporary Critical Theory and Technology* (Baltimore: Johns Hopkins University Press, 1994); David Kolb, *Socrates in the Labyrinth* (Cambridge, MA: Eastgate Systems, 1995) [hyertext diskette]; Kolb's essay by the same title in *Hyper/Text/Theory,* ed. George Landow, ed. (Baltimore: Johns Hopkins University Press, 1994); J. Yellowlees Douglas, "'How Do I Stop This Thing?': Closure and Indeterminacy in Interactive Narratives," also in *Hyper/Text/Theory.*

Chapter 5: From Cybernation to Interaction:
A Contribution to an Archaeology of Interactivity
1. Sir Leon Bagrit, *The Age of Automation: The BBC Reith Lectures 1964* (New York: Mentor Books, 1965), p. 33.

2.   Neither automation nor cybernation appears in the glossary or the index of John A. Barry's *Technobabble* (Cambridge, MA: MIT Press, 1991), a study of computer jargon.

3.   See Sherry Turkle, *The Second Self: Computers and the Human Spirit* (New York: Simon & Schuster, 1984) and *Life on the Screen: Identity in the Age of the Internet* (New York: Simon & Schuster, 1995).

4.   Bagrit, *The Age of Automation,* p. 38.

5.   See Seymour Papert, *The Children's Machine: Rethinking School in the Age of the Computer* (New York: Basic Books, 1993), especially chapter 1.

6.   Jacques Ellul, *The Technological Society,* John Wilkinson, trans. (New York: Vintage Books, 1964), p. 135. Ellul's idea about the fateful infiltration of the "technique," albeit in connection with mechanization, was interestingly preceded by George Orwell, who in *The Road to Wigan Pier* (1937) wrote: "The process of mechanization has itself become a machine, a huge glittering vehicle whirling us we are not certain where, but probably toward the padded Wells-world and the brain in the bottle." Quoted in *Of Men and Machines,* Arthur O. Lewis, Jr., ed. (New York: Dutton, 1963), p. 259.

7.   Ellul, *The Technological Society,* pp. 137–138.

8.   Clifford Stoll, *Silicon Snake Oil: Second Thoughts on the Information Highway* (New York: Doubleday, 1995), p. 136.

9.   See Simon Penny, "Machine Culture," in *SISEA Proceedings,* Wim van der Plas, ed. (Groningen, Netherlands: SISEA, 1991), pp. 184–191. For an extensive treatment, see Bruce Mazlich, *The Fourth Discontinuity: The Co-evolution of Humans and Machines* (New Haven: Yale University Press, 1993).

10.   Bagrit, *The Age of Automation,* p. 42.

11.   Daniel Bell, Preface to Bagrit, *The Age of Automation,* p. xvii.

12.   Quoted in Office of Charles and Ray Eames, *A Computer Perspective,* Glen Fleck, ed. (Cambridge, MA: Harvard University Press, 1973), p. 67.

13.   Quoted ibid.

14. Ibid., p. 148.

15. John Rose, *Automation: Its Uses and Consequences* (Edinburgh: Oliver & Boyd, 1967), p. 2.

16. The literature on automation is too vast to be listed here. Among the more interesting, albeit forgotten, books are Donald N. Michael, *Automation* (New York: Vintage Books, 1962); S. Deczynski, *Automation and the Future of Man* (London: Allen & Unwin, 1964); *Automation and Society,* Howard Boone Jacobsen and Joseph S. Roucek, eds. (New York: Philosophical Library, 1959); and Walter S. Buckingham, *Automation: Its Impact on Business and People* (New York: New American Library, 1963). The literature on cybernetics is also essential; see particularly Norbert Wiener, *The Human Use of Human Beings: Cybernetics and Society* (New York: Doubleday, 1954 [1950]).

17. Marshall McLuhan, *Understanding Media: The Extensions of Man* (London: Sphere Books, 1969 [1964]), p. 371.

18. Siegfried Giedion, *Mechanization Takes Command: A Contribution to Anonymous History* (New York: W. W. Norton, 1969 [1948]), p. 5.

19. Anson Rabinbach, *The Human Motor: Energy, Fatigue, and the Origins of Modernity* (New York: Basic Books, 1990).

20. Bagrit, *The Age of Automation,* p. 39. It is significant that in a sense Bagrit simply reversed the situation by speaking about "the slave services of automation," remaining strictly within the traditional polar opposition of master and slave (p. 45).

21. McLuhan, *Understanding Media,* pp. 371–372. The idea of automation as "thinking as much as a way of doing" seems to derive from John Diebold's *Automation: Its Impact on Business and Labor,* Planning Pamphlet no. 106 (Washington, DC: National Planning Association, 1959), p. 3. Quoted in Donald M. Michael, "Cybernation: The Silent Conquest," in Lewis, *Of Men and Machines,* p. 79.

22. See Bell's introduction to Bagrit, *The Age of Automation.*

23. Bagrit, *The Age of Automation,* pp. 41–42.

24. Ibid., p. 42.

25. Michael, "Cybernation: The Silent Conquest," p. 80 (original emphasis). Michael uses the formulation "we invent the term." Marshall McLuhan uses "cybernation" as synonymous with automation in *Understanding Media*, p. 370.

26. B. F. Skinner, the Harvard professor and behaviorist psychologist, was a pioneer in the field of teaching machines. His largely forgotten writings about the teaching machines he experimented with from the 1950s on were collected as *The Technology of Teaching* (New York: Appleton-Century-Crofts, 1968). The main influences for Skinner's machines were the testing-scoring machines devised in the 1920s by Sidney L. Pressey, who spoke about an "industrial revolution in education." Quoted in *The Technology of Teaching*, p. 30.

27. The phrase "automated Socrates" was coined by Desmond L. Cook. The historical predecessor of "automated teaching" is often considered to be Comenius and his "autopraxis." For more, see the useful handbook by Walter R. Fuchs, *Knaurs Buch vom neuen Lernen* (Munich: Th. Knaur Nachf; Zurich: Droemersche Verlagsanstalt, 1969).

28. The advertisement is reproduced in Ellen Lupton, *Mechanical Brides: Women and Machines from Home to Office* (New York: Princeton Architectural Press, 1993), p. 19. Another example is a publicity photograph analyzed by Adrian Forty. A housewife in a party dress stands by as her electric cooker prepares a complete meal. Forty comments: "No mess, no sweat—the cooker, it seems, produces meals of its own." Here the ideology of modernity means the complete replacement of human labor by elegantly designed, fully automated machines. The advertisement also implies the complete elimination of tactile relationship to work and tools. Adrian Forty, *Objects of Desire: Design and Society* (London: Thames & Hudson, 1986), p. 211.

29. There are many books about this topic. Particularly useful are *Robots Robots Robots,* Harry M. Geduld and Ronald Gottesman, eds. (Boston: New York Graphic Society, 1978); and *Robotics,* Marvin Minsky, ed. (New York: Anchor/Doubleday, 1985).

30. O. O. Binder, "Amazing Marvels of Tomorrow," *Mechanix Illustrated,* March 1955, p. 72. The text provides a typical example of the vagueness of the distinction between automation and mechanization: "You had the forerunners of this in your 1955 pilot plants . . . which were completely *mechanized"* (my emphasis).

31. Ibid., p. 210.

32. As far as I know, a complete "mental history of the computer" is yet to be written. There is plenty of material about its popular reception that has hardly been used. The early computer "appearances" on TV and in the cinema that I refer to, I have seen at the Computer Museum in Boston.

33. This priestly position resurfaced in the early 1990s, with the figure of the helper in a virtual reality demonstration. This is the person standing firmly beside the "virtual voyager" who tends to the apparatus, resetting the system after each user, calibrating and recalibrating the glove and the goggles, and even interpreting the blurry scenes "from the outside."

34. Robert Sherman Townes, "Problem for Emmy," in Lewis, *Of Men and Machines,* p. 90.

35. This theme continues, as can be seen in Josh Feldman's Quicktime digital narrative, "Consciousness," in which a computer comes to life and is then destroyed by its creators. "Consciousness" is included on the CD-ROM *New Voices, New Visions* (New York: Voyager, 1994).

36. Quoted in Les Brown and Sema Marks, *Electric Media* (New York: Harcourt Brace Jovanovich, 1974), p. 114.

37. Bagrit, *The Age of Automation,* p. 43.

38. Quoted in Brown and Marks, *Electric Media,* p. 98.

39. Lev Manovich, "The Engineering of Vision from Constructivism to Virtual Reality," Ph.D. dissertation, University of Rochester, 1993, p. 202. I would like to thank Manovich for giving me a copy. The "monitoring and regulation" functions also would fit well to the figure of the "automated housewife" staring at the "screen" of her automatic washing machine. This dissertation is being revised for publication by the University of Texas Press.

40. Ibid., p. 209.

41. Ibid., pp. 207–208.

42. Quoted in Stewart Brand, *The Media Lab: Inventing the Future at MIT* (New York: Penguin Books, 1988), p. 46.

43. Ted Nelson, *The Home Computer Revolution* (N.p.: Ted Nelson, 1977), p. 24.

44. Skinner, *The Technology of Teaching,* pp. 37–39.

45. The serious literature on coin-operated machines is scarce. See, however, Lynn F. Pearson, *Amusement Machines* (Princes Risborough, UK: Shire, 1992).

46. Karl Sims's computer installation *Genetic Images* (1993) combines an interactive interface (a line of monitors, with foot-triggered sensors) and a connection machine (to calculate generations of genetic images, based on the user's choices). Sims thus highlights the copresence and the interplay of the interactive and the automated features of computing.

47. See Howard Rheingold, *Tools for Thought: The People and Ideas Behind the Next Computer Revolution* (New York: Simon & Schuster, 1985).

48. This early history, including the development of Spacewar, the first computer game, is covered in Stewart Brand, *II Cybernetic Frontiers* (New York: Random House; Berkeley, CA: Bookworks, 1974).

49. Bagrit, *The Age of Automation,* p. 58. This proves that Seymour Papert is not right in his belief that Alan Kay was "the first person to use the words *personal computer*" (Papert, *The Children's Machine,* p. 42). Considering the popularizing nature of Bagrit's lectures, it is probable that he got the idea from someone else.

50. More than ten years later Ted Nelson elaborated in his *The Personal Computer Revolution:* "Before now, most computer systems have not been set up with ordinary people's use in mind. A certain class of experienced user was anticipated and so only these people used the system. . . . But that's about to change. Interactive systems will start appearing on little computers for every purpose" (p. 24).

51. McLuhan, *Understanding Media,* pp. 372–373.

52. Ibid., pp. 378–379.

53. E. M. Forster, "The Machine Stops," in Lewis, *Of Men and Machines,* pp. 283–284.

54. It seems significant to me that neither "interactivity" nor "interactive media" figures in Barry's *Technobabble,* published in 1991.

55. *Interactivity* (1995–) and *Interactive Week* (1994–) are two examples. The first edition of Tim Morrison's compendium *The Magic of Interactive Entertainment* (Indianapolis: SAMS Publishing, 1994) was soon followed by a second, updated edition (1995).

Chapter 6: Replacing Place

1. MUDs and MOOs, and their sociology, are extensively discussed in Howard Rheingold, *Virtual Community: Homesteading on the Electronic Frontier* (New York: HarperPerennial, 1993); and Sherry Turkle, *Life on the Screen: Identity in the Age of the Internet* (New York: Simon & Schuster, 1995).

2. Extensive information about the World Wide Web and its history can be found at the World Wide Web Consortium home page, <www.w3.org>.

3. <www.yahoo.com>.

4. <www.geocities.com>.

5. For a history and survey of these efforts from a mid-1990s vantage point, see Robert Rossney, "Metaworlds," *Wired* 4 (June 1996): 140–147, 202–212.

6. Slightly later, Neal Stephenson's novel *Snow Crash* (New York: Bantam, 1992) fictionally developed the idea of an avatar and gave it wide currency. For an extended discussion of electronic avatars and their history, see Jerry Michalski, "Avatars: Motion and Emotion Online," *Release 1.0* (May 29, 1996): 5–96.

7. For a discussion of the issues involved in creating comic strip worlds, see Scott McCloud, *Understanding Comics* (New York: HarperCollins, 1994).

8. <www.race.u-tokyo.ac.jp/RACE/TGM/Mud/habitat.html>.
The conclusion of "Agency and Proximity: Commmunities/CommuniTrees," the fifth chapter of Allucquère Rosanne Stone, *The War of Desire and Technology at the Close of the Mechanical Age* (Cambridge, MA: MIT Press, 1995), pp. 118–121, offers a detailed discussion of what happened to Fujistu's Habitat.

9. WorldsAway, <www.worldsaway.com>; ExploreNet, <longwood.cs.ucf.edu:80/ExploreNet/public_html>; The Palace, <www.thepalace.com>.

10. Oxygen, an experimental groupware program used by Chiat/Day Advertising, represented employees as face-only avatars who could meet in virtual offices. A col-

lection of press clippings and descriptions is maintained by the Art Technology Group at <www.atg.com>.

11. <www.is.ntts.com>.

12. <www.onlive.com>.

13. In particular, the film *Toy Story* pioneered the creation of an entire feature from 3D animated characters moving in 3D virtual sets.

14. Some of the still-active sites include: V-Chat, <www.microsoft.com/ie/chat/vchatmain.htm>; Point World, <www2.blacksun.com>; Alpha World and World's Chat, <www.worlds.net>; The Realm, <www.realmserver.com>.

15. <www.sics.se/dive/docs/description.html>.

16. <www.merl.com/projects/dp/index.html>.

17. See Robert Venturi, Denise Scott Brown, and Steven Izenour, *Learning from Las Vegas* (Cambridge, MA: MIT Press, 1972).

18. As of 1998, Netscape continues to organize its own "What's Cool" directory. It also offers a directory of "What's New" directories organized by others, Both "What's Cool" and "What's New" were buttons on the toolbar incorporated into Netscape's early interfaces. This use of the most premium of all locations indicates the value of novelty and buzz.

19. Often, these counters are implemented through outside services that offer guarantees of honesty.

20. <www.100hot.com>.

21. In Habitat and WorldsAway, which have virtual property and money, the complementary concept of theft quickly emerged.

22. Quoted in Jillian Burt, "Serfing the Net," *21 • C 2 • 96* (Spring 1996): 69. The garden, which has moved a number of times in both physical and virtual space, can be reliably accessed through Goldberg's home page, <www.ieor.berkeley.edu/~goldberg>.

23. On the historical evolution of these relationships, see Richard Sennett, *Flesh and Stone: The Body and the City in Western Civilization* (New York: Norton, 1994).

Chapter 7: The Medium Is the Memory

1. Marcel Proust, *Remembrance of Things Past,* C. K. Scott Moncrieff and Terence Kilmartin, trans. (New York: Random House, 1981), *Swann's Way,* p. 3, quoted after the Expanded Book version (New York: Voyager, 1993).

2. I draw my arguments from history and from my specific experiences designing electronic media. My thinking about these issues was particularly influenced by my work as the technical director of the Expanded Books project at the Voyager Company. This project was established to produce an interface to read books on the screens of laptop computers, thereby creating a new (electronic) publishing medium.

3. There are of course also the collectors who are more interested in the decorative effect of books on their walls ("They give the room such a warm ambience")—but, for them, book spines pasted on a board do the job nicely, and can also conceal a wet bar.

4. Walter Benjamin, "The Work of Art in the Age of Mechanical Reproduction," in *Illuminations,* Hannah Arendt ed., Harry Zohn, trans. (New York: Schocken Books, 1969), p. 233

5. Scott Bukatman, "There's Always Tomorrowland: Disney and the Hyper-cinematic Experience," *October* 57 (Summer 1991): 55–78.

6. As advertised by Microsoft in 1993 and 1994.

7. Ludwig Wittgenstein, *Philosophische Untersuchungen* (Frankfurt am Main: Suhrkamp, 1977), p. 43.

8. Gerald Unger, *fuse* # 3, 1995.

9. See *Wunschmaschine, Welterfindung: Eine Geschichte der Technikvisionen seit dem 18. Jahhundert,* Brigitte Felderer, ed. (Vienna: Springer, 1996).

10. "Long live the young muse of the cinema, for she has the mystery of dreams and makes the unreal real." This quotation was featured on a poster and invitation for the grand opening of the Vienna Film School in 1959.

11.   One that does, is *Le Livre de Lulu,* an electronic book for children that integrates text, images, and an interactive approach in an engaging enough manner that the reader can truly commit to becoming immersed in the story. There is such a richness of text and images—not in the above-noted encyclopedic mode, but rather in the depth of vision and effect—that *Le Livre de Lulu* offers the reader not a simulation of space but rather a sidereal space: a space to move around in and create the memory spaces needed to internalize the story. The readers/users build their own relationships to the story, their own unique memory spaces. In this cybernetic age, textual memory representation returns to the mind, where it resided before the technology of the book became ubiquitous. Romain Victor-Pujebet, *Le Livre de Lulu* (New York: Organa, 1995).

12.   Jorge Luis Borges, "The Library of Babel," in his *Labyrinths: Selected Stories and Other Writings* (New York: New Dimensions, 1962), p. 51.

13.   Frances Yates, *The Art of Memory* (Chicago: University of Chicago Press, 1966), p. 6.

14.   "The artificial memory is established from places and images." Quoted and translated in ibid.

15.   My thanks to UC Berkeley's Ken Goldberg for his contributions to these ideas.

16.   Bohumil Hrabal, *Too Loud a Solitude* (New York: Harvest/HBJ, 1992), p. 2.

17.   George Landow, *Hypertext: The Convergence of Contemporary Critical Theory and Technology* (Baltimore: Johns Hopkins University Press, 1992), p. 41. (Italics in original.)

18.   See Landow, *Hypertext;* and Jay David Bolter, *Writing Space: The Computer, Hypertext, and the History of Writing* (Hillsdale, NJ: Lawrence Erlbaum, 1991).

19.   Personal conversation with the author, 1978.

Chapter 8: Hypertext as Collage-Writing

1.   Difficult, possibly even illusory, as it is to pronounce origins, I can nonetheless point to several major stimuli for this essay. One of the most of important is Gregory L. Ulmer's "The Object of Post-Criticism," in *The Anti-Aesthetic: Essays on Postmodern Culture,* Hal Foster, ed. (Port Townsend, WA: Bay Press, 1983), pp. 83–110, which argues that "collage is the single most important innovation in artistic representa-

tion to occur in our century" (84). And to move one step farther back, I have to thank my daughter Shoshana for having given me the Foster volume to read some years ago. Although I had briefly touched upon collage and montage as an analogy in *Hypertext: The Convergence of Contemporary Critical Theory and Technology* (Baltimore: Johns Hopkins University Press, 1992), it was Pierre Joris's *Collage Between Writing and Painting,* which he posted on the discussion group Technoculture, that prompted me to produce the two webs from which this essay derives. Without William S. Shipp, Norman Meyrowitz, and the team that developed Intermedia at Brown University's now-closed Institute for Research in Information and Scholarship, I would have never had the opportunity to have worked with what remains the finest hypertext and hypermedia system thus far developed, and without J. David Bolter, Michael Joyce, John Smith, and Mark Bernstein, developers of Storyspace, distributed by Eastgate Systems, I would not have had the opportunity to have written the hypertext web, "Hypertext as Collage Writing."

2.   I have discussed the first year of Technoculture's existence in "Electronic Conferences and Samizdat Textuality: The Example of Technoculture," in *The Digital Word: Text-Based Computing,* George P. Landow and Paul Delaney, eds. (Cambridge, MA: MIT Press, 1993), pp. 237–249.

3.   The ideas of hypertext here presented derive from many of the standard writings on the subject, which readers can find in the bibliography of my *Hypertext.* I would cite in particular Vannevar Bush's writings on the memex, most conveniently found in *From Memex to Hypertext: Vannevar Bush and the Mind's Machine,* James M. Nyce and Paul Kahn, eds. (Boston: Academic Press, 1991); Theodor H. Nelson, *Computer Lib/Dream Machines* (Seattle: Microsoft Press, 1987); Jay David Bolter, *Writing Space: The Computer in the History of Literacy* (Hillsdale, NJ: Lawrence Erlbaum, 1991); and Nicole Yankelovich, Norman Meyrowitz, and Andries van Dam, "Reading and Writing the Electronic Book," *IEEE Computer* 18 (October 1985): 15–30.

4.   Those interested in the relation of contemporary critical theory and hypertext will want to consult Bolter's and my books cited in note 3, as well as the following: Terence Harpold, "Threnody: Psychoanalytic Digressions on the Subject of Hypertext," in *Hypermedia and Literary Studies,* Paul Delany and George P. Landow, eds. (Cambridge, MA: MIT Press, 1991), pp. 103–118; Michael Heim, *Electric Language: A Philsophical Study of Word Processing* (New Haven: Yale University Press, 1987); *Hyper/Text/Theory,* George P. Landow, ed. (Baltimore: Johns Hopkins University Press, 1994); and Richard A. Lanham, *The Electronic Word: Democracy, Technology, and the Arts* (Chicago: University of Chicago Press, 1994). For general issues involving

the relation of information technology to culture and thought, I would recommend the following as especially useful: William M. Ivins, *Prints and Visual Communication* (New York: DaCapo, 1969); Alvin Kernan, *Printing Technology, Letters & Samuel Johnson* (Princeton: Princeton University Press, 1987); Marshall McLuhan, *The Gutenberg Galaxy: The Making of Typographic Man* (Toronto: University of Toronto Press, 1962); Walter J. Ong, *Orality and Literacy: The Technologizing of the Word* (London: Methuen, 1982).

5.   H. W. Janson, *The History of World Art,* 3rd ed., rev. and enl. by Anthony F. Janson (New York: Harry N. Abrams, 1986), pp. 683–684.

6.   Shelley Jackson's *Patchwork Girl* (1995) and *The "In Memoriam" Web,* John Lanestedt and George P. Landow, eds. (1992), are available from Eastgate Systems, 134 Main St., Watertown, MA, as are other webs discussed above. Those by Nathan Marsh and Joshua Rappaport appear in *Writing at the Edge* (1995), also from Eastgate.

Chapter 9: What Is Digital Cinema?
This essay has greatly benefited from the suggestions and criticisms of Natalie Bookchin, Peter Lunenfeld, Norman Klein, and Vivian Sobchack. I also would like to acknowledge the pioneering work of Erkki Huhtamo on the connections between early cinema and digital media, which stimulated my own interest in this topic.

1.   Scott Billups, presentation during "Casting from Forest Lawn (Future of Performers)" panel at "The Artists Rights Digital Technology Symposium '96," Los Angeles, Directors Guild of America, February 16, 1996. Billups was a major figure in bringing Hollywood and Silicon Valley together by way of the American Film Institute's Apple Laboratory and Advanced Technologies Programs in the late 1980s and early 1990s. See Paula Parisi, "The New Hollywood Silicon Stars," *Wired* 3 (December 1995): 142–145, 202–210.

2.   "Super-genre" is a translation of the French *sur-genre.* Christian Metz, "The Fiction Film and Its Spectator: A Metapsychological Study," in *Apparatus,* Theresa Hak Kyung Cha, ed. (New York: Tanam Press, 1980): 373–409.

3.   Cinema, as defined by its "super-genre" of fictional live-action film, belongs to media arts, which, in contrast to traditional arts, rely on recordings of reality as their basis. Another term that is not as popular as "media arts," but perhaps is more precise, is "recording arts." For the use of this term, see James Monaco, *How to Read a Film,* rev. ed. (New York: Oxford University Press, 1981), p. 7.

4. Charles Musser, *The Emergence of Cinema: The American Screen to 1907* (Berkeley: University of California Press, 1990), pp. 49–50.

5. Ibid., p. 25.

6. C. W. Ceram, *Archeology of the Cinema* (New York: Harcourt, Brace & World, 1965), pp. 44–45.

7. The birth of cinema in the 1890s was accompanied by an interesting transformation: while the body as the generator of moving pictures disappeared, it simultaneously became their new subject. Indeed, one of the key themes of the early films produced by Edison is a human body in motion: a man sneezing, the famous bodybuilder Sandow flexing his muscles, an athlete performing a somersault, a woman dancing. Films of boxing matches played a key role in the commercial development of the Kinetoscope. See Musser, *The Emergence of Cinema,* pp. 72–79; David Robinson, *From Peep Show to Palace: The Birth of American Film* (New York: Columbia University Press, 1996), pp. 44–48.

8. Robinson, *From Peep Show to Palace,* p. 12.

9. This arrangement was previously used in magic lantern projections; it is described in the second edition of Althanasius Kircher's *Ars magna* (1671). See Musser, *The Emergence of Cinema,* pp. 21–22.

10. Ceram, *Archeology of the Cinema,* p. 140.

11. Musser, *The Emergence of Cinema,* p. 78.

12. The extent of this lie is made clear by the films of Andy Warhol from the first part of the 1960s—perhaps the only real attempt to create cinema without a language.

13. I have borrowed this definition of special effects from David Samuelson, *Motion Picture Camera Techniques* (London: Focal Press, 1978).

14. The following examples illustrate this disavowal of special effects; others can be easily found. The first example is from popular discourse on cinema. A section entitled "Making the Movies" in Kenneth W. Leish's *Cinema* (New York: Newsweek Books, 1974) contains short stories from the history of the movie industry. The

heroes of these stories are actors, directors, and producers; special effects artists are mentioned only once.

The second example is from an academic source: Jacques Aumont, Alain Bergala, Michel Marie, and Marc Vernet, in their *Aesthetics of Film,* trans. Richard Neupert (Austin: University of Texas Press, 1992), state that "the goal of our book is to summarize from a synthetic and didactic perspective the diverse theoretical attempts at examining these empirical notions [terms from the lexicon of film technicians], including ideas like frame vs. shot, terms from production crews' vocabularies, the notion of identification produced by critical vocabulary, etc." (p. 7). The fact that the text never mentions special-effects techniques reflects the general lack of any historical or theoretical interest in the topic by film scholars. David Bordwell and Kristin Thompson's *Film Art: An Introduction* (4th ed.; New York: McGraw-Hill, 1993), which is used as a standard textbook in undergraduate film classes, is a little better: it devotes 3 out of its 500 pages to special effects.

Finally, a relevant statistic: University of California, San Diego's library contains 4,273 titles cataloged under the subject "motion pictures" and only 16 under "special effects cinematography."

Two important works addressing the larger cultural significance of special effects by film theoreticians, are Vivian Sobchack, *Screening Space: The American Science Fiction Film,* 2nd ed. (New York: Ungar, 1987); and Scott Bukatman, "The Artificial Infinite," in *Visual Display,* Lynne Cooke and Peter Wollen, eds. (Seattle: Bay Press, 1995). Norman Klein is working on a history of special effects to be published by Verso.

15. For a discussion of the subsumption of the photographic to the graphic, see Peter Lunenfeld, "Art Post-History: Digital Photography & Electronic Semiotics," in the catalog *Photography After Photography: Memory and Representation in the Digital Age,* Hubertus von Amelunxen, Stefan Inglhaut, and Florian Rötzer, eds. (Sydney: G+B Arts, 1996), pp. 92–98.

16. For a complete list of people at ILM who worked on this film, see *SIGGRAPH '94 Visual Proceedings* (New York: ACM SIGGRAPH, 1994), p. 19.

17. In this respect 1995 can be called the last year of digital media. At the 1995 National Association of Broadcasters convention, Avid showed a working model of a digital video camera that records not on a videocassette but directly onto a hard drive. Once digital cameras become widely used, we will no longer have any reason to talk about digital media because the process of digitization will be eliminated.

18. Here is another, even more radical definition: digital film = f(x,y,t). This definition would be greeted with joy by the proponents of abstract animation. Since the computer breaks down every frame into pixels, a complete film can be defined as a function that, given the horizontal, vertical, and time location of each pixel, returns its color. This is actually how a computer represents a film, a representation that has a surprising affinity with certain well-known practices in the avant-garde vision of cinema! For a computer, a film is an abstract arrangement of colors and sounds changing in time, rather than something structured by "shots," "narrative," "actors," and so on.

19. See Barbara Robertson, "Digital Magic: Apollo 13," *Computer Graphics World* v. 18, no. 8 (August 1995): 20.

20. William J. Mitchell, *The Reconfigured Eye: Visual Truth in the Post-photographic Era* (Cambridge, MA: MIT Press, 1992), p. 7.

21. The full advantage of mapping time into 2D space, already present in Edison's first cinema apparatus, is now realized: one can modify events in time by literally painting on a sequence of frames, treating them as a single image.

22. See Robinson, *From Peep Show to Palace,* p. 165.

23. See "Industrial Light & Magic Alters History with MATADOR," promotion material by Parallax Software, SIGGRAPH 95 Conference, Los Angeles, August 1995.

24. The reader who followed my analysis of the new possibilities of digital cinema may wonder why I have stressed the parallels between digital cinema and the precinematic techniques of the nineteenth century but did not mention twentieth-century avant-garde filmmaking. Did not the avant-garde filmmakers explore many of these new possibilities? To take the notion of cinema as painting, Len Lye, one of the pioneers of abstract animation, was painting directly on film as early as 1935; he was followed by Norman McLaren and Stan Brackage, the latter extensively covering shot footage with dots, scratches, splattered paint, smears, and lines in an attempt to turn his films into equivalents of Abstract Expressionst painting. More generally, one of the major impulses in all of avant-garde filmmaking, from Leger to Godard, was to combine the cinematic, the painterly, and the graphic—by using live-action footage and animation within one film or even a single frame, by altering this footage in a variety of ways, or by juxtaposing printed texts and filmed images.

I explore the notion that the avant-garde anticipated digital aesthetics in my work, *The Engineering of Vision from Constructivism to Virtual Reality* (Austin: The University of Texas Press, forthcoming); here I would like to bring up one point particularly relevant for this essay. When the avant-garde filmmakers collaged multiple images within a single frame, or painted and scratched film, or revolted against the indexical identity of cinema in other ways, they were working against "normal" filmmaking procedures and the intended uses of film technology. Film stock, for example, was not designed to be painted on. Thus, they operated on the periphery of commercial cinema not only aesthetically but also technically.

One general effect of the digital revolution is that avant-garde aesthetic strategies became embedded in the commands and interface metaphors of computer software. In short, *the avant-garde became materialized in a computer.* Digital cinema technology is a case in point. The avant-garde strategy of collage reemerged as a "cut and paste" command, the most basic operation one can perform on digital data. The idea of painting on film became embedded in paint functions of film-editing software. The avant-garde move to combine animation, printed texts, and live-action footage is repeated in the convergence of animation, title generation, paint, compositing, and editing systems into single all-in-one packages. Finally, another move to combine a number of film images within one frame (for instance, in Leger's 1924 *Ballet Méchanique* or in Vertov's 1929 *A Man with a Movie Camera*) also become legitimized by technology, since all editing software, including Photoshop, Premiere, After Effects, Flame, and Cineon, by default assumes that a digital image consists of a number of separate image layers. All in all, what used to be exceptions for traditional cinema became the normal, intended techniques of digital filmmaking, embedded in technology design itself.

For the experiments in painting on film by Lye, McLaren, and Brackage, see Robert Russett and Cecile Starr, *Experimental Animation* (New York: Van Nostrand Reinhold, 1976), pp. 65–71, 117–128; and P. Adams Sitney, *Visionary Film,* 2nd ed. (Oxford: Oxford University Press), pp. 130, 136–227.

25. Paula Parisi reported: "A decade ago, only an intrepid few, led by George Lucas's Industrial Light and Magic, were doing high-quality digital work. Now computer imaging is considered an indispensable production tool for all films, from the smallest drama to the largest visual extravaganza." Parisi, "The New Hollywood Silicon Stars," p. 144.

26. Therefore, one way in which the fantastic is justified in contemporary Hollywood cinema is through the introduction of various nonhuman characters such as aliens, mutants, and robots. We never notice the pure arbitrariness of their colorful and mutating bodies, the beams of energy emanating from their eyes, the whirlpools

of particles spinning from their wings, because they are made perceptually consistent with the set, that is, they look like something that could have existed in a three-dimensional space and therefore could have been photographed.

27. Metz, "The Fiction Film and Its Spectator."

28. This twenty-eight-minute film, made in 1962, is composed of still frames narrativized in time, with one very brief live-action sequence. For documentation, see Chris Marker, *La Jetée: Ciné-roman* (New York: Zone Books, 1992).

29. Thomas S. Kuhn, *The Structure of Scientific Revolutions,* 2nd ed. (Chicago: University of Chicago Press, 1970).

30. *Flora petrinsularis* is included in the compilation CD-ROM, *Artintact 1* (Karlsruhe, Germany: ZKM/Center for Art and Media, 1994).

31. Steven Neale, *Cinema and Technology* (Bloomington: Indiana University Press, 1985), p. 52.

32. Natalie Bookchin, *The Databank of the Everyday,* artist's statement (1996), published by the author. Although I was the videographer on this project, I feel that Bookchin's piece is so fully resonant with the arguments I make here that I am willing to accept the risk of commenting on it at length.

33. It was Dziga Vertov who coined the term "kino-eye" in the 1920s to describe the cinematic apparatus's ability "to record and organize the individual characteristics of life's phenomena into a whole, an essence, a conclusion." For Vertov, it was the presentation of film "facts," based as they were on materialist evidence, that defined the very nature of the cinema. See *Kino-Eye: The Writings of Dziga Vertov,* Annette Michelson, ed., Kevin O'Brien, trans. (Berkeley: University of California Press, 1984). The quotation is from "Artistic Drama and Kino-Eye" (originally published in 1924), p. 47.

34. This is the third in a series of essays on digital cinema. See "Cinema and Digital Media," in *Perspektiven der Medienkunst/Perspectives of Media Art,* Jeffrey Shaw and Hans Peter Schwarz, eds. (Cantz Verlag Ostfildern, 1996); and "To Lie and to Act: Potemkin's Villages, Cinema and Telepresence," in *Mythos Information—Welcome to the Wired World. Ars Electronica 95,* by Karl Gebel and Peter Weibel, eds. (Vienna: Springler-Verlag, 1995), pp. 343–348. See also Erkki Huhtamo, "Encapsulated Bodies in Motion: Simulators and the Quest for Total Immersion," in *Critical Issues in Electronic Media,* Simon Penny, ed. (Albany: SUNY Press, 1995), pp. 159–186.

Chapter 10: "We Could Be Better Ancestors Than This": Ethics and First Principles for the Art of the Digital Age

1. Robert Hughes, "The Assault on Culture," *Time,* August 7, 1995.

2. Esther Dyson, "Friend and Foe: The Wired Interview," *Wired* 3 (August 1995), pp. 106–112; 160–162.

3. Neil Postman, *Amusing Ourselves to Death,* 1st electronic ed. (New York: Voyager Company, 1992; originally 1985, by arrangement with Viking Penguin), p. 3.

4. For more from this neo-Luddite, see Kirkpatrick Sale, *Rebels Against the Future: The Luddites and Their War on the Industrial Revolution. Lessons for the Computer Age* (Reading, MA: Addison-Wesley, 1995).

5. This sentiment is in the air, of course, as seen in Francis Fukuyama, *The End of History and the Last Man* (New York: Free Press, 1992).

6. The American Social History Project, Roy Rosenzweig, Steve Brier, and Josh Brown, *Who Built America?: From the Centennial Celebration of 1876 to the Great War of 1914* (New York: Voyager Company, 1993).

7. *First Person: Mumia Abu-Jamal* (New York: Voyager Company, 1995).

8. Mike Snider, "'Death Row' on Disc," *USA Today,* August 2, 1996.

Chapter 11: Musings on Amusements in America, or What I Did on My Summer Vacation

1. Dolphins often engage in sexual play when they are in contact with humans. In the early 1980s a young computer scientist who now works as a high-level executive with a Japanese video game company went on a pilgrimage to swim with John Lilly's dolphins. Shortly after he entered the pool one of them began masturbating on his leg. The man informed Lilly of the situation and asked if he could leave the pool. Lilly advised against it. "Best wait it out," he counseled, "or things could turn ugly." This may explain something.

2. When I met Ray Bradbury in the early eighties, he told me something of the plans he and Walt had cooked up for Epcot before the great man died. It was going to be a real residential community, an "experimental prototype community of to-morrow," with nonpolluting moving sidewalks and monorails and affordable hous-ing and community activities and uniformed bands playing in little gazebos on the

green like the last scene of *Yellow Submarine.* "Then the real estate people got a hold of it," Bradbury mourned.

3.   For example, "Would you rather slide down the edge a razor blade into a pool of alcohol, *or* suck all the snot out of a dog's nose until his head caves in?"

4.   For example, "What if there was an earthquake and you were left all by yourself and you had to decide whether to starve to death *or* eat the cat?"

5.   For example, "Which would you rather do, put on a hat full of chocolate syrup, *or* put on a pair of shoes with raw eggs tucked in the toes?"

Recommended Readings in New Media Theory

Adriaansens, Alex, Joke Brouwer, Rik Delhaas and Eugenie den Uyl, eds. *Book for the Unstable Media.* Amsterdam: Stichting V2, 1992.

Agre, Philip E. *Computation and Human Experience.* New York: Cambridge University Press, 1997.

von Amelunxen, Hubertus, Stefan Inglhaut and Florian Rötzer, eds. *Photography after Photography: Memory and Representation in the Digital Age.* Sydney: G+B Arts, 1996.

Aronowitz, Stanley, Barbara Martinsons and Michael Menser, eds. *Technoscience and Cyberculture.* New York: Routledge, 1996.

Baker, Robin. *Designing the Future: The Computer Transformation of Reality.* London: Thames & Hudson, 1993.

Balsamo, Anne. *Technologies of the Gendered Body: Reading Cyborg Women.* Durham, NC: Duke University Press, 1996.

Barrett, Edward, ed. *The Society of Text: Hypertext, Hypermedia, and the Social Construction of Information.* Cambridge, MA: MIT Press, 1989.

———. *Sociomedia: Multimedia, Hypermedia, and the Social Construction of Knowledge.* Cambridge, MA: MIT Press, 1994.

———. *Text, Context, and Hypertext.* Cambridge, MA: MIT Press, 1988.

Barry, John A. *Technobabble.* Cambridge, MA: MIT Press, 1991.

Bateson, Gregory. *Steps to an Ecology of Mind.* New York: Ballantine Books, 1972.

Baudrillard, Jean. *The Ecstasy of Communication.* Bernard Schutze and Caroline Schutze, trans. New York: Semiotext(e), 1988.

———. *Selected Writings.* Mark Poster, ed. Stanford: Stanford University Press, 1988.

———. *Simulations.* Paul Foss, Paul Patton, and Philip Beitchman, trans. New York: Semiotext(e), 1983.

Bellour, Raymond, Catherine David and Christine Van Assche, eds. *Passages de l'image*. Barcelona: Centre Cultural de la Fundacio Caixa de Pensions, 1991.

Bender, Gretchen and Timothy Druckrey, eds. *Cultures on the Brink: Ideologies of Technology*. Seattle: Bay Press, 1994.

Benedetti, Paul and Nancy DeHart, eds. *Forward Through the Rearview Mirror: Reflections on and by Marshall McLuhan*. Cambridge, MA: MIT Press, 1997.

Benedikt, Michael, ed. *Cyberspace: First Steps*. Cambridge, MA: MIT Press, 1991.

Benjamin, Walter. *Illuminations*. Hannah Arendt, ed. Harry Zohn, trans. New York: Schocken, 1969.

Bey, Hakim. *T.A.Z.: The Temporary Autonomous Zone, Ontological Anarchy, Poetic Terrorism*. Brooklyn, NY: Autonomedia, 1991.

Bierut, Michael et al., eds. *Looking Closer: Critical Writings on Graphic Design*. New York: Allworth Press: American Institute of Graphic Arts, 1994.

———. *Looking Closer 2: Critical Writings on Graphic Design*. New York: Allworth Press: American Institute of Graphic Arts, 1997.

Birkerts, Sven. *The Gutenberg Elegies: The Fate of Reading in an Electronic Age*. Boston: Faber & Faber, 1994.

Bogard, William. *The Simulation of Surveillance: Hypercontrol in Telematic Societies*. New York: Cambridge University Press, 1996.

Boigon, Brian, ed. *Culture Lab 1*. New York: Princeton Architectural Press, 1993.

Bolter, Jay David. *Writing Space: The Computer, Hypertext, and the History of Writing*. Hillsdale, NJ: Lawrence Erlbaum, 1991.

Bolter, Jay David and Richard Grusin. *Remediation: Understanding New Media*. Cambridge, MA: MIT Press, 1999.

Boyer, M. Christine. *CyberCities: Visual Perception in the Age of Electronic Communication*. New York: Princeton Architectural Press, 1996.

Bradford, Peter, ed. *Information Architects.* Zurich: Graphis Press, 1996.

Brand, Stewart. *How Buildings Learn: What Happens After They're Built.* New York: Viking, 1994.

———. *The Media Lab: Inventing the Future at MIT.* New York: Penguin Books, 1988.

Branwyn, Gareth. *Jamming the Media: A Citizen's Guide: Reclaiming the Tools of Civilization.* San Francisco: Chronicle Books, 1997.

Brook, James and Iain Boal, eds. *Resisting the Virtual Life: The Culture and Politics of Information.* San Francisco: City Lights Books, 1995.

Bukatman, Scott. *Terminal Identity: The Virtual Subject in Postmodern Science Fiction.* Durham, NC: Duke University Press, 1993.

Bynum, Terell Ward and James H. Moor, eds. *The Digital Phoenix: How Computers Are Changing Philosophy.* Cambridge, MA: Blackwell, 1998.

Cassell, Justine and Henry Jenkins, eds. *From Barbie to Mortal Kombat: Gender and Computer Games.* Cambridge, MA: MIT Press, 1998.

Castells, Manuel, ed. *The Rise of the Network Society.* The Information Age: Economy, Society, and Culture; vol. 1. Cambridge: Blackwell, 1996.

———. *The Power of Identity.* The Information Age: Economy, Society, and Culture; vol. 2. Cambridge: Blackwell, 1997.

———. *End of Millennium.* The Information Age: Economy, Society, and Culture; vol. 3. Cambridge: Blackwell, 1998.

Crary, Jonathan. *Techniques of the Observer: On Vision and Modernity in the Nineteenth Century.* Cambridge, MA: MIT Press, 1990.

Crary, Jonathan and Sanford Kwinter, eds. *Incorporations.* New York: Zone, 1992.

Critical Art Ensemble. *The Electronic Disturbance.* Brooklyn, NY: Autonomedia, 1994.

Cubitt, Sean. *Timeshift: On Video Culture.* New York: Routledge, 1991.

———. *Videography: Video Media as Art and Culture.* New York: St. Martin's Press, 1993.

Davis, Erik. *Techgnosis: Myth, Magic, and Mysticism in the Age of Information.* New York: Harmony Books, 1998.

Dawkins, Richard. *The Selfish Gene.* New York: Oxford University Press, 1976.

Debord, Guy. *Comments on the Society of the Spectacle.* Malcolm Imrie, trans. New York: Verso, 1990.

———. *The Society of the Spectacle.* Donald Nicholson-Smith, trans. New York: Zone Books, 1994.

Debray, Regis. *Media Manifestos: On the Technological Transmission of Cultural Forms.* Eric Rauth, trans. New York: Verso, 1996.

De Kerckhove, Derrick. *Brainframes: Technology, Mind and Business.* Utrecht: Bosh & Keuning BSO/Origin, 1991.

————. *Planetary Mind: Collective Intelligence in the Digital Age.* San Francisco: Hardwired, 1997.

————. *The Skin of Culture: Investigating the New Electronic Reality.* Christopher Dewdney, ed. Toronto: Somerville House, 1995.

De Landa, Manuel. *A Thousand Years of Nonlinear History.* New York: Zone Books, 1997.

————. *War in the Age of Intelligent Machines.* New York: Zone Books, 1991.

Delany, Paul and George Landow, eds. *Hypermedia & Literary Studies.* Cambridge, MA: MIT Press, 1991.

De Lauretis, Teresa and Stephen Heath, eds. *The Cinematic Apparatus.* New York: St. Martin's Press, 1980.

Deleuze, Gilles. *Cinema 1: The Movement-Image.* Hugh Tomlinson and Barbara Habberjam, trans. Minneapolis: University of Minnesota, 1986.

————. *Cinema 2: The Time-Image.* Hugh Tomlinson and Robert Galeta, trans. Minneapolis: University of Minnesota Press, 1989.

Deleuze, Gilles and Felix Guattari. *Anti-Oedipus: Capitalism and Schizophrenia.* Robert Hurley, Mark Seem, Helen R. Lane, trans. New York: Viking Press, 1977.

————. *A Thousand Plateaus: Capitalism and Schizophrenia.* Brian Massumi, trans. Minneapolis: University of Minnesota Press, 1987.

Dery, Mark. *Escape Velocity: Cyberculture at the End of the Century.* New York: Grove Press, 1996.

————, ed. *Flame Wars: The Discourse of Cyberculture.* Durham, NC: Duke University Press, 1994.

Dodsworth, Clark, Jr., ed. *Digital Illusion: Entertaining the Future with High Technology.* Reading, MA: Addison-Wesley, 1998.

Dreyfus, Herbert L. *What Computers Still Can't Do.* Cambridge, MA: MIT Press, 1992.

Droege, Peter, ed. *Intelligent Environments: Spatial Aspects of the Information Revolution.* Amsterdam: Elsevier Science, 1997.

Druckrey, Timothy, ed. *Electronic Culture: Technology and Visual Representation.* New York: Aperture, 1996.

————. *Iterations: The New Image.* Cambridge: MIT Press, 1993.

Dublin, Max. *Future Hype: The Tyranny of Prophecy.* New York: Dutton, 1989.

Duguet, Anne-Marie, Heinrich Klotz, and Peter Weibel. *Jeffrey Shaw: A User's Manual, From Expanded Cinema to Virtual Reality.* Karlsruhe, Germany: Edition ZKM, 1997.

Dyson, Esther. *Release 2.0: A Design for Living in the Digital Age.* New York: Broadway Books, 1997.

Edwards, Paul N. *The Closed World: Computers and the Politics of Discourse in Cold War America.* Cambridge, MA: MIT Press, 1996.

Ellul, Jacques. *The Technological Society.* John Wilkinson, trans. New York: Vintage, 1964.

Featherstone, Mike and Roger Burrows, eds. *Cyberspace/Cyberbodies/Cyberpunk: Cultures of Technological Embodiment.* London and Thousand Oaks, CA: Sage Publications, 1995.

Feenberg, Andrew. *Critical Theory of Technology.* New York: Oxford University Press, 1991.

Frampton, Hollis. *Circles of Confusion: Film, Photography, Video: Texts 1968–1980.* Rochester, NY: Visual Studies Workshop Press, 1983.

Frank, Thomas and Matt Weiland, eds. *Commodify Your Dissent: Salvos from The Baffler.* New York: W. W. Norton, 1997.

Friedberg, Anne, *Window Shopping: Cinema and the Postmodern.* Berkeley: University of California Press, 1993.

Gaggi, Silvio. *From Text to Hypertext: Decentering the Subject in Fiction, Film, the Visual Arts, and Electronic Media.* Philadelphia: University of Pennsylvania Press, 1997.

Goodman, Cynthia. *Digital Visions: Computers and Art.* New York: Harry Abrams, 1987.

Graham, Stephen and Simon Marvin. *Telecommunications and the City: Electronic Spaces, Urban Places.* New York: Routledge, 1996.

Gray, Chris Habels, ed. *The Cyborg Handbook.* New York: Routledge, 1995.

Grossman, Wendy M. *Net.Wars.* New York: New York University Press, 1997.

Grosswiler, Paul. *Method Is the Message: Rethinking McLuhan through Critical Theory.* Montreal: Black Rose Books, 1998.

Halberstam, Judith and Ira Livingston, eds. *Posthuman Bodies.* Bloomington: Indiana University Press, 1995.

Hall, Doug and Sally Jo Fifer, eds. *Illuminating Video: An Essential Guide to Video Art.* New York: Aperture, 1990.

Hanhardt, John G., ed. *Video Culture: A Critical Investigation.* Layton, UT: Peregrine Smith Books, 1986.

Haraway, Donna J. *Modest-Witness@Second-Millennium. FemaleMan-Meets-OncoMouse: Feminism and Technoscience.* New York: Routledge, 1997.

———. *Simians, Cyborgs, and Women: The Reinvention of Nature.* New York: Routledge, 1991.

Harvey, David. *The Condition of Postmodernity: An Enquiry into the Origins of Cultural Change.* Cambridge, MA: Blackwell, 1989.

Hayles, N. Katherine. *Chaos Bound: Orderly Disorder in Contemporary Literature and Science.* Ithaca: Cornell University Press, 1990.

Hayles, N. Katherine, ed. *Chaos and Order: Complex Dynamics in Literature and Science.* Chicago: University of Chicago Press, 1991.

Hayworth, Philip, ed. *Culture, Technology, and Creativity in the Late Twentieth Century.* London: John Libby, 1990.

Hayworth, Philip and Tana Wollen, eds. *Future Visions: New Technologies of the Screen.* London: British Film Institute, 1993.

Heim, Michael. *Electric Language: A Philosophical Study of Word Processing.* New Haven: Yale University Press, 1987, rev. ed. 1999.

———. *The Metaphysics of Virtual Reality.* New York: Oxford University Press, 1993.

———. *Virtual Realism.* New York: Oxford University Press, 1998.

Helfand, Jessica. *Six (+2) Essays on Design and New Media.* New York: William Drenttel, 1997.

Hershman-Leeson, Lynn, ed. *Clicking In: Hot Links to a Digital Culture.* Seattle: Bay Press, 1996.

Holzman, Steven R. *Digital Mantras: The Languages of Abstract and Virtual Worlds.* Cambridge, MA: MIT Press, 1994.

———. *Digital Mosaics: The Aesthetics of Cyberspace.* New York: Simon & Schuster, 1997.

Horn, Stacy. *Cyberville: Clicks, Culture, and the Creation of an Online Town.* New York: Warner Books, 1998.

Howard, Tharon W. *A Rhetoric of Electronic Communities.* Norwood, NJ: Ablex, 1997.

Hudson, David in association with eLine Productions. *Rewired: A Brief (and Opinionated) Net History.* Indianapolis, IN: Macmillan Technical Publishing, 1997.

Ihde, Don. *Technology and the Lifeworld: From Garden to Earth.* Bloomington: Indiana University Press, 1990.

Jacobson, Linda ed. *Cyberarts: Exploring Art & Technology.* San Francisco: Miller Freeman, 1992.

Jameson, Fredric. *Postmodernism, or, the Cultural Logic of Late Capitalism.* Durham, NC: Duke University Press, 1991.

Johnson, Steven. *Interface Culture: How New Technology Transforms the Way We Create and Communicate.* San Francisco: Harper Edge, 1997.

Jones, Steven G., ed. *Virtual Culture: Identity and Communication in Cybersociety.* London and Thousand Oaks, CA: Sage Publications, 1997.

Joyce, Michael. *Of Two Minds: Hypertext Pedagogy and Poetics.* Ann Arbor: University of Michigan Press, 1995.

Kahn, Douglas and Gregory Whitehead, eds. *Wireless Imagination: Sound, Radio, and the Avant-Garde.* Cambridge, MA: MIT Press, 1992.

Kinder, Marsha. *Playing with Power in Movies, Television, and Video Games: From Muppet Babies to Teenage Mutant Ninja Turtles.* Berkeley: University of California Press, 1991.

Kittler, Friedrich A. *Discourse Networks 1800–1900.* Michael Metteer, trans. Stanford, CA: Stanford University Press, 1990.

———. *Grammophon, Film, Typewriter.* Stanford: Stanford University Press, 1998.

———. *Literature, Media, Information Systems: Essays.* John Johnston, ed. Amsterdam: G+B Arts International, 1997.

———. *Materialities of Communication.* Hans Ulrich Gumbrecht and K. Ludwig Pfeiffer, eds. William Whobrey, trans. Stanford, CA: Stanford University Press, 1994.

Klein, Norman M. *The History of Forgetting: Los Angeles and the Erasure of Memory.* New York: Verso, 1997.

———. *Seven Minutes: The Life and Death of the American Animated Cartoon.* New York: Verso, 1993.

Klotz, Heinrich. *Contemporary Art. The Collection of the ZKM Centre for Art & Media, Karlsruhe.* Munich: Prestel, 1997.

Kroker, Arthur. *SPASM: Virtual Reality, Android Music, and Electric Flesh.* New York: St. Martin's Press, 1993.

Kroker, Arthur and Marilouise Kroker, eds. *Digital Delirium.* New York: St. Martin's Press, 1997.

———. *Hacking the Future: Stories for the Flesh-Eating 90s.* New York: St. Martin's Press, 1996.

Kroker, Arthur and Michael A. Weinstein. *Data Trash: The Theory of the Virtual Class.* New York: St. Martin's Press, 1994.

Krueger, Myron. *Artificial Reality II.* Reading, MA: Addison-Wesley, 1991.

Kuhn, Thomas S. *The Structure of Scientific Revolutions.* Chicago: University of Chicago Press, 1970.

Kurzweil, Raymond. *The Age of Intelligent Machines.* Cambridge, MA: MIT Press, 1990.

Landow, George P. *Hypertext 2.0: The Convergence of Contemporary Critical Theory and Technology.* Baltimore: Johns Hopkins University Press, 1997.

Landow, George P., ed. *Hyper/Text/Theory.* Baltimore: Johns Hopkins University Press, 1994.

Landow, George P. and Paul Delany, eds. *The Digital Word: Text-Based Computing in the Humanities.* Cambridge, MA: MIT Press, 1993.

Lanham, Richard A. *The Electronic Word: Democracy, Technology, and the Arts.* Chicago: University of Chicago Press, 1994.

Latour, Bruno. *Aramis, or, The Love of Technology.* Catherine Porter, trans. Cambridge, MA: Harvard University Press, 1996.

Laurel, Brenda. *Computers as Theater.* Reading, MA: Addison-Wesley, 1991.

Laurel, Brenda, ed. *The Art of Human-Computer Interface Design,* Reading, MA: Addison-Wesley, 1990.

Leary, Timothy Francis. *Chaos & Cyber Culture.* Michael Horowitz, ed. Berkeley, CA: Ronin, 1994.

Levidow, Les and Kevin Robins, eds. *Cyborg Worlds: The Military Information Society.* London: Free Association Books, 1989.

Levinson, Paul. *The Soft Edge: A Natural History and Future of the Information Revolution.* New York: Routledge, 1997.

Lévy, Pierre. *Becoming Virtual: Reality in the Digital Age.* Robert Bononno, trans. New York: Plenum Press, 1998.

————. *Collective Intelligence: Mankind's Emerging World in Cyberspace.* Robert Bononno, trans. New York: Plenum Press, 1997.

Lister, Martin, ed. *The Photographic Image in Digital Culture.* New York: Routledge, 1995.

Lovejoy, Margot. *Postmodern Currents: Art and Artists in the Age of Electronic Media.* Ann Arbor: UMI Research Press, 1989.

Ludlow, Peter and Loyd Blankenship. *High Noon on the Electronic Frontier: Conceptual Issues in Cyberspace.* Cambridge, MA: MIT Press, 1996.

Lyotard, Jean-François. *The Postmodern Condition: A Report on Knowledge.* Geoff Bennington and Brian Massumi, trans. Minneapolis: University of Minnesota Press, 1984.

Marchand, Philip. *Marshall McLuhan: The Medium and the Messenger.* Cambridge, MA: MIT Press, 1998.

Markley, Robert, ed. *Virtual Realities and Their Discontents.* Baltimore: Johns Hopkins University Press, 1996.

Marvin, Carolyn. *When Old Technologies Were New: Thinking About Electric Communication in the Late Nineteenth Century.* New York: Oxford University Press, 1988.

Massumi, Brian. *A User's Guide to Capitalism and Schizophrenia: Deviations from Deleuze and Guattari.* Cambridge, MA: MIT Press, 1992.

Masten, Jeffrey, Peter Stallybrass, and Nancy Vickers, eds. *Language Machines: Technologies of Literary and Cultural Production.* New York: Routledge, 1997.

McCaffery, Larry, ed. *Storming the Reality Studio: A Casebook of Cyberpunk and Postmodern Fiction.* Durham, NC: Duke University Press, 1991.

McCorduck, Pamela. *Aaron's Code: Meta-Art, Artificial Intelligence, and the Work of Harold Cohen.* New York: W. H. Freeman, 1991.

McCloud, Scott. *Understanding Comics: The Invisible Art.* New York: HarperCollins, 1994.

McKibben, Bill. *The Age of Missing Information.* New York: Plume, 1992.

McLuhan, Marshall. *Counter Blast.* New York: Harcourt, Brace & World, 1969.

————. *Culture Is Our Business.* New York: McGraw-Hill, 1970.

————. *Essential McLuhan.* Eric McLuhan and Frank Zingrone, eds. New York: BasicBooks, 1995.

————. *The Gutenberg Galaxy: The Making of Typographic Man.* Toronto: University of Toronto Press, 1962.

————. *The Mechanical Bride: Folklore of Industrial Man.* New York: Vanguard Press, 1951.

————. *Media Research: Technology, Art, Communication.* Michel A. Moos, ed. Sydney: G & B Arts, 1997.

————. *Understanding Media: The Extensions of Man.* Cambridge, MA: MIT Press, 1994 [orig. 1964].

McLuhan, Marshall and Quentin Fiore. *The Medium Is the Massage: An Inventory of Effects.* Produced by Jerome Agel. San Francisco: HardWired, 1996 [orig. 1967].

————. *War and Peace in the Global Village; An Inventory of Some of the Current Spastic Situations That Could Be Eliminated By More Feedforward.* Coordinated by Jerome Agel. New York, McGraw-Hill, 1968.

McLuhan, Marshall and Eric McLuhan. *Laws of Media: The New Science.* Toronto: University of Toronto Press, 1988.

McLuhan, Marshall and Bruce R. Powers. *The Global Village: Transformations in World Life and Media in the 21st Century.* New York: Oxford University Press, 1989.

Meyer, Pedro. *Truths and Fictions: A Journey from Documentary to Digital Photography.* New York: Aperture, 1995.

Mitchell, William J. *The Reconfigured Eye: Visual Truth in the Post-photographic Era.* Cambridge, MA: MIT Press, 1992.

————. *City of Bits: Space, Place, and the Infobahn.* Cambridge, MA: MIT Press, 1995.

Moser, Mary Anne and Douglas MacLeod, eds. *Immersed in Technology: Art and Virtual Environments.* Cambridge, MA: MIT Press, 1995.

Murray, Janet H. *Hamlet on the Holodeck: The Future of Narrative in Cyberspace.* New York: The Free Press, 1997.

Neale, Stephen. *Cinema and Technology: Image, Sound, Colour.* Bloomington: University of Indiana Press, 1985.

Negroponte, Nicholas. *Being Digital.* New York: Alfred A. Knopf, 1995.

Nelson, Theodor H. *Computer Lib/Dream Machines.* Seattle: Microsoft Press, 1987.

————. *The Home Computer Revolution.* N. p. Ted Nelson, 1977.

————. *Literary Machines.* Edition 93.1. Sausalito, CA: Mindful Press, 1992.

Norman, Donald A. *The Design of Everyday Things.* New York: Doubleday, 1988.

————. *Things That Make Us Smart: Defending Human Attributes in the Age of the Machine.* Reading, MA: Addison-Wesley, 1993.

————. *Turn Signals Are the Facial Expressions of Automobiles.* Reading, MA: Addison-Wesley, 1992.

Nyce, James M. and Paul Kahn, eds. *From Memex to Hypertext: Vannevar Bush and the Mind's Machine.* Boston: Academic Press, 1991.

Ong, Walter. *Orality and Literacy: The Technologizing of the Word.* New York: Routledge, 1982.

Pearce, Celia. *The Interactive Book: A Guide to the Interactive Revolution.* Indianapolis, IN: Macmillan Technical Publishing, 1997.

Penley, Constance. *NASA/Trek: Popular Science and Sex in America.* New York: Verso, 1997.

Penley, Constance and Andrew Ross, eds. *Technoculture.* Minneapolis University of Minnesota, 1991.

Penny, Simon, ed. *Critical Issues in Electronic Media.* Albany: SUNY Press, 1994.

————. *Machine Culture.* Computer Graphics: Visual Proceedings, Annual Conference Series. New York: The Association for Computing Machinery, Inc., 1993.

Perelman, Michael. *Class Warfare in the Information Age.* New York: St. Martin's Press, 1998.

Plant, Sadie. *Zeros and Ones: Digital Women and the New Technoculture.* New York: Doubleday, 1997.

Popper, Frank, *Art of the Electronic Age.* New York: Harry N. Abrams, 1993.

Porter, David, ed. *Internet Culture.* New York: Routledge, 1997.

Poster, Mark. *The Second Media Age.* Cambridge, MA: Blackwell, 1995.

Postman, Neil. *Amusing Ourselves to Death: Public Discourse in the Age of Show Business.* New York: Viking, 1985.

————. *Technopoly: The Surrender of Culture to Technology.* New York: Knopf, 1992.

Rawlins, Gregory J. E. *Moths to the Flame: The Seductions of Computer Technology.* Cambridge, MA: MIT Press, 1996.

————. *Slaves of the Machine: The Quickening of Computer Technology.* Cambridge, MA: MIT Press, 1997.

Raymond, Eric, ed. *The New Hacker's Dictionary, 3d ed.* Cambridge: MIT Press, 1996.

Renov, Michael and Erika Suderburg, eds. *Resolutions: Contemporary Video Practices.* Minneapolis: University of Minnesota Press, 1996.

Rheingold, Howard. *Tools for Thought. The People and Ideas behind the Next Computer Revolution.* New York: Simon & Schuster, 1985.

————. *The Virtual Community: Homesteading on the Electronic Frontier.* New York: HarperPerennial, 1993.

————. *Virtual Reality.* New York: Summit Books, 1991.

Ronell, Avital. *Finitude's Score: Essays for the End of the Millennium.* Lincoln: University of Nebraska Press, 1994.

———. *The Telephone Book: Technology, Schizophrenia, Electric Speech.* Lincoln: University of Nebraska Press, 1989.

Rosen, Phil, ed. *Narrative, Apparatus, Ideology: A Film Theory Reader.* New York: Columbia University Press, 1986.

Ross, Andrew. *Strange Weather: Culture, Science and Technology in the Age of Limits.* New York: Verso, 1991.

Rucker, Rudy, R. U. Sirius, and Queen Mu, eds. *Mondo 2000: A User's Guide to the New Edge.* New York: HarperPerennial, 1992.

Rushkoff, Douglas. *Cyberia: Life in the Trenches of Hyperspace.* San Francisco: Harper Edge, 1994.

Sale, Kirkpatrick. *Rebels Against the Future: The Luddites and Their War on the Industrial Revolution.* Reading, MA: Addison-Wesley, 1995.

Schivelbusch, Wolfgang. *Disenchanted Night: The Industrialization of Light in the Nineteenth Century.* Angela Davies, trans. Berkeley: University of California Press, 1988.

———. *The Railway Journey: The Industrialization of Time and Space in the 19th Century.* Berkeley: University of California Press, 1986.

Schroeder, Ralph. *Possible Worlds: The Social Dynamic of Virtual Reality Technology.* Boulder, CO: Westview, 1996.

Schwartz, Hillel. *The Culture of the Copy: Striking Likenesses, Unreasonable Facsimilies.* New York: Zone Books, 1996.

Schwarz, Hans-Peter. *Media Art History. ZKM Centre for Art & Media, Karlsruhe.* Munich: Prestel, 1997.

Shannon, Claude. *The Mathematical Theory of Communication.* Urbana: University of Illinois Press, 1949.

Shaw, Jeffrey and Hans Peter Schwarz, ed. *Perspectives of Media Art.* Cantz: Verlag Ostfildern, 1996.

Shields, Rob. *Cultures of the Internet: Virtual Spaces, Real Histories, Living Bodies.* London and Thousand Oaks, CA: Sage Publications, 1996.

Sinclair, Carla. *Net Chick: A Smart-Girl Guide to the Wired World.* New York: Henry Holt, 1996.

Slouka, Mark. *War of the Worlds: Cyberspace and the High-Tech Assault on Reality.* New York: Basic Books, 1995.

Smith, Merritt Roe and Leo Marx, eds. *Does Technology Drive History? The Dilemma of Technological Determinism.* Cambridge, MA: MIT Press, 1994.

Solomonides, Tony and Les Levidow. *Compulsive Technology: Computers as Culture.* London: Free Association Books, 1985.

Springer, Claudia. *Electronic Eros: Bodies and Desire in the Postindustrial Age.* Austin: University of Texas Press, 1996.

Stafford, Barbara Maria. *Artful Science: Enlightenment, Entertainment, and the Eclipse of Visual Education.* Cambridge, MA: MIT Press, 1994.

———. *Body Criticism: Imaging the Unseen in Enlightenment Art and Medicine.* Cambridge: MIT Press, 1991.

———. *Good Looking: Essays on the Virtue of Images.* Cambridge, MA: MIT Press, 1996.

Stoll, Clifford. *Silicon Snake Oil: Second Thoughts on the Information Highway.* New York: Doubleday, 1995.

Stone, Allucquère Rosanne. *The War Between Technology and Desire at the Close of the Mechanical Age.* Cambridge, MA: MIT Press, 1995.

Stork, David G., ed. *Hal's Legacy: 2001's Computer as Dream and Reality.* Cambridge, MA: MIT Press, 1997.

Talbott, Stephen L. *The Future Does Not Compute: Transcending the Machines in Our Midst.* Sebastopol, CA: O'Reilly & Associates, 1995.

Taylor, Mark C. *Hiding.* Chicago: University of Chicago Press, 1997.

Taylor, Mark C. and Esa Saarinen, *Imagologies: Media Philosphy.* New York: Routledge, 1994.

Teilhard de Chardin, Pierre. *The Future of Man.* Norman Denny, trans. New York: Harper & Row, 1964.

———. *The Phenomenon of Man.* Bernard Wall, trans. New York: Harper & Row, 1959.

Toffler, Alvin. *Future Shock.* New York: Random House, 1970.

———. *Powershift: Knowledge, Wealth, and Violence in the 21st Century.* New York: Bantam Books, 1990.

———. *The Third Wave.* New York: Morrow, 1980.

Toffler, Alvin and Heidi Toffler. *Creating a New Civilization: The Politics of the Third Wave.* Foreword by Newt Gingrich. Atlanta: Turner Publishing, 1995.

Tuchman, Maurice. *A Report on the Art and Technology Program of the Los Angeles County Museum of Art.* Los Angeles: Los Angeles County Museum of Art, 1971.

Tufte, Edward R. *Envisioning Information.* Cheshire, CT: Graphics Press, 1990.

———. *The Visual Display of Quantitative Information.* Cheshire, CT: Graphics Press, 1983.

———. *Visual Explanations: Images and Quantities, Evidence and Narrative.* Cheshire, CT: Graphics Press, 1997.

Turkle, Sherry. *Life on the Screen: Identity in the Age of the Internet.* New York: Simon & Schuster, 1995.

———. *The Second Self: Computers and the Human Spirit.* New York: Simon & Schuster, 1984.

Ullman, Ellen. *Close to the Machine: Technophilia and its Discontents.* San Francisco: City Lights, 1997.

Ulmer, Gregory L. *Teletheory: Grammatology in the Age of Video.* New York: Routledge, 1989.

VanderLans, Rudy and Zuzana Licko, with Mary E. Gray. *Emigre: Graphic Design into the Digital Realm.* New York: Van Nostrand Reinhold, 1993.

Virilio, Paul. *The Art of the Motor.* Julie Rose, trans. Minneapolis: University of Minnesota Press, 1995.

———. *Speed and Politics: An Essay on Dromology.* Mark Polizzoti, trans. New York: Semiotext(e), 1986.

———. *The Vision Machine.* Bloomington: Indiana University Press, 1994.

———. *War and Cinema: The Logisitics of Perception.* Patrick Camiller, trans. New York: Verso, 1990.

Wark, McKenzie. *Virtual Geography: Living with Global Media Events.* Bloomington: Indiana University Press, 1994.

Weibel, Peter, ed. *On Justifying the Hypothetical Nature of Art and the Non-Identicality within the Object World.* Cologne: Galerie Tanja Grunert, 1992.

Whitney, John. *Digital Harmony: On the Complementarity of Music and Visual Art.* Peterborough, NH: Byte Books, 1980.

Wiener, Norbert. *Cybernetics: Or Control and Communication in the Animal and the Machine.* Cambridge: MIT Press, 1948.

———. *The Human Use of Human Beings: Cybernetics and Society.* Boston: Houghton Mifflin, 1950.

Winner, Langdon. *Autonomous Technology: Technics-out-of-Control as a Theme in Political Thought.* Cambridge, MA: MIT Press, 1978.

———. *The Whale and the Reactor: A Search for Limits in an Age of High Technology.* Chicago: University of Chicago Press, 1986.

Wombell, Paul, ed. *Photovideo: Photography in the Age of Computers.* Concord, MA: Paul and Co., 1991.

Wooley, Benjamin. *Virtual Worlds: A Journey in Hype and Hyperreality.* Cambridge, MA: Blackwell, 1992.

Wurman, Richard Saul. *Information Anxiety: What to Do When Information Doesn't Tell You What You Need to Know.* New York: Doubleday, 1989.

Yates, Frances. *The Art of Memory.* Chicago: University of Chicago Press, 1966.

Youngblood, Gene. *Expanded Cinema.* New York: E. P. Dutton, 1970.

Index

Machines (*cont.*)
  replacement by, 66, 100
  Turing, 83–85
  vending, 231
  washing, 102
MacKay, Douglas, 74
McLuhan, Marshall
  on automation, 108–109
  on mechanization, 100, 101
  on nonlinear logic, 21
  on "The medium is the message," 130
Magic Kingdom, 218–223, 228–229
Magic lantern, 176
Manovich, Lev, 106
Man with a Movie Camera, A, 187–188
Mao Tse-tung, 212
Marks, Sema, 105
Marsh, Nathan, 161–163
Marx, Karl
  dialectic and, xvii–xviii, 25–26, 199
  on working class, 202
Marxian analysis, 39–40
Mass culture, 202. *See also* Globalism;
  World culture
Materiality and information, 69–94
Matter and spirit, 73
Maximum Entropy Formalism, 77, 78
Meanders, 9
Meaning
  cinema and, 172–192
  hypertext and, 150–170
  information and, 74
  memory and, 134–149
  new media and, 130–132
  usage and, 138
Mechanization, 100–101, 106, 107,
  110. *See also* Machines
Media, new. *See* New media
Media, the
  automation popularized by, 102–104

  cultural identity and, 51
  cyberspace backlash and, 31
  reality suppressed by, 32
  surrogate presence created by, 102
Medium and message, 130–132
  cinema and, 172–192
  hypertext and, 150–170
  memory and, 134–149
Memory
  art of, 142–143
  hypertext and, 164
  new media and, 134–149
  space, time, and, 139–140
Memory machines, 145
Memory technology, 142–148
Memory Theater, 142–143
Message and medium. *See* Medium and
  message
Message and signal, 73–74
Metalogue, 7
Metz, Christian, 173, 183
Michael, Donald N., 101
Midwest, the, 229–235
Mind Children, 72–73
Mind sphere, 35
Mitchell, William J., 80, 181
Mnemotechne, 142–143
Molecular biology, 69–72
Montage, 166, 169, 170. *See also*
  Collage
  cinema and, 187–188, 191
MOOs (object-oriented MUDs), 18,
  114, 126
Moral imagination, 61
Morality, 61, 62, 63
Moravec, Hans, 72–73, 75
Moulthrop, Stuart, 161
Moving pictures, archaeology of, 175–
  176. *See also* Cinema; Film
Mr. Tompkins Inside Himself, 70, 71